THE GENERALS' CIVIL WAR

CIVIL WAR AMERICA

Peter S. Carmichael, Caroline E. Janney,
and Aaron Sheehan-Dean, editors

This landmark series interprets broadly the history and culture of the Civil War era through the long nineteenth century and beyond. Drawing on diverse approaches and methods, the series publishes historical works that explore all aspects of the war, biographies of leading commanders, and tactical and campaign studies, along with select editions of primary sources. Together, these books shed new light on an era that remains central to our understanding of American and world history.

THE GENERALS' CIVIL WAR

WHAT THEIR MEMOIRS CAN TEACH US TODAY

Stephen Cushman

The University of North Carolina Press | Chapel Hill

Manufactured in the United States of America

Designed by April Leidig
Set in Garamond by Copperline Book Services, Inc.

The University of North Carolina Press has been a
member of the Green Press Initiative since 2003.

Cover illustration: Gen. U. S. Grant writing his memoirs,
Mount McGregor, June 27, 1885. Courtesy Library of Congress.

Library of Congress Cataloging-in-Publication Data
Names: Cushman, Stephen, 1956– author.
Title: The generals' Civil War : what their memoirs can teach us today /
Stephen Cushman.
Other titles: Civil War America (Series)
Description: Chapel Hill : The University of North Carolina Press, 2021. |
Series: Civil War America | Includes bibliographical references and index.
Identifiers: LCCN 2021009992 | ISBN 9781469665016 (cloth ; alk. paper) |
ISBN 9781469666020 (paperback) | ISBN 9781469665023 (ebook)
Subjects: LCSH: Biography as a literary form. | Generals—United States—
Biography—History and criticism. | United States—History—
Civil War, 1861–1865—Biography.
Classification: LCC CT21 .C87 2021 | DDC 973.7092/2—dc23
LC record available at https://lccn.loc.gov/2021009992

One would think that they were works of art.

—Ulysses S. Grant to Julia Dent Grant, May 7, 1848,
after his trip to the Cacahuamilpa Caverns of Mexico

CONTENTS

THE GENERALS' CIVIL WAR

1

WHY GENERALS?

WHY GENERALS? Why read their big books, except for pungent quotations and colorful anecdotes? In the beginning Civil War histories may have fallen under their spell, entranced by their exclusive views of events. But surely with the daybreak of various progressive movements we shook off that spell long ago. The lives of ordinary people in all their particularity—those who for any number of reasons never could have been generals during the American Civil War—have been commanding more and more attention for fifty, sixty, even a hundred years. And why generals now, when their statues have been vanishing since the June 2015 church shooting in Charleston, the August 2017 rally-turned-riot in Charlottesville, and the May 2020 killing of George Floyd in Minneapolis? In the aftermath of this last event a statue of Ulysses S. Grant, in Golden Gate Park, joined his Confederate counterparts among the toppled or removed. Why should we continue to engage with Civil War generals' public writings any more than with their public statues?

To answer that question this book considers a handful of Civil War generals' memoirs, printed by New York publishers between 1874 and 1888. Appearing in the last years of Reconstruction and first of Jim Crow, these works fell smack in the middle of the Gilded Age. During these years Ulysses S. Grant, Rutherford B. Hayes, James A. Garfield, Chester A. Arthur, and Grover Cleveland served as presidents. The first three, all Ohioans, commanded soldiers in battle; the lone Democrat, Cleveland, purchased a substitute to take his place in the army. During these years veterans' organizations held reunions, towns and cities unveiled monuments, regimental histories poured forth, and the Government Printing Office began its twenty-one-year publication of nearly 140,000 pages of the official records of the opposing armies. In 1890 the U.S. Congress created the Chickamauga and Chattanooga National Military Park, and counterparts at Shiloh, Gettysburg, and Vicksburg followed before the end of the century.

These and other developments have attracted closer scrutiny since the mid-1990s, when the term "Civil War memory" came into common use. That scrutiny has intensified against the backdrop of events fusing molten controversy about Confederate legacies with the divisive 2020 presidential campaign, during which such phrases as "another civil war" cropped up repeatedly in mainstream publications and on social media platforms. In 1855 Walt Whitman listed "the terrible significance of their elections" in a catalog of political and social Americana; the election of Abraham Lincoln to the presidency, with less than 40 percent of the popular vote, confirmed the poet's assessment. However the American experiment built the Civil War bomb, a presidential election detonated it. Heated national conversations have not ruled out the prospect of another one doing so.[1]

In such conversations "another civil war" can serve as secular shorthand for apocalyptic anxiety descended from end-of-the-world fantasies originating in the Middle East twenty-five hundred years ago. That this shorthand often has little to do with actualities of the nineteenth-century United States, or their replication in the twenty-first, does not make discussions of Civil War memory any less urgent. Quite the opposite; these discussions have become more urgent. They raise large questions about how Civil War memory has developed, how it has worked, and how it continues to develop and work. This book takes up these questions by looking closely at half a dozen of the best-known memoirs written by Civil War generals. In approaching the memoirs, the chapters that follow braid three strands: the relation of the memoirs to the postwar publishing boom of the late nineteenth century and its new Civil War memory market; the relations between and among memory, imagination, history, and literature; and the relations between audience expectations and first-person narratives by leading actors in historical events. Forerunners of our own recent memoir boom, Civil War generals did to memoir writing what Civil War photographers did to photography; they launched it quickly into public visibility on a newly vast scale. They did so by making public convulsion personal.

Many believe that general officers were the sole suppliers of Civil War recollections until the scales dropped from the eyes of readers who started paying attention to ordinary people. According to this model, Civil War remembering wandered through much of the nineteenth and twentieth centuries in the wilderness of top-down narratives, written by great men on lofty perches, until it passed safely to freedom in the promised land of other people's bottom-up perspectives awaiting discovery in archives, private collections, attics, and trunks.

The problem is, as Ulysses S. Grant put it in a sentence we shall meet again, "Like many other stories, it would be very good if it was only true."

As early as 1861 and 1862, publishers in New York, Boston, and Philadelphia, as well as in small places far from these centers, began publishing and marketing personal narratives by wartime authors who were not generals. Among the earliest, printed in 1861 by an unknown press in New Philadelphia, Ohio, was Alfred Edward Mathews's *Interesting narrative: being a journal of the flight of Alfred E. Mathews, of Stark Co., Ohio, from the State of Texas, on the 20th of April, and his arrival at Chicago on the 28th of May, after traversing on foot and alone a distance of over 800 miles across the States of Louisiana, Arkansas and Missouri, by the most unfrequented routes; together with interesting descriptions of men and things; of what he saw and heard; appearance of the country, habits of the people, &c., &c., &c.* A typesetter and artist serving in the Thirty-First Ohio Infantry, whose sketches of Vicksburg Grant later praised, Mathews dated his introduction July 1861.

This introduction sounded a note echoed by many wartime and postwar writers. "The undersigned, at the solicitation of many friends, has been induced to publish an account of his exodus from the South after the breaking out of the war between the United States and the so called Confederate States." Here Mathews followed a familiar convention of the day: excusing his bid for public attention by stating that others have asked him to write his book. Anticipating a recurrent motif in Civil War writing, Mathews continued, claiming to align his interesting narrative with "truth and justice," rather than with sectional partisanship or "local prejudice"—during the 1850s he had taught at a country school in Alabama. He closed with another particularly nineteenth-century touch: "He will therefore give a 'round unvarnished tale,' composed of facts, and leave each reader to draw his own conclusions therefrom." The allusion is to William Shakespeare's *Othello*, act 1, scene 3, and the title character's self-defense, before the Duke of Venice, for having married Desdemona secretly. Mathews's Shakespearean allusion signaled the level of literacy he assumed in his readership at the same time that it toyed with the distinction between the varnished and the unvarnished, a distinction the Civil War and the later nineteenth century would help to sharpen, separating fiction from nonfiction.[2]

Personal wartime narratives came from women as well as men, southerners as well as northerners, civilians as well as combatants, professional writers as well as amateurs. Often the narratives recounted ordeals in prisons or in hospitals. James Redpath in Boston published Louisa May Alcott's *Hospital Sketches* (1863), which pricked Walt Whitman with competitive envy and prompted the publication of his own book about the hospitals twelve years later. In the same year Boston publisher Ticknor and Fields, which had unveiled Henry David Thoreau's *Walden* in 1854, printed Frederick Law Olmsted's *Hospital Transports: A Memoir of the Embarkation of the Sick and Wounded from the Peninsula of Virginia in the Summer of 1862.* An especially successful wartime book, which added cross-dressing disguise to the hospital genre, was Sarah Emma Evelyn Edmonds's *Unsexed: or, The Female Soldier. The Thrilling Adventures, Experiences, and Escapes of a Woman, As Nurse, Spy, and Scout*, released in 1864. Subsequently reprinted in 1865 as *Nurse and Spy in the Union Army*, Edmonds's book sold so well that twenty years later Mark Twain would measure the sales of Ulysses S. Grant's *Personal Memoirs* (1885–86) against its achievement.[3]

The "Publisher's Notice" introducing Edmonds's book opens with a useful benchmark for surveying the writing and reading of personal Civil War narratives. "No APOLOGY is necessary for adding one more to the numerous 'War Books' which already fill a large space in American Literature; for, to the general reader, nothing connected with the Rebellion can be more interesting than the personal experiences of those who have been intimately associated with the different phases of military life, in Camp, Field, and Hospital." The notice shows that the publisher envisioned readers far enough from armies fighting, and disconnected enough from responsibility for the fighting, to enjoy the pleasures of dipping vicariously into others' personal experiences of war. It also shows that by 1864—year of Ulysses S. Grant's Overland Campaign in Virginia, William T. Sherman's capture of Atlanta and March to the Sea, and Abraham Lincoln's reelection—there were already many, many books about the war, and these books made up a part of some fledgling thing called American Literature. Finally, the notice shows that when generals began to write their books, they would have done so with full awareness that readers sought intimate accounts of personal experiences, at least if the generals-turned-amateur-authors wanted their books to sell. Not that they were always successful. When doing his background reading for *The Red Badge of Courage* (1895), Stephen Crane fumed impatiently about some generals' contributions to the *Century Magazine* "Battles and Leaders" series (1884–87), "I wonder that some of those fellows don't tell how they *felt* in those scraps. They spout enough of what they *did*, but they're as emotionless as rocks." Personal feelings were part of personal experience, at least for a readership schooled by Anglo-American sentimentalism, romanticism, and transcendentalism. Most of the generals knew it, and most delivered accordingly.[4]

Readers in the North would have also understood generals' writings in relation to the circulation of personal narratives written by people once enslaved. Initially, most were printed by minor firms in London or Boston, often privately for the author. Between 1840 and 1849, twenty-five such narratives were published; between 1850 and 1859, thirty-three, the most in any decade; between 1860 and 1869, twenty-one. With the appearance of Elizabeth Keckley's *Behind the Scenes, Or, Thirty Years a Slave and Four Years in the White House* (1868), the personal slave narrative and the personal Civil War narrative converged. Born in Virginia in 1818, Keckley purchased her freedom in St. Louis in 1852. An accomplished seamstress, she moved to Washington, where she made dresses for Varina Davis and Mary Custis Lee, eventually securing an interview with the new First Lady, Mary Todd Lincoln, and becoming her dressmaker, as well as her confidante. From this vantage point Keckley made special contributions to the growing body of Civil War narratives; chapters 7 through 11 of her book brim with details of life "behind the scenes" at the White House, a few of which, sometimes adapted, found their way into Steven Spielberg's film *Lincoln* (2012).[5]

When Ulysses S. Grant wrote his book, he was joining a bonanza in full swing, one which other generals, from both the loyal states and, more often, the seceding ones, had joined before him: Jubal Anderson Early in 1866, Joseph E. Johnston in 1874, William T. Sherman in 1875, Richard Taylor in 1879, John Bell Hood in 1880. Still other officers, below the rank of general, had made important contributions as well, among them two foreigners associated with the Confederate army, Arthur James Lyon Fremantle in 1864 and Heros von Borcke in 1866. What matters here is not only that the Civil War personal narrative was nearly twenty-five years old when Grant added his contribution; it matters that criticism of generals, in some cases outright scorn, was already well established, too. The debunking of great men and their top-down perspectives did not have to wait for progressive movements of the twentieth century; it had the strong brew of Protestant anti-authoritarianism, fermenting in North America since the seventeenth century, to encourage and embolden it long beforehand. Thinking otherwise is our historical mistake.

What conjured the twentieth-century mirage that generals' memoirs were the dominant product on the market was the growth and transformation of the postwar publishing industry. After the Civil War the world of print expanded rapidly on many fronts. During the 1870s the number of newspapers nearly doubled, the number of magazines doubled, and the book business soared. The price of paper dropped, mechanical typesetters sped up production, population increased, as did the literacy rate, and the number of public libraries grew, leading to the founding of the American Library Association in 1876. With greater demand for print, established publishers flourished and new ones appeared. Among the major ones selling Civil War books during the Gilded Age were D. Appleton, Charles Scribner, Harper and Brothers, and J. B. Lippincott. All these companies began in the North before the Civil War, and they had no equals in the antebellum South. Although the war disrupted bookselling in the South, these and other northern publishers dominated the trade before the war and after. Particularly interesting is the way in which these northern publishers both met and created demand by publishing personal narratives from both sides of the war, selling their wares in both the North and the South, as the number of bookstores in former Confederate states began to return to antebellum levels.[6]

Between 1865 and 1900 D. Appleton and Company published books by Confederates Joseph E. Johnston, Richard Taylor, and Walter Herron Taylor, lieutenant colonel and assistant adjutant general of the Army of Northern Virginia, while also publishing northerners William T. Sherman, David Dixon Porter, and Nelson Appleton Miles. Between 1881 and 1885 Charles Scribner published sixteen volumes in the series *Campaigns of the Civil War*, all authored by northerners, then followed with Confederate John B. Gordon's *Reminiscences of the Civil War* in 1903 and Edward Porter Alexander's *Military Memoirs of a Confederate* in 1907. In the first years of postwar peacetime Harper and Brothers also worked both sides, as did the Philadelphia firm J. B. Lippincott and Company, best known for major Confederate titles while also publishing books by northern authors with connections to Pennsylvania.[7]

There was one large exception to the postwar pattern of publishing books from both sides. A newcomer firm, founded in 1884 as a publisher by subscription, Charles L. Webster and Company of New York had an office at 658 Broadway, near its corner with Bond Street. Charles L. Webster served as business director of the firm, which in 1891 brought out a forgotten minor novel by Matt Crim titled *Adventures of a Fair Rebel*. Otherwise, Webster and Company stuck to Civil War books written from a northern perspective, mostly by U.S. generals. The nearly exclusive northern focus did not result from the tastes of Charles L. Webster, however. He had to answer to the founder of the firm, his wife's uncle, whose pen name was Mark Twain.

Mark Twain founded Webster and Company to publish himself, and he started with a bang, *The Adventures of Huckleberry Finn* (1885). But it was the second Webster publication that changed everything. It changed the fortunes of Webster and Company, and it changed the Civil War memory market, which watched as December 1885 and March 1886 launched in succession the two volumes of *Personal Memoirs of U. S. Grant.* With sales surpassing 60 percent of the 500,000 mark for the top best sellers of the 1880s—Lew Wallace's *Ben-Hur, or a Tale of the Christ* (1880) and Edward Bellamy's *Looking Backward, 2000–1887* (1888), both novels, were two of them—Grant's book achieved a level of commercial success that set the always entrepreneurial Twain a-bragging. In a letter to William Smith, dated February 3–4, 1887, he reeled off numbers with shameless pleasure: "We have printed & sold 610,000 single volumes, at an average of $4 each; using 906 tons of paper; & in the binding, 35,261 sheep, goat, & calf skins, & 25 ¼ miles of cloth a yard wide. There were 276 barrels (69,000 pounds) of binder-paste used, & the gold-leaf on the backs of the books cost $21,639.50; 41 steam-presses were employed day & night, & together they turned out a complete book at every revolution. The books was issued 14 months ago, & we have thus far paid Mrs. Grant two checks for royalties: one for $200,000, & the other for $150,000—& more is still due her." Adjusted for inflation, the amount Mark Twain eventually paid Julia Dent Grant eventually reached the equivalent of ten to eleven million dollars today. The tipsy pleasures of his boasting aside, Twain's inventory takes a compressed peek into details of postwar publishing.[8]

Along with this commercial success, Mark Twain relished Grant's mixture of memory, imagination, history, and literature. Never out of print, *Personal Memoirs of U. S. Grant* is available today in many editions, some of them abundantly annotated. It also has eclipsed, at least in the sight of many readers now, the majority of personal narratives published before and after it. Although Mary Chesnut's diary suggests a possible exception, thanks in part to the appearance of C. Vann Woodward's 1981 edition *Mary Chesnut's Civil War*, nothing else comes close to Grant's memoirs. For this reason it is easy to understand why some might think that generals' narratives dominate Civil War remembering. A formulation by British military historian John Keegan points to part of the problem in historical perspective. In *The Mask of Command* (1987) Keegan ventured, "If there is a single contemporary document which explains 'why the North won the Civil War,' that abiding conundrum of American historical enquiry, it is the *Personal Memoirs of U. S. Grant.*" Whether or not one cares to debate Keegan's choice of Grant for this distinction, the notion that any single document can explain why the North won the Civil War already reveals a habit of mind behind the illusion that generals dominated until they were displaced. Keegan's own quotation marks, around "why the North won the Civil War," suggest that he wished to put some distance between himself and the abiding conundrum of American history. Even so, his statement shows how ready many readers are, or the memory market is, to let the part tyrannize the whole.[9]

When people speak of Civil War memory now, they are really speaking about remembrance or commemoration, accumulated over more than a century and a half, of past events unavailable to their own brains for firsthand neurological storage and retrieval. Used this way, the word "memory" has a shimmery, shifting quality. In some contexts it suggests a synonym for "annals," in others "tradition," in others "myth," in others "spin." Whatever its connotations at a particular moment, for a particular group of people, the persistence of Civil War memory depends heavily on writing. Photography, visual art, songs, battlefield parks, material artifacts, and roadside markers make contributions, too, but without writing Civil War memory could never have become or remain as powerful as it is. This book focuses on personal narratives by influential men, in high-ranking positions of authority, who did have firsthand experience of the Civil War. For a variety of reasons, their personal narratives, usually called memoirs, helped to shape the way many people have thought about the Civil War ever since.

What is a memoir, particularly a general's memoir that became part of public language in the United States between 1874 and 1888? In an 1887 dinner speech, Mark Twain declared *Personal Memoirs of U.S. Grant* a literary masterpiece, anticipating by one hundred years the addition of Grant's book, in 1990, to the Library of America collection of "America's greatest writing." When it comes to reading Grant's book, or any of the books by generals discussed in this one, both Twain and the Library of America prompt further thinking about underlying assumptions. Twain called Grant's book a literary masterpiece, unique and unapproachable, "in its peculiar department"; the Library of America includes it with America's greatest writing by "pushing the boundaries of the American canon." But where did this peculiar department or these canonical boundaries come from? And why do they matter?[10]

Anyone searching for *Personal Memoirs of U. S. Grant* in a library will find the book classified under the specific heading American history. Originating in the same century, and the same part of the century, that gave us the American Library Association and the American Historical Association and the Civil War publishing boom, library classification systems, such as the one the Library of Congress began to develop in 1897, did not come out of nowhere; they have histories at least as old as the Library of Alexandria in the third century BCE. But their immediate precursor was the classification system used by

Thomas Jefferson for his own library, which by 1815 numbered between six and seven thousand volumes.

"Books may be classed according to the faculties of the mind employed on them: these are—I. MEMORY. II. REASON. III. IMAGINATION." So Jefferson introduced the classification scheme he devised for his collection. He borrowed the scheme from Francis Bacon's *Advancement of Learning* (1605), later adopted and modified by the twenty-eight-volume *Encyclopédie* edited by Denis Diderot and, until 1759, Jean le Rond d'Alembert (1751–72). Following the *Encyclopédie*, Jefferson mapped the three mental faculties onto three areas of knowledge, so that Memory, Reason, and Imagination corresponded respectively to History, Philosophy, and Fine Arts. He then proceeded to subdivide History, Philosophy, and Fine Arts. The result was forty-four classes of books, each a numbered "chapter" in his scheme.[11]

Western debates about the one and the many are as old as the pre-Socratic philosophers Parmenides and Heraclitus, and most systems of classification that attempt to parse the many lead back to Aristotle. What is so special about the Library of Congress classification system beginning to develop in the late nineteenth century, and what does it have to do with Civil War generals' memoirs? A geological model suggests the beginnings of an answer. We can think of the areas Memory, Reason, and Imagination, paired respectively with History, Philosophy, Fine Art, as working like tectonic plates, particularly where plate boundaries are spreading apart, forming midocean ridges as magma upwells from the mantle through cracks and vents to cool as new crust. As new knowledge upwells, all plates adjust, and new classifications form new crust. We can see this process at work in the specific case of American literature, which had no chapter of its own in Thomas Jefferson's classification scheme and no Library of Congress call number of its own until the library began reclassification of general literary studies, along with English and American literature, in 1909, finishing in 1912, nearly one hundred years after Jefferson's 1815 catalog. We look back now and know that those hundred years produced an abundance of writing read around the world as American literature, but we can see and know these things only because the late nineteenth and early twentieth centuries ground and polished the appropriate lens through which we now look. When Mark Twain called *Personal Memoirs of U. S. Grant* a great work of literature, he was sending up a little bit of new magma through a small crack between knowledge plates.[12]

At stake in the classifying of books is nothing less than how to read them fully and well. Or to put it another way, at stake in the classification of books is how that classification prepares us to receive the knowledge books have to give. How we receive the knowledge books have to give affects how we use that knowledge in shaping our pictures of the past; our pictures of the past affect our debates in the present. Should we read *Personal Memoirs of U. S. Grant* or the other memoirs considered here as History or Literature? Do we assume that the faculty most important to the creation of these books was Memory or Imagination? For that matter, when we speak of Civil War memory, are we also, or really, speaking about Civil War imagination? How do these books mix neurological information stored in the brains of generals with their authorial manipulations or modifications? "In all narratives," retired general in chief Winfield Scott wrote in the introduction to his 1864 memoirs, "the art of selecting, rejecting, and grouping incidents" is "one of difficult attainment." The art Scott described is one that recalls the history of the word "fiction," derived from a Latin verb meaning to shape, fashion, form, or mold. How do these books mix the varnished and the unvarnished; how do they shape and mold; how do they blend fiction and nonfiction? In the Library of Congress catalog the earliest book with the phrase "creative nonfiction" in its title appeared in 1987; now the titles in which it appears are legion. Are we witnessing the upwelling of another classification, like the invention by the Library of Congress of the American Literature classification a hundred years ago? Are the Civil War memoirs of generals a species of creative nonfiction before the species had a classification? If so, what are the implications for how we should read them in order to receive all the knowledge they have to give?[13]

If a general officer wanted to reproduce his memories of the Civil War for readers buying books in the 1870s and 1880s, then imagination had to play a part in that reproduction, even if the general determined to tell nothing but the truth of real events, as far as he could discern it. Because the general spoke and wrote American English, his understanding of the term "imagination" would have had something in common with Noah Webster's, as defined in *An American Dictionary of the English Language* (1828): "The power or faculty of the mind by which it conceives and forms ideas of things communicated to it by the organs of sense." For this primary definition—"conceit; an unsolid or fanciful opinion" is Webster's fourth one—the 1828 dictionary gave several illustrative quotations, among them one especially relevant here: "We would define *imagination* to be the will working on the materials of memory; not satisfied with following the order prescribed by nature, or suggested by accident, it selects the parts of different conceptions, or objects of memory, to form a whole more pleasing, more terrible, or more awful, than has ever been presented in the ordinary course of nature." If we think of imagination as the will working on the materials of memory, we can deepen our understanding of generals' memoirs, debates about Civil War memory, and the connections among them.[14]

Between Thomas Jefferson's first library inventory and the eruption of the American Civil War, European Romanticism migrated to the New World, bringing with it transformative ideas about the power of individual imagination. Romanticism has many connotations that can make twenty-first-century historians nervous, especially those among them who insist that history is a social science. At the same time, prominent literary histories of the United States have used 1865 to draw a boundary between American Romanticism and American realism, causing any discussion of romanticism in relation to Civil War memoirs to risk sounding quaint or obsolete, as though one were suffering from a lingering case of what Mark Twain called Sir Walter Disease, referring to the medieval romances of Walter Scott and their deleterious influences on nineteenth-century southern writers in particular.

If a boundary between American Romanticism and American realism exists, Civil War generals' memoirs straddle it. Their popularity in the late nineteenth-century publishing market of the United States depended on this straddling, as does the fervor of many debates now. One of the richest legacies romanticism bequeathed to nineteenth-century memoirs was the rhetorical technology of first-person narrative. This bequest has affected readers of generals' memoirs and their expectations.

First-person narrative is so pervasive now, so naturalized by the contemporary market for memoir into the mode we associate with telling candid stories about ourselves, that we can easily forget it has a history of its own and has not always dominated. "In most books, the *I*, or first person, is omitted; in this it will be retained; that, in respect to egotism, is the main difference." This is Henry David Thoreau in the second paragraph of *Walden*, published in 1854, twenty years before Joseph E. Johnston's *Narrative of Military Operations during the Civil War.* That Thoreau could make such a statement halfway through the nineteenth century shows how first-person narrative had not yet come into its kingdom, as it would by the end of the century. "We commonly do not remember that it is, after all, always the first person that is speaking," he added, before closing with characteristic wit, "I should not talk so much about myself if there were anybody else whom I knew as well."[15]

Yes, it is always the first person speaking, but the first person has not always spoken comfortably in the first person. In his *Anabasis*, fourth-century BCE forerunner of American Civil War generals' memoirs, Xenophon referred to himself in the third person when narrating his march into Persia. Julius Caesar likewise wrote about himself in the third person in his first-century BCE *Commentaries*. In the learned introduction to his memoirs, Winfield Scott cited both Xenophon and Julius Caesar as antecedents of his own book, which he likewise narrated in the third person. Only a little more than a hundred years ago, Henry Adams chose third-person narrative for his autobiography *The Education of Henry Adams* (1918), and in his 1945 manuscript of the posthumously published *War as I Knew It* (1947), George S. Patton Jr. felt compelled to "apologize for the frequent appearance of the first personal pronoun."[16]

Despite the norm sketched by these examples, first-person narrative had reared several monuments more lasting than bronze by the beginning of the nineteenth century. Among them was *The Confessions of J.-J. Rousseau*, which in an early manuscript added the subtitle *Containing the Circumstances of the Events of His Life, and of His Secret Feeling in All the Situations in Which He Found Himself.* Jean-Jacques Rousseau's opening two sentences mark a significant development in the history of the first person: "I am forming an undertaking which has no precedent, and the execution of which will have no imitator whatsoever. I wish to show my fellows a man in all the truth of nature; and this man will be myself." Rousseau's first-person undertaking anticipated many aspects of the romantic endeavor. In showing himself to others in all the truth of his nature, however, the Geneva-born thinker and writer revealed more than some people cared to see. Eventually translated by William Swinton, Civil War correspondent and English professor at the University of California, and published in New York in 1856 by Calvin Blanchard, 76 Nassau Street, the *Confessions* circulated legally in the United States through the nineteenth century and the first decades of the twentieth, until the book was banned in 1929 by the U.S. Customs Department for threatening public morals.[17]

Rousseau's *Confessions* gave nineteenth-century writers a model for more than the verbal workings of first-person narrative; it gave them an imaginative precedent for what a first-person speaker might do with memory. A writer coming after Rousseau did not have to reproduce his confessional frankness, of course. First-person narrative did not have to lead to making private things public. Ulysses S. Grant did not talk about his drinking. William T. Sherman chose to strike from the manuscript he sent to D. Appleton and Company a few lines about the history of insanity in his family. If Joseph E. Johnston's narrative indulged in anything unseemly, it was only his persistent resentment of Jefferson Davis. Richard Taylor acknowledged that he swore in front of Stonewall Jackson, George B. McClellan admitted his uncertainty to his wife in private letters, and Philip H. Sheridan, who made it clear he could swear too, owned up to his insubordinate behavior. But these disclosures, hardly sensational confessions, fell well within the boundaries patrolled by respectable northern publishers, such as the Appletons and Mark Twain.[18]

In the end, though, what made these books important and makes them important still is the convergence of first-person storytelling with the most extensive violence yet visited, in a compressed period of a few years, on people living in the United States. No one aware of that violence, suffered firsthand or witnessed from a distance, could comprehend the whole of it; each could know it only in his or her own person or from his or her point of view. What made generals' memoirs of the 1870s and 1880s especially effective in the Civil War memory market was their innovative application of the personal to the impersonal, of private sensibility to public events. All memoirs fall somewhere on a spectrum of combining the personal with the impersonal, the private with the public. Writing a book that tried to tally an individual personality with the momentous spirit and fact of Civil War America was a new, or a very recent, undertaking.

When northern publishers brought out the memoirs of Civil War generals, they were hoping to make money by selling the American book-buying public a paradox. The paradox was one Abraham Lincoln recognized a year before the war ended. In a letter dated April 4, 1864, written to Albert G. Hodges, editor of the *Frankfort (Ky.) Commonwealth*, the president put it neatly: "I claim not to have controlled events, but confess plainly that events have controlled me." The paradox is that those invested with the highest authority, appearing to wield the greatest power, are those most exposed to the countervailing vicissitudes of contingency. The more things you have under your command, the more chances you have for things beyond your command to affect them. Five years after Lincoln's letter to Hodges, Leo Tolstoy published *War and Peace*, which challenged the so-called Great Man Theory, advanced by Thomas Carlyle in lectures that became *On Heroes, Hero-Worship, and the Heroic in History* (1841). In the first lecture, "The Hero as Divinity," delivered Tuesday, May 5, 1840, Carlyle contended that "Universal History, the history of what man has accomplished in this world, is at bottom the History of the Great Men who have worked here." Following in the spirit of his friend Carlyle, as Carlyle followed in the spirit of Plutarch's second-century *Parallel Lives*, Ralph Waldo Emerson gathered seven lectures into his book *Representative Men* (1850). One of Emerson's representative men was Napoleon, whom he called the Man of the World and whom Tolstoy would treat differently.[19]

It was not only humility making Lincoln disavow his Great Man control over events; it was his pragmatic recognition, after three tumultuous years in office, of all he had not controlled and could never control. The higher one's position, the wider one's view of the uncontrollable. The corresponding paradox of Civil War generals' memoirs is that they grafted what Henry James called the romantic privilege of the first person onto unromantic constraints imposed by wartime events no one person could comprehend fully, let alone control. Many American readers of the late nineteenth century had a particular use for such grafting, as do many readers today, whether they drive the market for memoirs by prominent figures or follow their microblogging during periods of social or political turbulence.

If recent debates about Civil War legacies show us anything, it is that for many people the only way to face the past is to take it personally. Here "take it personally" means both to view historical records from the perspective of one's own identity and to take offense at them. This double meaning helps explain the furor debates about the Civil War still produce in the United States, one often baffling to foreign observers. The memoirs of Civil War generals established most visibly the precedent for taking public disruption personally. In doing so, they appeared to render comprehensible the vast welter of recent events by subjecting those events to familiar conventions of first-person control. The personal story of someone with power—someone exceptional—could and can serve those with less or no power—those who were and are unexceptional—as a manageable microcosm of, and a handy substitute for, the overwhelming, unknowable total. It could and can also encourage the less powerful to read the past, and the present, in exclusively personal terms.[20]

2

SURRENDER ACCORDING TO JOSEPH E. JOHNSTON AND WILLIAM T. SHERMAN

WHY DO MOST students of the Civil War know less about the surrender of Joseph E. Johnston to William T. Sherman, at the farmhouse of James and Nancy Bennett, on the road between Hillsborough and Durham Station, North Carolina, than they do about the surrender of Robert E. Lee to Ulysses S. Grant in Wilmer McLean's parlor at Appomattox Court House? The negotiations initiated by Johnston—in a letter written April 13, 1865, and received by Sherman the next day, which was also Good Friday and the same day John Wilkes Booth shot Abraham Lincoln in Ford's Theatre—led to the largest surrender of the war. Totals for the number of men paroled first at Appomattox and then, three weeks later, at Greensboro, North Carolina, vary from source to source, but *The War of the Rebellion: A Compilation of the Official Records of the Union and Confederate Armies* (1880–1901) gives them as 28,231 and 39,012, respectively. Even if we take for paroles at Greensboro the lower total of 36,817 officially reported by U.S. brevet major general John M. Schofield, commander of the Department of North Carolina, in fact the terms signed by Johnston and Sherman also disbanded Confederate units in South Carolina, Georgia, and Florida, adding another 52,453 soldiers paroled, as reported by U.S. brevet major general James H. Wilson, commander of the Cavalry Corps of the Military Division of the Mississippi, and bringing the total to 89,270.[1]

Why the disparity in memory of the two surrenders? Some may say that it reflects the greater importance of Robert E. Lee and the Army of Northern Virginia to the existence of the Confederacy and its institutions; yet it does not necessarily follow that Lee's greater importance should have wholly eclipsed the North Carolina surrender for so long. There is extensive writing about Civil War campaigns in which Lee took no part. Some may say that the disparity underscores the Virginia-centric historiography of the war, and there may be partial truth to this claim, but it cannot be the whole truth. Virginia-centrism has not produced similar acoustic shadows in the cases of Shiloh, Chickamauga, and Sherman's March to the Sea, for example, and, for that matter, Johnston was a Virginian, too. Others may say that whereas Appomattox offers the pathos, dignity, and catharsis of Aristotelian tragedy, all neatly contained in one small, picturesque place during a handful of days, the surrender in North Carolina was too scattered, protracted, confused, and messy to offer the stuff of clean closure and marketable narrative. Again, there may be partial truth here, but again, it cannot satisfy fully. The Battle of the Wilderness was also scattered, confused, and messy, as well as inconclusive, and yet it has been studied carefully by many historians.

Johnston's negotiations with Sherman at the Bennett farmhouse and the subsequent surrender at Greensboro were controversial and belated in ways that events at Appomattox were not. For one thing, Abraham Lincoln was assassinated between the two surrenders, and the assassination disrupted everything. In a letter dated May 5, 1865, Sherman confessed as much to Schofield, whom he had left in charge of North Carolina: "I feel deeply the embarrassment that is sure to result from the indefinite action of our Government. It seems to fail us utterly at this crisis." Had Booth's plot been foiled, the Lincoln plot would have continued; Lincoln almost certainly would have treated Sherman more diplomatically than did his successor, Andrew Johnson, and his secretary of war, Edwin M. Stanton, when the redheaded general exceeded his military authority in initial negotiations with Johnston; and the surrender at Greensboro might have taken another form, one characterized by a bit more of the mythmaking pomp and circumstance associated with Appomattox.[2]

For another thing, once the controversial negotiations between Johnston and Sherman concluded, attention immediately scattered elsewhere. With the departure of Lincoln's funeral train from Washington on April 21 and his burial at Springfield, Illinois, on May 4, many northern eyes were not focused on North Carolina at all during this time. In the same letter to Schofield, Sherman described the minds of U.S. government authorities as "so absorbed with the horrid deformities of a few assassins & southern Politicians that they overlook the wants and necessities of the great masses." At the same time, many southern eyes were turning grimly toward the urgent challenges of those same wants and necessities. Most of the U.S. soldiers who had ended their war in North Carolina in late April were being marched to Washington, across much of the eastern theater warscape, for the Grand Review held there in late May; most Confederate soldiers were on their ways home, between seven and eight thousand of them having deserted, according to Johnston, in the interval between announcement of the surrender and the subsequent delivery of their arms. Whether northern or southern, these soldiers and their families likely had no more thoughts for the cleanup crews in Greensboro than participants in weddings or funerals do for those who close up after them.[3]

Last of all there is the matter of history writing. As it has taken the historiography of World War II some time to focus popular attention on the often overlooked war in Italy, as, for example, volume 2 of Rick Atkinson's Liberation Trilogy (2002–13) has helped to do, so it has taken Civil War historiography a while to pay closer attention to events largely overlooked during its first century and a half. Despite this lag, no memoir-writing generals gave to the Civil War memory market what Joseph E. Johnston and William T. Sherman did with their books and their postwar friendship. Their contribution to public imagination began with the surrender of Johnston to Sherman in North Carolina in late April 1865, two weeks after Robert E. Lee surrendered to Ulysses S. Grant at Appomattox.

The surrender of Lee to Grant furnished abundant material for Lost Cause and reconciliationist mythmaking, but it did so without the former enemies working together in public, whereas it was the public performance of their mutual respect and admiration, up until their deaths only five weeks apart in early 1891, that distinguished the postwar association of Johnston and Sherman. For all Lee and Grant gave to Civil War memory, much of which continues to be debated, they could not provide the public with the same emotional engagement or the same subsequent legacy as Johnston and Sherman. Recent historians have debunked postwar myths of reconciliation, criticizing them for ignoring the racism that persisted through Reconstruction; yet in the wake of the Truth and Reconciliation Committee, active in South Africa from 1996 to 2003, the language, and the ideal, of reconciliation persist in the twenty-first century. Imperfect and unfinished as the work of the Truth and Reconciliation Committee may have been, it offers one model for defusing high-explosive divisions among fellow citizens. At the end of the nineteenth century Joseph E. Johnston and William T. Sherman offered another.[4]

The Two Big Books

The surrender at Appomattox may eclipse the later and larger surrender of Johnston to Sherman in North Carolina in part because the Appomattox surrender starred the two legendary generals-in-chief and because it conveniently obeyed the neoclassical dramatic unities of time and place, generating in one place on two days such fictions as the story of the famous apple tree, dismissed by Grant in his *Personal Memoirs*. The surrender at Appomattox also combined the two historical meanings of "surrender," and the surrender at Bennett House did not. One meaning is to "give up," and the other is to "give back" or "give over" or "deliver" something. What distinguishes "surrender" from any of its familiar synonyms, formal or colloquial—yield, submit, capitulate, concede, cry uncle, throw in the towel—is that, in a military context, it implies two steps or stages: first, the verbal or written acknowledgment of defeat, and second, the action of delivering or giving something over. In the surrender by Lee to Grant at Appomattox, the two steps or stages took place on April 9 and April 12, 1865, and the sesquicentennial anniversaries of these dates recalled to popular attention, in various media, the familiar and mythologized outlines of each. For the first, which was also Palm Sunday, there are the details of Grant in his "rough garb" with "a soldier's blouse for a coat," as he recollected in his *Personal Memoirs*, meeting Lee in his elegant dress uniform in the parlor of Wilmer McLean's house and offering him magnanimous terms. For the second, four years to the day after the firing on Fort Sumter, details often come from U.S. general Joshua Lawrence Chamberlain's many accounts of his reconciliatory salute to the soldiers led by Confederate general John Brown Gordon into the village for the formal ceremony of handing over their arms, equipment, and flags.[5]

But in the literary history of the Civil War, or the literary-military history of Civil War memory, the surrender at Appomattox has one colossal liability: Lee did not write and publish his memoirs, so we have no public narration by him of the second week of April 1865. The great memoir melee of the late nineteenth and early twentieth centuries gave us narratives by Lee's counterpart, Grant, and by fellow Confederates Jubal Anderson Early, Richard Taylor, Jefferson Davis, John Bell Hood, James Longstreet, John B. Gordon, and Edward Porter Alexander, among others. But we cannot hear from Lee himself, at least not in memoir form. Two weeks after the surrender at Appomattox, he gave Thomas M. Cook of the *New York Herald* his only formal postwar interview—the interview resulted in a paraphrase by Cook, not a word-for-word transcript—and in February 1866 he appeared in Washington to give testimony before the Joint Congressional Committee on Reconstruction. Otherwise, we must rely on Lee's private letters and statements to others, later reported by them.[6]

By contrast the North Carolina surrender found its way into two big books, each of the principals authoring his own. First, in 1874, came Johnston's, with an original title page reading, rather drily, *Narrative of Military Operations, / Directed, / During the Late War Between the States / By / Joseph E. Johnston, / General, C.S.A.* The next year came Sherman's *Memoirs of General William T. Sherman*, a second edition of which, with new first and last chapters, appeared in 1886. Lee and Grant at Appomattox may have captured most of the limelight in popular imagination of Civil War closure, but the relations between Johnston's and Sherman's books, as well as between the men who wrote them, tell a significant story of their own, one with no counterpart at Appomattox.

To begin with, the two books were published by the same New York publisher, D. Appleton and Company, located at 549–51 Broadway in 1874. Representing a partnership formed by the sons of Daniel Appleton, who published his first book in 1831 and died in 1849, this famous house published a long list of prestigious titles that included the first American edition of Lewis Carroll's *Alice's Adventures in Wonderland* (1865), Joel Chandler Harris's *Uncle Remus* (1880), Stephen Crane's *The Red Badge of Courage* (1895), and works by Noah Webster, James Fenimore Cooper, William Cullen Bryant, Charles Darwin, Florence Nightingale, Benjamin Disraeli, Herbert Spencer, Thomas Huxley, Hamlin Garland, and Edith Wharton.[7]

Two points arise here. First, publication of Johnston's and Sherman's books by the same prominent publisher gives us a vivid image of commercial pragmatism during postwar Reconstruction and reconciliation. The rest of us are free to debate the political and social complexities and nuances of Reconstruction and reconciliation, but the Appleton brothers had their eyes on the marketplace, and obviously they believed that the public differences and self-justifications of Civil War generals were good business for them, however much they might complicate public remembrance and reconciliation. In 1879, five years after Johnston's book appeared and four years after Sherman's, Appleton and Company followed with Confederate general Richard Taylor's memoir *Destruction and Reconstruction: Personal Experiences of the Late War*. In 1893, two years after Johnston's death, the company published in its Great Commanders series *General Johnston*, a biography by Virginian Robert M. Hughes—the biography of Johnston preceded those of Lee, Grant, and Sherman in the same series—and in 1913 it brought out Thomas F. Dixon's *The Southerner: A Romance of the Real Lincoln*, this title by the author of the Ku Klux Klan trilogy (1902–7) confirming that once again the complexities of reconciliation were not necessarily opposed to, and might even enhance, the economics of publishing.

Second, the evidence suggests that in the eyes of the Appleton brothers, or their subordinates, Johnston's and Sherman's books were connected from the start. As it turns out, someone at Appleton and Company overestimated the appeal of Johnston's book, which sprang from the author's desire to settle scores with other Confederates, especially Jefferson Davis, and not with Sherman, his wartime opponent. Johnston's *Narrative* sold poorly and was a financial disappointment for Appleton. To boost sales of the troubled volume, which served up too much of its author's resentment of Davis, whose two-volume *Rise and Fall of the Confederate Government* Appleton published in 1881, and not enough of anything resembling Sherman's more artful, readable prose, the publishers resorted to a singular and telling strategy: on the first page following the end of volume 1 in the first edition of Sherman's far more successful *Memoirs*, which sold ten thousand copies the month it was published, they printed a "Letter from General Sherman" as part of a full-page advertisement for Johnston's book. Headed and dated "Headquarters Army of the United States / Washington, D.C., October 31, 1873" and addressed to "Messrs. D. Appleton & Co., / 549 Broadway, New York," Sherman's endorsement read this way:

> DEAR SIRS: I have your favor of the 30th, repeating what you said to me in person yesterday, that you have for publication the manuscript of General Johnston's "Narrative of the Military Operations directed by him during the late War between the States."
>
> Without the least hesitation I advise its immediate publication, for I believe it will have a most extensive sale at the North, as well as the South, and even in Europe.
>
> General Johnston is most favorably known to the military world, and is regarded by many as the most skillful general on the Southern side. He is also ready with his pen, and whatever he records will receive the closest attention by students of the art of war on this continent, and will enter largely into the future Military History of the Civil War.
>
> With great respect, your obedient servant,
> W. T. Sherman, General[8]

An intriguing document for many reasons, Sherman's letter now appears a hybrid of a perfunctory reader's report, dashed off by someone who appears not to have read the manuscript, and a retroactive blurb, marshaled belatedly by the publisher more than a year after the appearance of the book it describes. Appleton could have printed Sherman's letter the previous year at the back of Johnston's book, after all, but instead the advertisements placed there are for Appleton's International Scientific Series; a translation from the French of

Professor Deschanel's *Natural Philosophy: An Elementary Treatise*; textbooks on botany, arithmetic, geography, and U.S. history; *Popular Science Monthly*; a title on ovarian tumors; and many novels now consigned to oblivion, among them *Doctor Vandyke*, by Lost Cause apostle John Esten Cooke, "a well-conceived story of colonial life in Virginia," according to the *Charleston News*.

By late October 1873 Sherman was already writing his own memoirs, and although he had no formal contract with Appleton at this point, his endorsement of Johnston's *Narrative* could not help but enhance his connection with the people who two years later would bring out his own book. During late 1871 and most of 1872 Sherman had traveled extensively throughout Europe, Egypt, and Turkey, his travels no doubt accounting in part for the assurance with which he prophesied good sales for Johnston abroad. Promoted to general after Grant's first election to the presidency, and now Grant's successor as commanding general of the army, Sherman framed his letter to suggest that he met in person with Messrs. D. Appleton and Company in New York on October 29, 1873, a Wednesday, and then traveled back to Washington in time to locate his imprimatur at "Headquarters Army of the United States" two days later. In fact, however, he merely may have written out his letter on a piece of official stationery he happened to have with him in New York. As for the face-to-face meeting with Appleton in New York, it is certainly possible that the only item on the agenda was the manuscript of Johnston's *Narrative*, but the commanding general of the army was a busy man, who could have corresponded about that manuscript by letter. Perhaps he was discussing the prospects for his own manuscript, and the request for an endorsement of Johnston's was a secondary transaction.

Johnston in Sherman's Book

Whatever the truth, it is clear that Sherman composed the second volume of his *Memoirs*, and subsequently revised the whole, with Johnston's *Narrative* before him. At the end of his chapter titled "Atlanta Campaign—Nashville and Chattanooga to Kennesaw," which opens volume 2, Sherman referred to Johnston's book as "just published (March 27, 1874)," not quite five months after his letter to Appleton, and then took issue with Johnston, who was "greatly in error, in his estimates on page 357, in stating our loss, as compared with his, at six or ten to one." As at so many moments in his *Memoirs*, Sherman's meticulously logistical and rhetorically forensic sides emerge clearly here, as he converted to statistical tables the figures usually given by Johnston in complete sentences and then scrupulously referred to the latter by page number to make his case in the manner of a lawyer or professor, both of which he had been before the war.[9]

Despite the corrective tone Sherman adopted here, elsewhere in his *Memoirs* he treated Johnston very well. In fact, he treated him so well that one does not have to be a cynic to wonder about his motives. The October 1873 letter to Messrs. Appleton and Company contained a sentence that foreshadowed what was to come in the *Memoirs*: "General Johnston is most favorably known to the military world, and is regarded by many as the most skillful general on the Southern side." So much for the popular estimation of Robert E. Lee, whom this sentence demoted by omitting altogether. Although Sherman and Johnston served in the regular army together for thirteen years, they did not meet until April 17, 1865, at the Bennett farmhouse. As Sherman put it in his lengthy official report, dated May 9, 1865, "At noon of the day appointed I met General Johnston for the first time in my life, although we had been interchanging shots constantly since May, 1863." Sherman was thinking of interchanging shots in Mississippi during the Vicksburg and Jackson Campaigns, but actually he and Johnston had faced each other at First Manassas–Bull Run as well. Unlike Grant and Lee, Sherman and Johnston squared off at various points throughout the war. As a result, Johnston would have been a frequent subject of Sherman's *Memoirs*, even if Sherman had not been consulting Johnston's narrative while composing his own. With Johnston's book also before him, the Confederate leader's presence in Sherman's *Memoirs* became all the more interesting.[10]

All his life Sherman loved attending plays and reading novels, and if his own book had been either one instead, we might have credited him with managing the entrances and exits of Johnston with particular deftness. After a passing assessment of "the reports of the opposing commanders, McDowell and Johnston," on July 21, 1861, as "fair and correct," Sherman brought Johnston back on stage in his Vicksburg chapter, this time with additional commentary that echoed the sentence in the letter to Appleton: "Even then the ability of General Johnston was recognized, and General Grant told me that he was about the only general on that side whom he feared." Again, no mention of Lee. One could argue that in context Sherman understood that Grant was referring only to "that side" of the Vicksburg Campaign, not of the entire war, so Lee would have had no relevance. But the stronger argument would seem to be that Sherman was working throughout his *Memoirs* to cast Johnston in superlative terms not so much for Johnston's benefit as for his own. If he were successful in his elevation of Johnston to the preeminent place among Confederate generals, the surrender negotiations at the Bennett farmhouse could no longer be viewed as mere postscripts or sideshows to Appomattox.[11]

When Sherman's *Memoirs* introduce Johnston for the final time, now in North Carolina in March 1865, Jefferson Davis having relieved John Bell Hood and returned the Army of Tennessee to Johnston in February, they bestow on him a distinguishing epithet: "I then knew that my special antagonist, General Jos. E. Johnston, was back, with part of his old army; that he would not be misled by feints and false reports, and would somehow compel me to exercise more caution that I had hitherto done." "My special antagonist": it is an apt and accurate phrase, one that describes the relationship between the two soldiers, as well as between the two authors they became. At least twice in his *Memoirs* Sherman turned aside from his narrative present to tell stories that established the tone of this special antagonism, one which distinguishes the relationship of Sherman and Johnston from that of Grant and Lee.[12]

The first digression appears in the opening chapter of volume 2, which narrates the Atlanta Campaign through Kennesaw Mountain. In his narrative present Sherman had brought his readers up to the events of May 19 and 20, 1864, when Johnston ordered an attack from his position at Cassville, Georgia, but then went on the defensive and crossed the Etowah River. Confessing that he "could not then imagine why [Johnston] had declined battle," Sherman added that he "did not learn the real reason till after the war was over."[13]

In the next sentence, which opens a new paragraph, Sherman's narrative suddenly flashes forward to the autumn of 1865: "Taking a steamer for Cairo, I found as fellow-passengers Generals Johnston and Frank Blair [commander of Sherman's Seventeenth Corps]. We were, of course, on the most friendly terms, and on our way up we talked over our battles again, played cards, and questioned each other as to particular parts of our mutual conduct in the game of war." Whether or not the card-playing reminiscences included drinking bourbon, as had the surrender negotiations in the Bennett farmhouse the previous spring, one can find nothing comparable in Grant's narration of his relationship with Lee in his *Personal Memoirs*. More to the point, it is nearly impossible even to imagine something comparable between the two principals at Appomattox, and contemporary descriptions of their very brief meeting at the White House on May 1, 1869, reinforce this impossibility, representing that meeting as simple, dignified, and restrained.[14]

As for Sherman and Johnston playing cards en route to Cairo, what is most remarkable is not what Sherman learned and subsequently narrated about tensions between Johnston and his subordinates, Hood and Leonidas Polk (the flash forward includes Sherman's later conversation with Hood, at the St. Charles Hotel in New Orleans in the spring of 1870, during which Hood gave Sherman a different version of events as Cassville, the difference "very natural," according to Sherman, as "subsequent events estranged these two officers"); what is most remarkable is the narrative bravado of Sherman's "of course" in the statement that he and Johnston "were, of course, on the most friendly terms." Of course? The "most friendly" terms? The meeting on the steamer to Cairo, the fourth one in their lives, was their first since they concluded negotiations at the Bennett farmhouse on April 26, 1865, and although they would go on to become quite close, their families exchanging dinner invitations when both had houses in Washington, D.C., this closeness had to grow throughout the 1870s, culminating in the latter part of the decade. No reader of Johnston's *Narrative* could take such superlative friendliness so confidently for granted on the basis of his book alone, and no reader of Sherman's *Memoirs* up to this point would necessarily do so either, although signs of Sherman's high estimation of Johnston are readily available. In a small but characteristically skillful touch, Sherman's "of course" does not remind his reader of anything already said or confirm anything inevitably known; it provides new information about his subsequent relationship with Johnston under the guise of treating the reader as an informed insider.[15]

The second digression, which appears in the fifth chapter of volume 2, "Atlanta and After—Pursuit of Hood," is not as long as the first, but it has a distinct flavor of its own, as it describes Johnston's inquiring of Sherman after the war the name of his chief railroad engineer. Johnston's curiosity was not merely idle, as he worked with railroads throughout his life. An army topographic engineer assigned to survey a possible route through Texas before the war, and briefly the president of a railroad company after it, Johnston wound up as U.S. railroad commissioner in the first administration of Grover Cleveland. On learning that Sherman's chief railroad engineer was Colonel W. W. Wright, a civilian, Johnston expressed his surprise and admiration before turning to an anecdote obviously relished by Sherman in the retelling. Johnston's anecdote revealed that about the time one of Sherman's trains was reaching him at Big Shanty on tracks recently repaired by his men, Confederates were reporting to Johnston at Marietta that the break they had made in those tracks, near Tilton Station, would take Sherman's people another two weeks to repair.[16]

Sherman in Johnston's Book

Johnston would not have seen these most friendly representations of his special antagonism with Sherman until he read them in his antagonist's *Memoirs*, and he may have been gratified by what he read or somewhat surprised or wryly amused by Sherman's typically unguarded warm-bloodedness. But Sherman would have read what Johnston had written of him by the time he was writing. What did he find when he looked in the mirror of Johnston's *Narrative*? If he was hoping to find himself complimented, as he would go on to compliment Johnston, Sherman would have had a long wait and a long time to call on the patience for which he was never famous. Twenty-nine times in Johnston's narrative Sherman's name comes and goes with perfunctory matter-of-factness before the narrative begins to inch toward greater intimacy in a section of the eleventh chapter, when Johnston gave his reasons for leaving Dalton, Georgia: "I supposed, from General Sherman's great superiority of numbers, that he intended to decide the contest by a battle." At this point, when Johnston finally ventured into his opponent's thinking, with his narrative nearly three-quarters finished, the movement into Sherman's psyche was neither deep nor colorful. But having subsisted on such a meager narrative diet up to this point, Sherman would have found himself thrown his first nourishing crumb on the next page. There Johnston commented on the high quality of U.S. soldiers and added, with reference to Sherman, "It was not to be supposed that such troops, under a sagacious and resolute leader, and covered by intrenchments [sic], were to be beaten by greatly inferior numbers." True, it is faint praise; to be "sagacious and resolute" is not quite the same thing as being the most skillful and feared soldier on his side, and Sherman's resolute sagacity gets somewhat discounted by the mention of his covering entrenchments and Johnston's inferior numbers. But as Johnston moved toward the denouement, he became more liberal with praise, although he tended to direct that praise toward Sherman's soldiers and thus only indirectly toward their leader.[17]

In his account of his first meeting with Sherman, at the Bennett farmhouse on April 17, 1865, Johnston once again hinted at a deeper portrait of his antagonist. Narrating in the muted register of indirect discourse, he briefly recounted Sherman's showing him news of Lincoln's assassination, noting, "I told General Sherman that, in my opinion, the event was the greatest possible calamity to the South." He then summarized his desire for an armistice to give "the civil authorities" an opportunity to negotiate; Sherman's objection that the United States did not recognize the existence of a Southern Confederacy or its civil authorities; Sherman's counteroffer of the same terms that Grant offered Lee; and his, Johnston's, countering response that "we might do more than he proposed" and "arrange the terms of a permanent peace," citing as precedent Napoleon's belief that "the civic crown earned by preserving the life of one citizen confers truer glory than the highest achievement merely military."[18]

In light of subsequent events, in which Sherman was publicly chastised and humiliated for exceeding his "merely military" authority, it is easy to see this moment in Johnston's *Narrative* as the temptation scene in which Johnston plays Satan to Sherman's Eve. If Sherman had stuck to the merely military, he would have saved himself, and many others, much distress. But there is no suggestion by Johnston that he thought of himself as luring Sherman into difficulty, and in the pages that followed he did not describe or take any responsibility for the controversy he helped create for Sherman. It is not hard to imagine that Sherman, reading Johnston's account in 1874, would have felt vindicated by it, since it showed the controversial suggestion that the U.S. government recognize existing governments in the Confederate states originated with Johnston, not with him. Instead of any hint of controversy, what Johnston's narrative of the first meeting does give is one suggestive glimpse into Sherman's interior: "General Sherman replied, with heightened color, that he appreciated such a sentiment, and that to put an end to further devastation and bloodshed, and restore the Union, and with it the prosperity of the country, were to him objects of ambition."[19]

Johnston's understated phrase "with heightened color" has the ring of truth about it, as it describes succinctly the flushed face Sherman showed to the world on many occasions, both in war and in peace. No doubt, negotiations with him at the Bennett farmhouse included many moments of Sherman's heightened coloring and provided a sharp contrast with the unbroken dignity of negotiations between Grant and Lee in Wilmer McLean's parlor. Sherman's heightened coloring is not remarkable; what is remarkable is that throughout his account of the surrender negotiations Johnston represented himself as both coolly rational and in control while he was advancing initiatives that put Sherman on the defensive.

Two Views into the Bennett House

When Sherman came to write his version of the negotiations, he made no reference to the specifics of Johnston's account, which he summarized as "quite accurate and correct," but he reciprocated in kind, fully turning the tables and casting himself as the coolly shrewd one, whose skillful management of the situation put Johnston on the defensive and got an emotional rise out of him. Having described his arrangement of a private interview with his adversary at the Bennett farmhouse, Sherman continued in a new paragraph: "As soon as we were alone together I showed him the dispatch announcing Mr. Lincoln's assassination, and watched him closely." The four-word phrase "and watched him closely" moved Sherman's observation of Johnston closer to that of a detective or a psychotherapist, someone whose study of his subject was particularly keen and charged. In the draft of Sherman's manuscript in the Library of Congress, the first version of Johnston's reaction read this way: "The perspiration came out on his forehead, and he did not attempt to conceal his distress." The detail of Johnston's anxious sweating at noon on an April day in North Carolina was a small but compelling one, but Sherman was not yet content with it. His manuscript shows that he chose to insert over a caret mark after "out," the prepositional phrase, which appeared in the published version, "in large drops": "The perspiration come out in large drops on his forehead." In a work of eight hundred pages, this one prepositional phrase would be easy for a reader to miss. But it certainly suggested that at this extraordinary moment Johnston was in the grip of intense feelings and not at all as cool as his own narrative suggested.[20]

Small as Sherman's detail of Johnston sweating large drops may seem, it was large enough to prompt a published response from Johnston once he had read Sherman's *Memoirs*. In an article entitled "My Negotiations with General Sherman," published in the *North American Review* in 1886, the same year the second edition of Sherman's *Memoirs* appeared, Johnston objected to Sherman's depiction of him in the Bennett farmhouse: "From his account of this interview, it is evident that General Sherman's memory confounds, I think, occurrences in Raleigh with those in Mr. Bennett's house. The idea that the Confederates should be suspected of such a crime [the assassination of Lincoln] never entered my mind, and the amount of sensibility ascribed to me is unnatural; nor is General Sherman capable of the rudeness of speaking to me in such terms of my President as he attributes to himself."[21]

Johnston protested a little too much in rejecting the very idea that the outspoken Sherman could possibly be capable of rudeness to Davis, Johnston's own very public grudge against his president often veering in that direction. But this quibble aside, Johnston's statement that the amount of sensibility attributed to him by Sherman "is unnatural" again has the ring of truth to it. Any reader of Sherman's *Memoirs* can easily imagine its author both coloring and sweating large drops at various points in his career, but few readers of Johnston's temperate prose could imagine the same of him. Johnston's rejection of Sherman's description not only asserts his own coolness; it reads like a fastidious critic's judgment against what he sees as sensational overwriting, a fault of which Johnston himself could never be accused. But if Sherman overstepped here, perhaps projecting his own heightened sensibility onto his special antagonist, this moment in his *Memoirs* had a long foreground. In 1868, seven years before the publication of his book, Sherman narrated the same moment for his friend John W. Draper, a founder of the New York University School of Medicine and author of the three-volume *History of the American Civil War* (1867–70). Draper's papers include Sherman's earlier version of the moment at the Bennett farmhouse: "The perspiration came in heavy blots on his high forehead as he was reading [the dispatch about Lincoln's assassination], and he made many ejaculations, such as 'Great God!' 'Terrible!' &c.&c. . . . He declaimed against it in terms harsher than I did, and I believed him sincere. I still believe he was sincere."[22]

Johnston's reaction was even more dramatic in this version, and if he could have seen it, he would have been even more displeased than he was with the toned-down version eventually published in Sherman's *Memoirs*. Admittedly, Sherman may have been absolutely truthful in his recounting of Johnston's reaction. It is perfectly possible that in the privacy of the Bennett farmhouse, with both generals' staff officers waiting in the yard, in contrast to well-populated surrender scenes in the McLean parlor at Appomattox, Johnston may have dropped both his guard and his mask in reacting quite naturally to the shocking news of the first assassination of a U.S. president. One can only imagine what Lee and Grant might have said to one another if they, too, had been left alone for a few minutes. But they were not, and after the private moment in the Bennett farmhouse neither were Sherman and Johnston.

What is at stake here is public perception of a private moment between the special antagonists, one with no counterpart at Appomattox. Different points of view will see the same situation differently, and Sherman may have seen Johnston as agitated by news of the assassination, while Johnston was seeing himself as relatively calm under the circumstances. More important, at least to these two soldiers and authors, was the narrative staging of the moment in their respective books. On one level, quite understandably, each man wanted to look composed and self-possessed, especially in the face of all the public criticism and controversy each one encountered, both during the war and after. Military surrender was one thing, but surrender to what Johnston called an unnatural amount of sensibility would have been another thing altogether, one that violated codes of masculinity and conduct becoming an officer. In his official report of May 9, 1865, Sherman showed clearly that in the rhetoric of a military report, he, too, subscribed to these codes, as he described his first interview with Johnston as "frank and soldier-like." No signs of distress, no great drops of perspiration, no agitated ejaculations marked by unsoldierlike exclamation points. These would have to wait for his memoirs.

Friendship Commences

But something else may have been going on, particularly on Sherman's end. Reading the two books side by side, one suspects that Sherman's representation of their special antagonism was an attempt to invent the friendship it purported to describe. In other words, on reading Johnston's rather constrained version of the relationship, Sherman may have been moved, consciously or unconsciously, to extend himself toward Johnston and in doing so attempt to move the relationship up a notch. Sherman's feelings for Johnston appeared in the official records as early as April 23, 1865, when he wrote to his enemy during the tense, unsettled, six-day interval between the signing of their first agreement on Tuesday, April 18, and Monday, April 24, when Grant visited Sherman with the news that the terms of the agreement were rejected and the truce must end immediately. During this fretful interval, also without counterpart at Appomattox, the two opposing generals had to work hard to maintain the status quo and keep their respective lines from changing, in violation of the truce agreement. In particular, Sherman had to rein in his cavalry commander, James H. Wilson, whom he had described to Johnston, in a letter written April 20, the same day Wilson occupied Macon, Georgia, as "impetuous and rapid." Having added, in a letter written to Johnston the next day, that Wilson "seems to have his blood up and will be hard to hold," Sherman returned to the subject of checking his cavalry commander again on April 23, by which date Wilson also had occupied Talladega, Alabama. But this time Sherman added something extra for his special antagonist: "Indeed, I have almost exceeded the bounds of prudence in checking him without the means of direct communication, and only did so on my absolute faith in your personal character."[23]

This was an extraordinary declaration for one human being to make to another, let alone a combatant to his adversary in the midst of especially fraught surrender negotiations. Yet it was pure Sherman, a signature mixture of abiding commitment to an ethos of moral integrity and a trusting, impulsive guilelessness that many might consider imprudent indeed under the circumstances. One has only to recall Sherman's heated correspondence with John Bell Hood about the treatment of the civilians of Atlanta to realize that there was nothing formulaic or perfunctory about his declaration of faith in Johnston's character; Sherman did not make such statements lightly. In fact, readers of his *Memoirs* will find them rare, with Grant the prominent exception eliciting from Sherman such direct second-person expressions of respect and admiration.

Sherman often exceeded the bounds of prudence, especially when it came to talking and writing, but to his credit he often knew it, and if his lack of prudent restraint frequently caused him problems, most spectacularly and painfully in his negotiations toward the rejected first agreement with Johnston, it also produced results with lasting benefits that spread beyond their postwar friendship. Sherman's side of the correspondence with Johnston during the six-day interval between their first agreement and news of its rejection by Washington reads like nothing else in the paper trail left by either the surrender at Appomattox or the one in North Carolina. In his letter of April 21, for example, the same in which he referred to Wilson as having his blood up and being hard to hold, Sherman included the kind of visionary meditation that would have infuriated anyone, such as Edwin M. Stanton, who wanted him to stick to the merely military: "I believe, if the South would simply and publicly declare what we all feel, that slavery is dead, that you would inaugurate an era of peace and prosperity that would soon erase the ravages of the past four years of war." Turning to the subject of the labor force available in freedmen and freedwomen, Sherman slipped into an informal tone more appropriate to subsequent dinner conversations of the late 1870s: "Negroes would remain in the South and afford you abundance of cheap labor which otherwise will be driven away, and it will save the country the senseless discussions which have kept us all in hot water for fifty years." Then, in the next sentence, Sherman's prudence made a token attempt to check him, producing results that testify, with sad irony, to his naïveté: "Although strictly speaking this is no subject of a military convention, yet I am honestly convinced that our simple declaration of a result will be accepted as good law everywhere." A final sentence only compounded the irony: "Of course I have not a single word from Washington on this or any other point of our agreement, but I know the effect of such a step by us will be universally accepted."[24]

The official records do not contain any direct response by Johnston to Sherman's dizzying dilation into personal opinions about the proper course of reconstruction, a dilation well beyond the bounds of a military convention, but clearly Sherman's letters, and the actions they announced, had a profound effect on him. On April 23 Sherman addressed an unofficial letter, accompanying a bundle of papers with the latest news about the assassins and their victims, to both Johnston and Confederate lieutenant general William J. Hardee, a letter that included his views on the negative effects the assassination would have on the South, as well as the bald statement, "I am thus frank with you and have asserted as much to the War Department." Sherman's next long letter to Johnston came on April 27, after three short, terse ones of April 23–24, in which he conveyed the arrival of the reply from Washington, the rejection of their first agreement, and his demand for Johnston's surrender on the same terms offered to Lee "pure and simply." On April 27, with the final agreement of April 26 now signed and behind them, Sherman sent Johnston copies of his Field Orders Nos. 65 and 66, empowering Schofield to carry out the surrender terms, along with an offer of ten days' rations for twenty-five thousand men. This magnanimous gesture might well have been enough to stir Johnston's gratitude, but for good measure Sherman threw in another memorable example of his unguarded frankness: "Now that the war is over, I am as willing to risk my person and reputation as heretofore to heal the wounds made by the past war, and I think my feeling is shared by the whole army."[25]

In reading over Sherman's often effusive side of the correspondence, one may be tempted to ascribe to him a certain amount of strategic calculation, as though he knowingly weighed everything he wrote to Johnston with fully prescient anticipation of the eventual publication of their correspondence by the Government Printing Office. But although Sherman had learned the hard way, beginning as early as his service in Kentucky in 1862, that he was a public figure whose statements were subject to critical scrutiny by a national audience, a full reading of his letters and his *Memoirs* leads to the conclusion that his intelligence, which was both quick and deep, did not necessarily include this kind of calculation. In contrast with Abraham Lincoln, who had an unusual capacity to see a given situation from multiple points of view, Sherman tended to see things from his own perspective, credit others with seeing the world as clearly as he did, and then wince in bewildered and indignant astonishment when it turned out otherwise. In the negotiations with Johnston at the Bennett farmhouse, he encountered someone who did see many things as he did, or so he believed, and the correspondence that accompanied and followed those negotiations reflected Sherman's immediate, instinctive trust in what he took to be a congruence of visions, not his shrewdly far-sighted performance before the audience of posterity.

The proof that Sherman's instincts were sound, at least about Johnston, if not at all about Washington, came the next day in Johnston's answer of April 28. For a dutiful reader of Johnston's *Narrative*, and his side of the official correspondence with Sherman, the moving mixture of professional utterance with private feeling makes his response stand out: "The enlarged patriotism manifested in these papers reconciles me to what I had previously regarded as the misfortune of my life—that of having had you to encounter in the field. The enlightened and humane policy you have adopted will certainly be successful. It is fortunate for the people of North Carolina that your views are to be carried out by one so capable of appreciating them. I hope that you are as well represented in the other departments of your command; if so, an early and complete pacification in it may be expected." Having demonstrated in this well-crafted blending of complex and simple sentences the ready pen with which Sherman credited him in the later letter to the Appletons, Johnston "very gladly" accepted Sherman's "generous offer" of food for his troops and then went on to confirm the like-mindedness of the special antagonists: "The disposition you express to heal the wounds made by the past war has been evident to me in all our interviews. You are right that similar feelings are entertained by the mass of the army. I am sure that all the leading men in it will exert their influence for that object."[26]

As it turned out, Johnston was no better than Sherman at seeing the end of the war from points of view radically different from his own. Among the leading men of the Confederate army who did not entertain similar feelings, Jubal A. Early and Nathan Bedford Forrest immediately come to mind as counterexamples. But his April 28 letter to Sherman marked the written beginning of their friendship and anticipated the public performance of that friendship, along with the mythologizing of it that culminated, and continues to this day, in the public narration of Johnston's presence at Sherman's funeral services in New York on February 19, 1891.

Johnston at Sherman's Funeral

Front-page coverage of the funeral procession in the *New York Times* (Sherman would be buried in St. Louis on February 21) helped set the dominant tone, beginning with a rhythmic catalog of warriors that echoed English translations of Homeric epic: "Then came the pallbearers. An added sense of melancholy confronted the sightseer as the veterans came into view: the brave Schofield; Howard, who gave an arm to the cause while commanding Sherman's right wing; Braine, whose shells crashed against Forts Fisher and Anderson; Greer, who fought beside Porter at Vicksburg; Sickles, Dodge, and Corse; Swayne, Woodford, Wright, and Moore, brave men and true—these did the last honors beside the bier of their lamented chieftain." Then, after this long and resonant sentence, came the dramatic turn with all its rolling, sonorous parallelism:

"There was another face among them—that of Johnston, the same Joseph E. Johnston who threw himself and his army before Sherman in the march to the sea—the same Johnston, who in April, 1865, surrendered to the soldier whose corpse he was following in sorrow." The heightened language was certainly compelling, even if some of the facts were wrong, Johnston having been relieved of command four months before Sherman began his March to the Sea.[27]

Serving as an honorary pallbearer was nothing new to Johnston at this point. Six years earlier, in 1885, he had performed the same service at the funerals of Grant and his old friend George B. McClellan. But the coverage of his presence at Sherman's funeral set it apart. The mythmaking began with obituaries printed after Johnston died in Washington, D.C., four weeks later on March 21, 1891. On this occasion the *New York Times* stated that "the General had been suffering for the past three weeks with an affection of the heart, aggravated by a cold he caught soon after Gen. Sherman's funeral in New-York." The same sentence appeared in the *Chicago Sunday Tribune*, and the *Washington Post* also mentioned Johnston's cold, "supposed to have been contracted while he was in attendance on the Sherman obsequies." The *Los Angeles Times* did not mention the cold or Sherman's funeral, but the subheading of its obituary echoed the emerging tenor: "The Confederate General Who Became Sherman's Friend." Two weeks later *Harper's Weekly* drove the point home with a rhetorical flourish: "The day of the funeral pageant was cold and raw, and the ex-Confederate soldier suffered so far from the exposure that he died of it, and so gave up his life in showing this last respect to the memory of the man whose forces he had once tried to cut to pieces."[28]

With the appearance of Robert M. Hughes's biography of Johnston two years later, the causal link between Johnston's service as a pallbearer for Sherman and his own death was firmly established: "Though unusually feeble at the time, Johnston attended the obsequies; and the bad weather which prevailed gave him a cold, which greatly enfeebled him." Although the nineteenth century believed that cold weather could cause colds, a belief embedded in the continuing use of "cold" to mean "a viral infection characterized by inflammation of the mucous membranes of the respiratory passages and accompanying fever, chills, coughing, and sneezing," as defined by the *American Heritage Dictionary*, the present does not concur. In the words of the *Merck Manual of Medical Information*, "Becoming chilled doesn't by itself cause colds or increase a person's susceptibility to infection by a respiratory virus. A person's general health or eating habits don't seem to make any difference either." What is noteworthy here is not that the present thinks differently from the past about the common cold; what is noteworthy is that despite its different thinking the present continues to repeat the discredited causality in the case of Johnston at Sherman's funeral, as in, for example, Craig L. Symonds's biography of Johnston (1992) or Edward G. Longacre's *Worthy Opponents* (2006). The myth is too attractive and compelling to discard.[29]

Making the myth more attractive and more compelling was Oliver Otis Howard's account of Sherman's funeral in his two-volume *Autobiography*, published in 1907. There Howard put words into Johnston's mouth, words that do not appear in the original newspaper coverage or in Hughes's biography but that nevertheless continue to be repeated as frequently as any quotable lines associated with Civil War memory. Howard's full account went this way: "The weather was exceedingly cold. Some one said to General Joseph E. Johnston, one of the bearers: 'General, put on your hat, you will take cold.' Johnston answered: 'If I were in his place and he standing here in mine he would not put on his hat.'" Howard then went on to moralize Johnston's utterance in case anyone had missed the point: "Thus delicately he signified his deep regard for Sherman. In fact, these two, after their campaign was over, behaved always toward each other as brothers."[30]

Here was the myth of reconciliation much of the country wanted and needed. It took the familiar image of "the brothers' war" or of "brother against brother"—referring literally to families divided by the war, especially in the border states and Upper South, as well as figuratively to fellow citizens pitted against each other in civil war—and extended it. Strangers to each other in the regular army, Johnston and Sherman were not antebellum brothers sadly divided by the war; it was the war itself that made them brothers. In their case the war was not the occasion for tragic fratricide; it was the agent of their postwar fraternity. Magnanimous and dignified as Lee and Grant had been at Appomattox, they could offer the popular imagination nothing comparable.

Those who have repeated and continue to repeat what Johnston supposedly said at Sherman's funeral either quote and cite Howard's 1907 version of the famous statement made sixteen years earlier—if not others who quote and cite Howard—or a slightly varied version that appeared a quarter-century after Howard's in Lloyd Lewis's biography *Sherman: Fighting Prophet* (1932). Because of the citation conventions Lewis adopted in his endnotes, his source for Johnston's famous reply is not clear; he simply cited "newspapers of the time," which did not contain it. In his version of the funeral, however, Lewis introduced another perspective, that of Sherman's son-in-law, Alexander Montgomery Thackara, from whom Lewis did receive a statement, according to his endnotes, although he did not make clear whether Thackara's statement was the source for Johnston's words. At any rate, Lewis's version of the famous moment went like this:

> The day was raw and cold. Bareheaded stood the honorary pallbearers. One was seen by Thackara to bend toward the oldest of the group, a man who had celebrated his eighty-second birthday twelve days earlier. He said:
>
> "General, please put on your hat; you might get sick."
>
> Joe Johnston turned. "If I were in his place and he were standing here in mine, he would not put on his hat." From this last meeting with Sherman, Johnston would not retreat. In his breast as he went home were the seeds of the pneumonia that killed him ten days later.[31]

Although Lewis had a flare for readable narrative, the calendar does not seem to have been his specialty. Johnston had turned eighty-four sixteen days earlier, not eighty-two twelve days earlier, and he died thirty days later, not ten. Although Thackara would seem from internal evidence to be Lewis's source here, his bibliography did include Howard's *Autobiography*, even if the relevant endnote did not. Perhaps Lewis got his version from Howard; perhaps he got it from Thackara, who had gotten it from Howard. Either way, what is telling is that Lewis's slight variant introduced into Howard's version, along with a comma, a second "were" that bolstered even further Johnston's suspiciously metrical reply, one that, broken into lines of verse, suggests an iambic sound shape, alternating stressed and unstressed syllables: "If *I* were *in* his *place* / and *he* were *stand*ing *here* in *mine*, / *he* would *not* put *on* his *hat*."

The response Howard attributed to Johnston came ready-made for admission into public imagination. Did an eighty-four-year-old man standing bareheaded in cold, raw weather, with the seeds of pneumonia in his lungs and with no record in print of any previous tendency toward metrical composition, suddenly erupt spontaneously into such resonant elegance? It is not very likely. But it is believable that Johnston said something similar, and simpler, and if Howard's recollection burnished the response a decade and a half later, one should not attribute to him any motives less than honorable. Howard, too, was a writer with a ready pen, one who turned to writing in the 1870s because he "was forced to do something to earn money over and beyond my pay." But unlike some writers, he did not direct his ready pen toward promoting postwar images of fraternal reconciliation intended to reassure only the white populations of the formerly opposed sections, images that ignored or suppressed the concurrent realities of life for many Black people. Commissioner of the

Freedmen's Bureau, as well as founding president of Howard University, the so-called Christian General was anything but indifferent to the racial dimensions of reconciliation. If the words he transmitted from Johnston's mouth to the reading public were somewhat new and improved—there is no statement in his *Autobiography* that he was necessarily the first recipient of Johnston's words, so they may have come to him already secondhand—that improvement certainly did not reflect any self-serving motive on his part or any devious scheme to harmonize some people while excluding others.[32]

Whatever size the grain of salt should be to acknowledge the inevitable vicissitudes of oral transmission and later recollection, Howard's account of Johnston at Sherman's funeral in February 1891 finally completed the surrender in North Carolina that began nearly twenty-six years before. Whereas the requisite two parts of the Appomattox surrender occurred within days of each other and did so with a fictive, mythic potential subsequently fulfilled by the writings and speeches of Joshua Lawrence Chamberlain and John Brown Gordon, the second part of the North Carolina surrender, the one that involved delivering or handing over, did not come into its fully fictive, mythic force until, in the words of *Harper's Weekly*, Johnston "gave up his life in showing this last respect to the memory of the man whose forces he had once tried to cut to pieces." The soldiers remaining in the Army of Tennessee may have sporadically handed over their arms, without pageantry or fanfare, to the small body of U.S. soldiers detailed to receive them near the railroad depot in Greensboro during late April and early May 1865, but the ceremonial and richly symbolic handing over occurred when the public began to imagine, with the help of various writers, both anonymous and named, that Joseph Eggleston Johnston self-sacrificingly handed over his life to the memory of William Tecumseh Sherman, thereby effecting a closure, in the eyes of warriors and civilians, that approached, even reached, the sublime.

3

DESTRUCTION AND RECONSTRUCTION IN RICHARD TAYLOR'S HAPPY VALLEY

Having published William T. Sherman's memoirs in 1875, D. Appleton and Company did not follow with another book by a top U.S. commander until it brought out Admiral David Dixon Porter's *Incidents and Anecdotes of the Civil War* in 1885. During the ten years between Sherman's book and Porter's, Appleton continued to publish major Confederate titles in the wake of Joseph E. Johnston's 1874 *Narrative of Military Operations*, among them Richard Taylor's *Destruction and Reconstruction: Personal Experiences of the Late War*, which appeared in 1879, shortly before the former Confederate lieutenant general died of dropsy at the age of fifty-three. Douglas Southall Freeman included both Confederate generals' memoirs in the "Controversy and Apologia" chapter of *The South to Posterity* (1939). But though the two books have controversy and apologia in common, as they do with other Confederate titles on Freeman's list of "Distinguished Personal Narratives" in his bibliographic finale, "A Confederate Book Shelf," they are very different books, as Freeman himself recognized.[1]

"Had the beam of fate been tipped in the opposite direction, he probably would have risen high," Freeman mused about Zachary Taylor's son. The same might be true of other Confederate generals who wrote memoirs; yet Taylor and his book stand out from the rest. In *The Cotton Kingdom* (1861), Frederick Law Olmsted described Richard Taylor, at home on his Louisiana plantation, as "a man of more than usual precision of mind, energetic and humane." Olmsted hid Taylor's identity behind the abbreviated pseudonym "Mr. R.," so few readers would have recognized him, especially in the North, but they might have recognized the statement about slavery Olmsted attributed to Mr. R., if they knew Thomas Jefferson's earlier pronouncements on the subject. "Mr. R. himself also acknowledged Slavery to be a very great evil, morally and economically," Olmsted reported. "It was a curse upon the South; he had no doubt about it at all: nothing would be more desirable than its removal, if it were possible to be accomplished," the New England visitor to the Lower Mississippi continued before adding, "But he did not think it could be accomplished without instituting greater evils than those sought to be remedied."[2]

Whatever Olmsted's 1861 readers thought of such sentiments, or whatever Freeman's 1939 readers thought of his image of the fateful beam tipping in the opposite direction, many twenty-first-century readers will resist separating Richard Taylor's unusual precision of mind from his status as a wealthy slaveholder; had there been statues of him, they might well have come down. Whereas Joseph E. Johnston did not mention slavery once in his *Narrative of Military Operations,* Taylor named it in his first paragraph and several times afterward. But this was not the only difference between Johnston's book and Taylor's; Taylor's book shows that he was deliberately, self-consciously literary in his ambitions. For all that his book shared with other examples of Confederate literature that had, according to Freeman, sufficient conviction, sincerity, and human appeal to interest a new generation of Americans in the southern perspective, Taylor's literary ambitions distinguished him among Confederate generals who published memoirs. Although those ambitions may not sway a new generation toward a southern point of view, they produced a significant book for the Civil War memory market. Its significance does not depend wholly on its place in Lost Cause mythmaking.[3]

"'Tis dangerous to be out of harmony with the practices of one's time." This warning appears in a late chapter of *Destruction and Reconstruction* titled "Closing Operations of the War—Surrender." Taylor's sentence concludes a story about an unnamed Bank of Tennessee official arrested by U.S. authorities in the spring of 1865. At the insistence of former Tennessee governor Isham Harris, the unnamed official had traveled to Nashville to return the coin of the bank, removed by Harris three years earlier when he withdrew from Nashville on the retreat of Albert Sidney Johnston's Army of Central Kentucky from that city. The bank official was "incarcerated for his fidelity" despite the protective escort detailed by U.S. major general Edward Canby, to whom Taylor surrendered the forces of the Department of Alabama, Mississippi, and East Louisiana in May 1865. Commenting on the fate of the official, the author of *Destruction and Reconstruction* observed wryly, "Had he betrayed his trust, he might have received rewards instead of stripes." Fully adequate to the task of closure as this penultimate sentence would have been, Taylor chose to nudge the moral of the story up one more notch with the additional warning about falling out of harmony with the practices of one's times.[4]

In Richard Taylor's version of Reconstruction, few honorable deeds of postwar southern fidelity went unpunished, and the implicit rhyming of his own situation with that of the incarcerated bank official must have motivated, at least in part, the moralizing sentence he distinguished with the archaic "'Tis." Much as he relished flamboyant displays of literariness and erudition, Taylor resorted to the archaic "'tis" only four other times in his book. It appears three times within direct quotations (twice from French general Pierre Bosquet and once from Richard Ewell, Confederate major general at the time) and once in a similarly moralizing moment based on the maxims of French marshal Thomas Robert Bugeaud: "Moral: 'Tis easier to watch and defend one bridge than many miles of fordable water." Evidently Taylor reserved this archaism for special occasions, and the final one, "'Tis dangerous to be out of harmony with the practices of one's times," was the most special of all. It could serve as the epigraph for *Destruction and Reconstruction*.[5]

In many ways *Destruction and Reconstruction* is about disharmony, most obviously the violent disharmonies of the "late war" and the volatile period of Reconstruction that followed. In addition to the collective, public disharmony of 1860 to 1877 in the United States, however, there are the many ways in which Richard Taylor himself was out of harmony with the practices of his times. Son of a U.S. president, brother-in-law of the Confederate States president, graduate of Yale, successful member of the Louisiana plantation class, state senator, delegate to the national Democratic convention in Charleston in the spring of 1860, the young aristocrat seemed to have set all the bells ringing. Impending shifts and changes across nineteenth-century North America would soon render their chiming discordant.[6]

Elsewhere in his memoir, much of which he drafted during 1877 in Winchester, Virginia, where he took up residence to be near his sister Betty (Mrs. Philip Dandridge) after the death of his wife, Myrthe (Mimi), in 1875, Taylor employed the same telling phrase to describe himself that he used for the Bank of Tennessee official. The Louisiana convention on secession having voted in January 1861 "by an immense majority" to leave the Union, Taylor, with a dash of the irony he kept ready to hand, "marveled at the joyous and careless temper in which men, much my superiors in sagacity and experience, consummated these acts." He then followed this remark, which appears only five pages into his narrative, with the first of many allusions to military history that stud his writing, as they apparently studded his charismatic conversation. This one pointed to the "*gaîté de coeur* that M. Ollivier [French premier Émile Ollivier] claimed for the Imperial Ministry when war was declared against Prussia" in July 1870. With the humiliating defeat of the French by the Prussians fresh in the minds of his 1879 readers, Taylor's allusion to the gay hearts of warmongers would have been especially effective in characterizing the naive ardor of southern secessionists. He then turned to the formulation that at this early moment in the story, instead of moralizing on what had transpired, foreshadowed what was to come. "As soon as the Convention adjourned, finding myself out of harmony with prevailing opinion as to the certainty of war and necessity for preparation, I retired to my estate, determined to accept such responsibility only as came to me unsought."[7]

Richard Taylor found himself out of harmony with his times in 1861 and at many moments afterward. He had outspoken, often insubordinate disagreements with his superior, Lieutenant General Edmund Kirby Smith, about the conduct of operations in Louisiana, especially during the Red River Campaign of spring 1864. His initial efforts during the summer of 1865 to win the release of Jefferson Davis from Fort Monroe, Virginia, efforts he made in meetings with President Andrew Johnson, Secretary of State William Seward, Thaddeus Stevens, Charles Sumner, and other government officials, were tense and fraught. But for all these disharmonies, to which we could add the disharmony of Taylor's practices and worldview with prevailing attitudes toward the Civil War era in our own time, *Destruction and Reconstruction* stands out in the literary-military history of the Civil War for several reasons.

One is that it offers readers much more than unalloyed self-justification of the kind that, in combination with ongoing grievance and feuding, soured Joseph E. Johnston's *Narrative of Military Operations*. Taylor could certainly marshal biting invective in his own defense, as he demonstrated deftly in his first footnote, which closes the third chapter, "After Manassas." In response to former Confederate vice president Alexander Stephens's charge that a piece Taylor published in the *North American Review* in 1878 had been guilty of a "Munchausenism," or an extravagant fiction like the ones concocted by the eponymous protagonist of Rudolf Erich Raspe's *Baron Munchausen's Narrative of his Marvelous Travels and Campaigns in Russia* (1785), Taylor fired off this volley: "Like other ills, feeble health has its compensations, especially for those who unite restless vanity and ambition to a feminine desire for sympathy. It has been much the habit of Mr. Stephens to date controversial epistles from 'a sick chamber,' as do ladies in a delicate situation. A diplomatist of the last century, the Chevalier D'Eon, by usurping the privileges of the opposite sex, inspired grave doubts concerning his own." The elaborate artfulness of this put-down, elusively recondite as it may be to twenty-first-century readers, barely softens the viciousness intended. Taylor first linked Stephens's sickliness—from which Taylor himself, suffering from chronic rheumatoid arthritis, was not always free—to vanity and unmanliness. He then compared Stephen's unmanly vanity to the condition of a woman either pregnant or menstruating. Finally, he alluded to the sexual ambiguity of a cross-dressing French diplomat and spy, who because of his androgynous appearance successfully infiltrated the Russian court dressed as a woman, afterward spending his last thirty-three years identifying as one and prompting Havelock Ellis to coin the term "eonism" for transgender behavior.[8]

This is a singular example, rare in a narrative otherwise generous with praise and encomia for friends and enemies alike. The rhetorical theatricality behind it points to another reason *Destruction and Reconstruction* stands out in the literary-military history of the Civil War: in Douglas Southall Freeman's often-quoted formulation, Richard Taylor was "the one Confederate general who possessed literary art that approached the first rank." Had Freeman known Edward Porter Alexander's *Fighting for the Confederacy*, not published until 1989, he might have admitted a second Confederate general to this elite distinction. Without that comparative knowledge, however, Freeman focused his brief assessment of Taylor's book on praising the "literary charm" of a writer who was "so observant an analys[t] of character," one whose "remarkable book" is "fascinating, rich in historical allusion and written with the unmistakable touch of cultured scholarship."[9]

Twenty-three years later in *Patriotic Gore* (1962), Edmund Wilson supplemented Freeman's assessment with eight eccentric pages, five of which go to Stonewall Jackson and Taylor's "unique and piquant" portrait of him. In these pages Wilson can sound as though he echoed Freeman's Lost Cause notes, but for the Marxist-pacificist northerner the truth was more complex. Whereas Freeman, the Virginia newspaperman, had his own reasons for defending Confederate legacies, Wilson railed against Lincoln and what he saw as northern suppression of the South not because he defended slavery but because he saw northern hard-war policy as the forerunner of aggressive U.S. militarism in World War II and the Cold War. In the three pages he devoted to Taylor himself, Wilson described *Destruction and Reconstruction* as "the masculine document that, from the point of view of realistic intelligence, is most nearly comparable to Mary Chesnut's diary." Wilson also commented on Taylor's allusions to literature and military history, which "show a wide range of reading." But his most incisive and useful formulation remains this one: "Richard Taylor is conscious, and a little vain, of being a *rara avis*; he is a connoisseur of soldiers and battles; he plays his fine role with a shade of disdain, even, perhaps, with a shade of enjoyment—vain, also, and almost perverse—of its gratuitousness and ultimate futility."[10]

The literary art of *Destruction and Reconstruction* will be one of the strands that runs through this discussion, but it is important from the outset to state explicitly that Taylor's literary artfulness is not identical with his compulsive alluding to literature and military history. To begin with, he did not always get the allusions right. In the sketch of Joseph E. Johnston that opens the chapter entitled "The Valley Campaign," for example, Taylor spoke of the general this way: "To the East, as his great namesake Albert Sidney to the West, he was 'the rose and fair expectancy' of our cause." In alluding to Ophelia's speech in *Hamlet*, act 3, scene 1, Taylor did what most of us have done, quoting from memory without checking the original. Had he done so, he would have found Ophelia struggling to absorb the feigned madness of her erstwhile lover, the Prince of Denmark, who has just exited the stage, having recommended she get herself to a nunnery: "O, what a noble mind is here o'er-thrown!— / The courtier's, soldier's, scholar's, eye, tongue, sword, / The expectancy and rose of the fair state." Minor as the mistake may seem, it can be harder to overlook in the case of someone "sharp-tongued and rather arrogant with his equals," as Edmund Wilson put it. This particular slip of the pen could lead, moreover, to deeper reading by those inclined to make something of Taylor's transference of the adjective "fair" from the state—toward which, in the case of a confederacy based on secession, he had his ambivalences—to the hopeful expectation for its success.[11]

Taylor's allusions reveal assumptions about literacy that differ radically from our own. Between, on the one hand, distracted, skimming readers who increasingly prize brevity and user-friendliness above all things and, on the other, a writer steeped in European military history through the nineteenth century, as well as in English literature up through Sir Walter Scott, yawns a vast and widening gulf. Taylor's relentless exhibition of his reading and learning will not endear him to many readers now; yet the irony is that our own moment, though not so well read, is better equipped to decipher Taylor than many of the contemporaries he set out to impress and intimidate with his erudition. If ever a writer lent himself to the swift demystifications afforded by digital search engines, it is Richard Taylor. What a few good reference books cannot solve, a few taps on a screen or keyboard can.

Even with all allusions decoded and defanged, the question is, Why allude at all? Some of the answers that follow overlap with yet another reason *Destruction and Reconstruction* stands out: Taylor's fifth chapter, "The Valley Campaign," which is the longest in his book and unanimously considered the best. Edmund Wilson's tunnel-vision concentration on Taylor's influential portrait of Stonewall Jackson speaks for the way many readers remember *Destruction and Reconstruction*, and Douglas Southall Freeman's remark that "the earlier chapters on Taylor's service with Jackson are more thrilling than his later narrative of his checkmating campaigns in Louisiana" confirms the appraisal. Five years after Freeman's statement appeared in print, he acknowledged the influence of Taylor's view of Jackson's Valley Campaign, claiming that it helped establish the pattern of subsequent narratives through G. F. R. Henderson's *Stonewall Jackson and the American Civil War* (1898). Because Jackson and his Valley Campaign occupy a large place in Lost Cause memory, Taylor's portrait of the Confederate icon still figures in controversial debates, though the source of the portrait often goes unrecognized or unidentified. Douglas Southall Freeman's own narrative of the Valley Campaign in the first volume of *Lee's Lieutenants* (1942) frequently refers to and quotes from *Destruction and Reconstruction*, albeit with healthy detachment. Nearly half a century later, Taylor's influence surfaced again in a prominent place, this time in James McPherson's *Battle Cry of Freedom* (1988), which recycled, without acknowledgment, Taylor's memorable description of Richard Ewell, a portrait that blends affection, admiration, sympathy, and caricature in the mode of Charles Dickens.[12]

Taylor as Instructor

Even a brief comparison of "The Valley Campaign" with, for example, Taylor's ninth chapter, which bears the elongated title "Attacked by the Federals—Attempt to Relieve Vicksburg—Capture of Berwick's Bay," underscores the unique achievement of the former. By contrast with "The Valley Campaign," Taylor's ninth chapter contains no piquant portraits of fellow officers, no observant analysis of character, no enlarging digressions, no entertaining anecdotes, no thrilling battle narrative, no self-deprecating humor, or for that matter little humor of any kind, unless one includes biting sarcasm. Except for two brief, relatively accessible allusions late in the chapter—one to the rowdy brawling associated with the Irish at Donnybrook Fair and one to Leonidas and the Spartans at Thermopylae—the whole could have been written by Joseph E. Johnston. Taylor knew Johnston's method of appealing for exoneration to documentary evidence from reading the older man's *Narrative*, and on occasion Taylor borrowed Johnston's method, three times invoking the "Report on the Conduct of the War," as well as the report of a U.S. major after he was exchanged.[13]

What we do get in the ninth chapter, and what may appear to account for much of its lackluster flatness, is a vulnerable and moving paragraph in which Taylor recounted the news that two of his sons had died of scarlet fever. The paragraph closes this way: "I was stunned by this intelligence, so unexpected, and it was well perhaps that the absorbing character of my duties left no time for the indulgence of private grief; but it was sad to think of the afflicted mother, alone with her dead and dying, deprived of the consolation of my presence. Many days passed before we met, and then but for an hour." One could argue that the flatness of the narrative in the later chapter reflects the stunning of the narrator or the solemnity appropriate to the news Taylor had received. But such an argument quickly shows its limitations when one considers that he was just as recently bereaved—having lost Mimi, too, by the time of writing—when he sat down to draft "The Valley Campaign."[14]

Taylor's allusions to English literature reveal that when he sat down to draft his book, most often he invoked writers of the eighteenth century. In "The Valley Campaign," for example, we encounter echoes of or references to Horace Walpole, Richard Steele, Laurence Sterne, and Samuel Johnson. If we back up to the previous chapter, "Opening of the Peninsular Campaign," we find Thomas Gray. In the chapter before that one, "After Manassas," we encounter a phrase from the opening lines of Alexander Pope's translation of Homer's *Iliad* (1715–20), "the spring of woes unnumbered," which Taylor borrowed to compare the debilitating rift between Joseph E. Johnston and Jefferson Davis to the destructive wrath of Achilles. "The Valley Campaign" alludes to writings and writers from other centuries as well, among them the book of Genesis, Rabelais, and Shakespeare, but references to John Bunyan's *Pilgrim's Progress* (1678) and Walter Scott's *Guy Mannering* (1815) meanwhile fall within the penumbra of what some might call the long eighteenth century.[15]

Another disharmony for Taylor was one between his eighteenth-century literary sensibility, in one corner, and, in the other, the contemporary literary worlds of nineteenth-century Great Britain and the United States, which having passed through romanticism were exploring various versions of what often gets lumped into the baggy category "realism." With reference to "The Valley Campaign," what matters is that Taylor's inclination toward the British eighteenth century, which literary histories habitually designate the Augustan Age, neoclassicism, the Enlightenment, the Age of Reason, or the Age of

Satire, aligned his sense of aesthetics with a well-known dictum from Horace's *Ars poetica* (ca. 19 BCE). Subsequently transmitted through French writers to Alexander Pope and other eighteenth-century Britons, Horace's Latin, *Omne tulit punctum qui miscuit utile dulci*, could be translated, "The one who has mixed the useful with the delightful has carried every vote."[16]

For neoclassicists influenced by Horace's line, the more familiar formulation is usually something like "Good writing should delight and instruct." In his skillful mixing of delight with instruction, Richard Taylor revealed his deep commitment to the neoclassical worldview of eighteenth-century literariness. That he set out in *Destruction and Reconstruction* to instruct his readers is evident from the beginning of the book. At the opening of his second chapter, "First Scenes of the War," for example, Taylor described an invitation from Braxton Bragg, at the time Confederate brigadier general, to come to Pensacola, Florida, "where he commanded the southern forces, composed of volunteers from the adjacent States." Of these southern volunteers Taylor had this to say: "Full of enthusiasm for their cause, and of the best material, officers and men were, with few exceptions, without instruction, and the number of educated officers was, as in all the southern armies, too limited to satisfy the imperious demands of the staff, much less those of the drill-master."[17]

Various forms of the word "instruct" recur through *Destruction and Reconstruction*, suggesting the high value Taylor placed on proper instruction combined with discipline, but the clearest statement of his didactic intention to instruct others appears in the final paragraph of "Opening the Peninsular Campaign," the chapter that precedes "The Valley Campaign":

> These observations are not for the "heaven-born," who from their closets scan with eagle glance fields of battle, whose mighty pens slay their thousands and their tens of thousands, and in whose "Serbonian" inkstands "armies whole" disappear; but it is hoped that they may prove useful to the young adopting the profession of arms, who may feel assured that the details of the art of war afford "scope and verge" for the employment of all their faculties. Conscientious study will not perhaps make them great, but it will make them respectable; and when the responsibility of command comes, they will not disgrace their flag, injure their cause, nor murder their men.[18]

In moving through this paragraph, a reader has to fight through a thicket of allusions to the Homeric epithet "heaven-born" (διογένης or *diogenes*); to 1 Samuel 18:7 in the King James Version ("Saul hath slain his thousands, and

David his ten thousands"); to book 2 of John Milton's *Paradise Lost* (1674; "A gulf profound as that Serbonian bog / Betwixt Damiata and Mount Casius old, / Where armies whole have sunk"); and to Thomas Gray's *The Bard: A Pindaric Ode* (1757; "Give ample room, and verge enough / The characters of hell to trace," misquoted by Horace Walpole in a letter of June 26, 1778, apparently Taylor's source, as "ample scope and verge enough"). Once the thicket has been cleared, however, the point of Taylor's paragraph appears to be straightforward enough: this book is intended to be "useful" (Horace's *utile*) to "the young adopting the profession of arms" because if they study this instruction conscientiously, they will acquit themselves respectably, not disgracefully.

Was Richard Taylor's aim really so didactically straightforward? One does not need Sigmund Freud or the theory of the Oedipus complex to suspect that Taylor's preoccupation with reading and alluding to military history had something to do with finding himself the grandson of a lieutenant colonel in the American Revolution and the son of a Mexican War hero. Taylor spent about eight years of his young life at military posts, first at Fort Snelling in Minnesota and then at Fort Crawford in Wisconsin. Having graduated from Yale in August 1845, he set out in June of the following year, at the age of twenty, to discuss his career prospects with his father, then camped in Mexico at Matamoros after victories at Palo Alto and Resaca de la Palma had brought him national fame. Despite an attack of rheumatoid arthritis in New Orleans while in route, Taylor joined his father in July 1846 and remained with him until August, when General Taylor sent him home because of his ill health. During their time together in Mexico, Old Rough and Ready firmly rejected suggestions that his son be appointed to his staff, believing the appointment inappropriate after other qualified young officers had applied for such positions.[19]

These bare biographical facts go a long way toward accounting for Richard Taylor's interest in military history, but in themselves they do not explain the intensity of his preoccupation with it, nor do they immediately clarify the complicated literary role that military history played in the shaping of *Destruction and Reconstruction* in general and of "The Valley Campaign" in particular. It is worth noting, for example, that Taylor's index, which is both idiosyncratic and revealing, contains no entry for his father, although his father appears at least ten times in the book. His first two appearances introduce Taylor *père* unceremoniously in passing as "Colonel Zachary Taylor" commanding in Florida during the Second Seminole War at the Battle of Okeechobee, December 25, 1837, and "General Zachary Taylor" commanding the U.S. Army near Matamoros in the early summer of 1846. Not until "The Valley Campaign" does the man whose military achievements got him elected twelfth president of the United States become "my father," and then only twice, in connection with memorable vignettes to be considered soon. After his second appearance in "The Valley Campaign," he reverts to General Zachary Taylor, who disappears from the narrative, except for one brief mention in a paragraph about Braxton Bragg, until a final cluster of late invocations, in the context of antebellum Whig politics, in the chapter "Criticisms and Reflections."[20]

Beyond his apparent ambivalence toward his father, it is also worth noting that the author of *Destruction and Reconstruction*, who stoutly maintained the necessity of studying military history for proper instruction in the profession of arms, did not have anything favorable to say about West Point, which his father never attended. When the younger Taylor referred to the United States Military Academy, he usually did so neutrally, merely noting particular officers' education there, among them, in order of appearance, fellow Confederates William H. T. Walker, Richard Ewell, Richard Garnett, Thomas J. Jackson, Jefferson Davis, Braxton Bragg, Albert Sidney Johnston, and Edmund Kirby Smith, as well as Union general Andrew Jackson Smith. Taylor's reference to A. J. Smith's West Point education cut with an implicit edge, as from Taylor's point of view neither the West Point education nor long service in the regular army prevented Smith's "outrages" against "weeping women and children" when he burned Alexandria, Louisiana, on May 13, 1864, although Taylor laid the ultimate blame for this destruction on Smith's superior, William T. Sherman.[21]

It was when he came to Ulysses S. Grant, about whom he also had mixed feelings, that Taylor offered his most negative assessment of a West Point education. Having praised the Republican president twenty pages earlier for "his modesty and his generosity," in the phrasing of his index entry on Grant, Taylor was not so kind to him subsequently in a passage bristling with allusions to *Twelfth Night* and *Othello*, caliph Harun al-Rashid and tyrant Phalaris of Akragas. "Though he had wasted but little time on books since leaving West Point, where in his day the curriculum was limited, he had found out to the last shilling the various sums voted by Parliament to the Duke of Wellington, and spoke of them in a manner indicating his opinion that he was another example of the ingratitude of republics." Grant graduated twenty-first out of thirty-nine in the class of 1843. If the curriculum at West Point was limited then, then it was also probably limited during the educations of the other West Pointers mentioned by Taylor, all of whom preceded Grant, with the exceptions of Jackson (1846) and Kirby Smith (1845). Even more damning, if Grant wasted little time on books since leaving West Point, and if the curriculum was limited when he was there, the implication is that he learned precious little from books at all, at least according to Taylor, who by this point had been working tirelessly for nearly three hundred pages to establish himself as the exact opposite of such an unlettered person.[22]

Taylor's 1862 Valley Campaign

The subtotal of the above is that *Destruction and Reconstruction* announced itself explicitly as a source of military instruction for young soldiers and offered itself implicitly as a preferable alternative, or at the very least a necessary supplement, to the limitations of a West Point education. Extravagant as these claims may sound, Taylor was not the only Civil War officer whose particular gifts enabled him to read his way from private citizenship into the path that led to high command; Joshua Lawrence Chamberlain did so, too. But beyond its instructional mission, Taylor's book set out to delight and give pleasure, at least in "The Valley Campaign." The word "delight" may sound strange when it comes to narration of a military campaign that produced about 8,500 casualties in killed, wounded, captured, and missing men. It may sound especially strange and repellent to historians now focused on the Civil War as the Dark War, the monstrous brutality of which eclipses all other considerations; yet Douglas Southall Freeman chose to describe Taylor's narrative in "The Valley Campaign" as "thrilling," and many others have testified to the pleasure-giving aspects of this chapter.[23]

If "delight" is the wrong word, the fault began with Stonewall Jackson himself, as Taylor depicted him at the opening of the Battle of Port Republic, early on June 9, 1862: "Jackson was on the road, a little in advance of his line, where the fire was hottest, with reins on his horse's neck, seemingly in prayer. Attracted by my approach, he said, in his usual voice, 'Delightful excitement.' I replied that it was pleasant to learn he was enjoying himself, but thought he might have an indigestion of such fun if the six-gun battery was not silenced. He summoned a young officer from his staff, and pointed up the mountain." Free of self-consciously arch allusions to literature or military history, this spare little sketch, with its deft balancing of direct and indirect discourse, anticipated the tonal achievements of Ambrose Bierce's *Tales of Soldiers and Civilians* (1891) or Ernest Hemingway's *In Our Time* (1925), in which this short excerpt would be set in italics and appear alone on a page of its own. In Taylor's hands, however, it is part of the braid of continuous narration, which includes other strands, among them Taylor's mistaken identification of Monday, June 9, 1862, as a Sunday, a mistake he might not have made had he paused to consider that the Sabbath-minded Jackson could be less likely to indulge in savoring aloud the delightful excitement of battle on the Lord's Day.[24]

The mistake appeared in "Stonewall Jackson and the Valley Campaign," which Taylor published in the *North American Review* in 1878, and it remained uncorrected in *Destruction and Reconstruction*, which altered the passage above with the insertion of two commas and a "that" alongside the deletion of the adjective "low" from the original phrasing, "he said in his usual low voice," a change not necessarily for the better. What makes the mistake more interesting, and more telling, is that it marks the gap between the staunchly pious Presbyterianism of Jackson and the secular urbanity of Taylor, to whom Jackson said with "reproachful surprise . . . in a gentle voice," after Taylor had sworn at his men for ducking under fire, "'I am afraid you are a wicked fellow.'" This is a charming, funny moment, one for which Taylor prepared with a reference to the innocuous swearing of "the delightful 'Uncle Toby'" in Laurence Sterne's comic masterpiece *Tristram Shandy* (1759–67). It is also a rhetorically winning moment, of the kind that is rare later in *Destruction and Reconstruction*, as the narrator steps outside himself to poke fun, without censure or judgment, at the incongruity of the situation.[25]

The gap between Jackson and Taylor has other significance, too, particularly with respect to the delightful excitement of battle. Whereas Bierce or Hemingway created fictional and nonfictional worlds in which a soldier in the midst of battle could not say "Delightful excitement" without causing readers to suspect the subversive stirrings of irony, Taylor represented the humorless Jackson as wholly without the propensity to say one thing and mean another, describing him at one point as having "no more capacity for jests than a Scotchman." Jackson's "Delightful excitement" conveys no grisly underside in Taylor's narration, and for that reason it may prove a stumbling block for twenty-first-century readers committed to a view of the Civil War as wholly dark. Through its Latin root "delight" inherits the meaning "entice from" or "allure away," and if Taylor's fifth chapter conveys anything to us now, whether military historians or casual readers, it conveys that the Valley Campaign was often enticing and alluring, thrilling and pleasurable, to Stonewall Jackson, to Richard Taylor, probably to many readers of the *North American Review* in 1878, and to many readers of *Destruction and Reconstruction* down to our own day. That people who are reading "The Valley Campaign" retrospectively through the intervening wars of the last century and a half may find themselves unable to participate in Taylor's delight is beyond question; that their inability may arise from blinding anachronism may be, too.[26]

One way to follow and appreciate Taylor's narrative braid is to consider the passages he added to "Stonewall Jackson and the Valley Campaign" in expanding the piece into the fifth chapter of *Destruction and Reconstruction.* Readers of the 126th volume of the *North American Review*, published by D. Appleton and Company in 1878, would have found "Stonewall Jackson and the Valley Campaign" in the company of George B. McClellan's "Capture of Kars, and Fall of Plevna," James A. Garfield's "Army of the United States," and, from the January number, Taylor's own "Reminiscences of the Civil War," over which he later crossed swords with Alexander Stephens. Appearing in the March–April issue, "Stonewall Jackson and the Valley Campaign" opened with memorable, often repeated images of Jackson in "a pair of cavalry-boots covering feet of gigantic size, a mangy cap, with visor drawn low, a heavy, dark beard, and weary eyes—eyes I afterward saw filled with intense but never brilliant light." From this sketch in its second paragraph, the piece continued to Jackson's "contemplative suck on a lemon"; his "ungraceful" horsemanship; an encounter with "a young, rather well-looking woman—afterward widely known as Belle Boyd," Confederate spy; the engagement at Front Royal (May 23); the Battle of Winchester on "a lovely Sabbath morning" (May 25); various skirmishes; the Battle of Cross Keys (June 8); the Battle of Port Republic (June 9), to which Taylor devoted more space than any other fight of the campaign; and final meditations on Jackson's ambition and his death.

What is significant here is that Edmund Wilson could have written his pages on Richard Taylor using nothing more than what appeared in the *North American Review.* He did not need "The Valley Campaign" in *Destruction and Reconstruction* to make any of his observations. If we add a sentence from Taylor's well-known portrait of Richard Ewell, which appeared only in *Destruction and Reconstruction*, not in either of his contributions to the *North American Review*, we have the bulk of what many readers recall and quote from him: "Bright, prominent eyes, a bomb-shaped, bald head, and a nose like that of Francis of Valois, gave him a striking resemblance to a woodcock; and this was increased by a bird-like habit of putting his head on one side to utter his quaint speeches." There is certainly much to delight in here, as there is in the "piquant" details about Jackson. But in expanding "Stonewall Jackson and the Valley Campaign," Taylor showed that he had other designs in mind, some of them pleasure-giving, some of them instructional, and some of them neither.[27]

Take Taylor's addition of this verbal equivalent of eighteenth-century landscape painting to the original 1878 article:

> But the glory of the Valley is Massanutten. Rising abruptly from the plain near Harrisonburg, twenty-five miles north of Staunton, this lovely mountain extends fifty miles, and as suddenly ends near Strasburg. Parallel with the Blue Ridge, and of equal height, its sharp peaks have a bolder and more picturesque aspect, while the abruptness of its slopes gives the appearance of greater altitude. Midway of Massanutten, a gap with good road affords communication between Newmarket and Luray. The eastern or Luray valley, much narrower than the one west of Massanutten, is drained by the east branch of the Shenandoah, which is joined at Front Royal, near the northern end of the mountain, by its western affluent, whence the united waters flow north, at the base of the Blue Ridge, to meet the Potomac at Harper's Ferry.

This excerpt briefly samples a three-page aside on the topography of the Shenandoah Valley, its transportation networks, and the "inhabitants of this favored region," the whole a full-throated aria that opens, "The great Valley of Virginia was before us in all its beauty." Adding this lyrical appreciation of the Shenandoah Valley had nothing to do with the instruction of young military professionals; it had everything to do with conveying to readers the author's delight in the landscape. Joseph E. Johnston's *Narrative of Military Operations*, which contains not a single instance of the words "beauty" or "lovely" and "picturesque," offered Taylor no precedents or models for this kind of writing; William T. Sherman's *Memoirs* offered him some. But the true precursors of this passage are travel writings, which, though ancient in origin, emerged abundantly in Taylor's beloved eighteenth century, with examples supplied by, among others, Daniel Defoe, Henry Fielding, Thomas Jefferson, Samuel Johnson, and Jonathan Swift, if we take *Gulliver's Travels*, first published in 1726, as in part a send-up of the genre.[28]

The other precursors are visual rather than verbal, with Taylor's choice of the word "picturesque" pointing to eighteenth-century aesthetic debates about painting. According to one explicator of the picturesque mode, whereas images of the sublime tended toward "vastness and obscurity" and images of the beautiful toward "smoothness and gentleness," the picturesque occupied a middle zone between them and inclined toward "roughness and sudden variation joined to irregularity of form." Taylor's description of the "abruptness" of the slopes of Massanutten fulfills the expectation of "roughness and sudden variation joined to irregularity of form" associated with the picturesque. But beyond the immediate context of landscape description, Taylor's attraction to the picturesque gives us a way to think about his crafting of "The Valley Campaign." More inclusive than the categories "delight" and "instruction," the category of the picturesque enables us to account for the sudden variations and abrupt irregularities that emerged more sharply as Taylor revised his original material on Stonewall Jackson into the best chapter of *Destruction and Reconstruction*. It also explains why *Destruction and Reconstruction* would find itself out of harmony with the dark turn of recent Civil War historiography, which tends toward the unmitigated horrors of negative sublimity rather than toward the sudden variations of the picturesque.[29]

Taylor and the 1864 Valley Campaign

One kind of sudden variation Richard Taylor included throughout *Destruction and Reconstruction* was digression. In the midst of narrating events of June 1, 1862, after a reference to Louisiana slaves who accompanied his brigade, Taylor turned to a two-page digression about his "servant," Tom Strother, "who deserves honorable and affectionate mention at my hands, and serves to illustrate a phase of Southern life now passed away." As interesting as the digression itself is Taylor's rationale for indulging in it at all: "My readers have had so much fighting lately, and are about to have so much more, as to render unnecessary an apology for introducing Tom's history." This is the only appearance in the whole of *Destruction and Reconstruction* of the phrase "my readers" and the only moment when Taylor commented so explicitly and so baldly on the machinery of his own narrative. We have seen that Taylor knew *Tristram Shandy*, and in his digression on Tom Strother we hear an echo of Sterne's self-conscious literary artifice, often extravagantly digressive. Digressions may not be the soul of reading for all readers, especially pragmatic ones who want to get to the point as quickly as possible, but they are certainly a distinct feature of the picturesque in Richard Taylor's "Valley Campaign." What abruptness is to the picturesque in painting, digression is to his military-historical narrative. In this example it gives them a break from "so much fighting lately" and "so much more" they are about to have.[30]

In context the "so much more" fighting about to come was the fighting of Sunday, June 1, 1862 (Taylor did get this Sunday right), with Jackson near Strasburg, Virginia, as well as the fighting of the later battles of the campaign during the following eight days. Then there was all the fighting in Louisiana, after Taylor's transfer there in July 1862 as major general, still to be narrated and still to be read. But Taylor's reference to future fighting pointed in another direction, too. The foreshadowing of the following paragraph, also a digression, inserted immediately after the pages on the beauties of the Shenandoah Valley, and also appearing in *Destruction and Reconstruction* but not in the earlier *North American Review* article, suddenly turned "The Valley Campaign" into a chronological palimpsest, the narrative equivalent of double-exposure or time-lapse photography:

> Ere the war closed, the Valley was ravaged with a cruelty surpassing that inflicted on the Palatinate two hundred years ago. That foul deed smirched the fame of Louvois and Turenne, and public opinion, in what has been deemed a ruder age, forced an apology from the "Grand Monarque." Yet we have seen the official report of a Federal general wherein are recounted the many barns, mills, and other buildings destroyed, concluding with the assertion that "a crow flying over the Valley must take rations with him." In the opinion of the admirers of the officer making this report, the achievement on which it is based ranks with Marengo. Moreover, this same officer, General Sheridan, many years after the close of the war, denounced several hundred thousands of his fellow citizens as "banditti," and solicited permission of his Government to deal with them as such. May we not well ask whether religion, education, science and art combined have lessened the brutality of man since the days of Wallenstein and Tilly?[31]

Considered as an isolated strand apart from the braid of "The Valley Campaign," this singular paragraph might give aficionados of the Dark War approach abundant grist for grinding. There is nothing delightful or charming or humorous or picturesque about Taylor's appalled revulsion from U.S. major general Philip H. Sheridan's operations in the Shenandoah Valley from mid-August through mid-October of 1864. There is, however, much about Taylor's dense layering of references to seventeenth-century European military history that is both complicated and illuminating. Following the lead of *New York Times* correspondent William Swinton in *Campaigns of the Army of the Potomac* (1866), which may well have been his source, Taylor adopted the rhetorical strategy of likening Sheridan's destruction of food and supplies in the Shenandoah Valley to military operations carried out by the French under orders from Louis XIV, the "Grand Monarque." But already there are problems, or at least complexities, as Taylor conflated two separate campaigns against the Palatinate, in what is now southwestern Germany, the first during the Franco-Dutch War (1672–78), the second an episode of the Nine Years' War or War of the Grand Alliance (1688–97), during which French troops destroyed more than twenty substantial towns and numerous villages in the spring months of 1689.[32]

Even this much tracking down of Taylor's historical references makes it hard to believe that he was in full control of his material or was shaping it with anything like the dispassionate detachment of the scholar he pretended to be. The swerving accumulation of widely disparate historical comparisons begins to feel uncharacteristically undisciplined, especially when it comes to the reference to the supposed apology by Louis XIV for his scorched-earth policy, a detail that did not appear in the Swinton's long footnote comparing Sheridan to the French in the Palatinate. One wonders how much such an apology could be worth, at least in the minds of those few readers who knew or know the history to which Taylor referred, if the French king pursued the same destructive strategy against the same region in campaigns separated by fifteen years. Apparently his apology, if actual, did not lead to lasting amendment of his ways.[33]

The point is not to catch Richard Taylor out on the details of his use of seventeenth-century European military history; the point is to recognize that in Philip H. Sheridan's operations against the Shenandoah Valley, two years after the delightful excitements of Stonewall Jackson's campaign there, Taylor confronted large problems, and the sudden piling up of historical comparisons may have been his conscious or unconscious method for trying to manage those problems. First, there is the problem of who was responsible for the destruction of the Shenandoah Valley during 1864. In laying the blame on Sheridan, Taylor made the error of mistaking the agent for the principal, an error still common in many Civil War circles. Although it is understandable that an elite southern aristocrat like Richard Taylor might find repulsive most things about a rough-mannered northern son of Irish immigrants—as other members of the Confederate officer corps also found Sheridan—it is less understandable that he did not recognize the hand of Ulysses S. Grant behind the strategy pursued in the Shenandoah. Taylor certainly understood the chain of military command, and he understood, or should have understood, that Sheridan in the Shenandoah Valley could not have been operating wholly autonomously. True, Sheridan fully endorsed the wisdom and efficacy of Grant's Shenandoah Valley "programme," as he called it in his memoirs, but his instructions clearly came from Grant. Those instructions, reproduced in Sherman's memoirs, came in five installments from mid-August through early November 1864. As Sheridan put it, "Grant's instructions to destroy the valley began with the letter of August 5 to [U.S. major general David] Hunter," whom Sheridan replaced:

> In pushing up the Shenandoah Valley, as it is expected you will have to go first or last, it is desirable that nothing should be left to invite the enemy to return. Take all provisions, forage, and stock wanted for the use of your command; such as cannot be consumed destroy. It is not desirable that buildings should be destroyed; they should rather be protected, but the people should be informed that so long as any army can subsist among them recurrences of these raids must be expected, and we are determined to stop them at all hazards.[34]

Three weeks later, after Sheridan had replaced Hunter, Grant repeated himself in unequivocal terms: "If the war is to last another year we want the Shenandoah Valley to remain a barren waste." As for Sheridan's infamous line, "A crow flying over the Valley must take rations with him," its source is also Grant, who wrote Major General and Chief of Staff Henry W. Halleck, in a letter of July 14, 1864, "If the enemy has left Maryland, as I suppose he has, he should have upon his heels veterans, militiamen, men on horseback, and everything that can be got to follow to eat out Virginia clear and clean as far as they go, so that crows flying over it for the balance of this season will have to carry their provender with them." Whether or not Sheridan saw this letter, written while Hunter was still commanding in the valley, in carrying out the orders of the man who penned it, Sheridan could not have helped absorbing Grant's destructive vision, along with, perhaps, the figurative language in which he voiced it.

In fact, however, Richard Taylor never saw anything in an official report by Philip Sheridan about a crow carrying its own rations. The closest Sheridan came to saying such a thing was this sentence from his official report of October 7, 1864: "When this is completed the Valley, from Winchester up to Staunton, ninety-two miles, will have but little in it for man or beast." The infamous line attributed to Sheridan by Taylor and many others, past and present, is apocryphal; the self-reliant crow of the Shenandoah Valley was wholly Grant's invention. As it turns out, Taylor himself may well have been the source, or at least the conveyor, of Sheridan's apocryphal line, seen by thousands of readers in the pages of the *Southern Historical Society Papers*, which published "Advanced Sheets of 'Reminiscences of Secession, War, and Reconstruction,' by Lieutenant-General Richard Taylor" in March 1878. The first selection from the advanced sheets consisted of five paragraphs subtitled "The Valley of Virginia," opening with the sentence, "The great Valley of Virginia was before us in all its beauty," and closing with Taylor's question, "May we not well ask whether religion, education, science and art combined have lessened the brutality of man since the days of Wallenstein and Tilly?"[35]

This question leads to the second large problem posed for Taylor by Sheridan's so-called destruction of the beautiful valley that furnished the setting for his 1862 triumphs as a brigade commander under Richard Ewell and Stonewall Jackson. It is not difficult to understand why Taylor found Sheridan loathsome. In the process of defeating Jubal A. Early, Sheridan not only damaged the capacity of the Shenandoah Valley to support the Confederate war effort, thereby helping the reelection campaign of Abraham Lincoln; he compounded his loathsomeness as commander of the Fifth Military District, comprising Texas and Taylor's paradisiacal Louisiana, during a tumultuous six-month tenure running from March through August 1867. Nor is it difficult to understand why Taylor might have shied away from charging Ulysses S. Grant with brutality he attributed to Sheridan instead. Even if he had had access to such documents as Grant's July 14, 1864, letter to Henry W. Halleck in the years before the Government Printing Office began publishing *The War of the Rebellion: A Compilation of the Official Records of the Union and Confederate Armies* (1880–1901), Grant was a great admirer of Zachary Taylor, under whom he served in Mexico. Although Richard Taylor died before Grant put his admiration on record in *Personal Memoirs of U. S. Grant* (1885–86), presumably Grant made his admiration of the father clear to the son during their Washington meetings of summer 1865, in the event that Taylor had not seen it firsthand during his brief 1846 visit to Mexico. Grant's connection to his father may have tempered Taylor's attitude toward him, prompting him to flay Sheridan instead.[36]

The larger challenge is to plumb the implications of Richard Taylor's question, prompted by his image of what Sheridan had wrought in the Shenandoah Valley, "May we well not ask whether religion, education, science and art combined have lessened the brutality of man" since the early seventeenth century? In posing such a question, Taylor opened his knowledge, or at least his use, of military history to more exacting scrutiny. From the vantage point of the twenty-first century, few would be likely to say that any combination of religion, education, science, and art has lessened the brutality of human beings toward one another. Counterexamples from the twentieth and early twenty-first centuries are so numerous that the question itself is hard to take seriously. But what could someone have seen from the vantage point of 1877 or thereabouts? What could Taylor have seen apart from the American Civil War and what he thought of as the singular brutality of Sheridan in the Shenandoah Valley?

If he looked all the way back to the classical and biblical antecedents he occasionally invoked in *Destruction and Reconstruction*, he would have seen the sacking of Troy and the uncompromising policy of *herem* in the book of Joshua. The sacking of Troy included such widely depicted moments as the rape of Cassandra by Ajax the Lesser, the throwing of Hector's infant son from the walls, and the burning of the city itself; in the book of Joshua the destruction of Jericho culminated in this verse from the King James Version: "And they utterly destroyed all that was in the city, both man and woman, young and old, and ox, and sheep, and ass, with the edge of the sword" (Joshua 6:21). Sheridan's conduct in the Shenandoah Valley approached neither of these precedents in kind or degree, as Mark Neely has demonstrated, nor did it come close to the "moral enormity" of the French campaign against civilians of the Palatinate, as Mark Grimsley has argued in his criticism of William Swinton's "learned analogy" from 1866.[37]

As for Taylor's own present, he had only to look a little more closely at the Franco-Prussian War (1870–71) and the Russo-Turkish War (1877–78) to see abundant evidence of what he might have considered brutality. Alluding to both these conflicts in his first twenty pages, Taylor chose to focus on leaders and their strategies, but he could have focused on the thousands of civilian casualties during the Siege of Paris, in the first case, or on massacres of both Muslim and Christian populations, in the second. If he needed evidence of continuing brutality closer to home, he had the Bear River Massacre of 1863, the Sand Creek Massacre of November 1864, the Washita Massacre of November 1868, and the Marias Massacre of January 1870. He would not be alive for the Wounded Knee Massacre of 1890.[38]

Richard Taylor had overwhelming evidence, then, that the answer to his question, "May we not well ask whether religion, education, science and art combined have lessened the brutality of man since the days of Wallenstein and Tilly?" was clear: We may well ask indeed, and the answer is, No, religion, education, science, and art have done nothing to lessen the brutality of human beings. The rhetorical shaping of his question suggests that he knew the answer perfectly well; yet his highly selective use of military history also suggests that whereas there was nothing at all anomalous about Sheridan's treatment of the Shenandoah Valley in 1864—which in fact was restrained compared to the examples above—Taylor chose to view it as an exceptional lapse. Instead of seeing events in the 1864 Shenandoah Valley as continuous with events from Troy or Jericho down to the Russo-Turkish War, Taylor opted for marshaling the righteous indignation of Enlightenment belief in human improvement, if not perfectibility. Framed this way, Sheridan in the Shenandoah Valley represented the failure of the civilized standards of refinement and cultivation, of which Taylor himself was the self-appointed apostle. Unlike a twenty-first-century student of history who might find Taylor's question pathetically quaint, Taylor himself, in posing the question for the readership he apparently had in mind, staunchly affirmed the values underlying it.

Taylor and Stonewall Jackson

The drama of "The Valley Campaign"—or the source of its picturesque irregularity and abruptness—is that Richard Taylor was trying to hold two opposed ideas in his mind at the same time. One idea centered on the tactical victories of Stonewall Jackson's Valley Campaign of 1862, the other on the strategic defeat inflicted by Philip Sheridan's Valley Campaign of 1864. The first idea was an idea of how war should be waged by civilized combatants; the second was an idea of what war really was and had been all along, no matter how hard one tried to pretend otherwise. In his narrative Taylor worked to keep the first idea front and center, the second one backstage. But the second idea intruded into the foreground at least twice, once quite explicitly in the digressive paragraph about Sheridan and the Palatinate, the other time in a way somewhat harder to see:

> I have written that he was ambitious; and his ambition was vast, all-absorbing. Like the unhappy wretch from whose shoulders sprang the foul serpent, he loathed it, perhaps feared it; but he could not escape it—it was himself—nor rend it—it was his own flesh. He fought it with prayer, constant and earnest—Apollyon and Christian in ceaseless combat. What limit to set to his ability I know not, for he was ever superior to occasion. Under ordinary circumstances it was difficult to estimate him because of his peculiarities—peculiarities that would have made a lesser man absurd, but that served to enhance his martial fame, as those of Samuel Johnson did his literary eminence. He once observed, in reply to an allusion to his severe marching, that it was better to lose one man in marching than five in fighting; and, acting on this, he invariably surprised the enemy—Milroy at McDowell, Banks and Fremont in the Valley, McClellan's right at Cold Harbor, Pope at second Manassas.[39]

The ambitious "he" is Stonewall Jackson. In the 1878 *North American Review* version, this excerpt takes up two paragraphs; the second, beginning with "He once observed," is the antepenultimate of the article. If we add to the opening sentence another from the previous page, "Yet, in that moment, I saw an ambition, boundless as Cromwell's, and as merciless" (with only the final comma in *Destruction and Reconstruction*), we find in this strange eulogy more than a third of all the appearances of the words "ambitious" (two times) and "ambition" (six times) in Taylor's book, none of them suggesting he thought of ambition as a virtue. In the early footnote excoriating Alexander Stephens, for example, Taylor placed the former vice president among "those who unite restless vanity and ambition to a feminine desire for sympathy." By contrast, a paragraph praising Robert E. Lee closed with the sentence, "He was without ambition, and, like Washington, into whose family connection he had married, kept duty as his guide."[40]

In his remarks on *Destruction and Reconstruction*, Edmund Wilson took Taylor's characterization of ambitious Jackson at face value and continued with a discussion about southerners, who, "as a rule, did not entertain this kind of ambition." While many details of Taylor's piquant portrait of Jackson have lodged themselves in popular imagination of the Civil War, the detail about Jackson's ambition has not, or at least not to the extent it has in popular imagination of, say, U.S. major general Joseph Hooker, thanks in part to Abraham Lincoln's widely reprinted January 26, 1863, letter to him: "You are ambitious, which, within reasonable bounds, does good rather than harm." But something is odd about Taylor's attribution to Jackson of Cromwellian ambition. Setting aside the comparison of Jackson's peculiarities to those of Samuel Johnson, one that splices the military and the literary in a way that says more about Taylor's own dual identity and ambition than it does about either Jackson or Johnson, a reader has to wonder how Taylor suddenly gained access to the inmost spiritual and psychological combat of the habitually taciturn and remote Jackson: "He loathed it, perhaps feared it; but he could not escape it—it was himself—nor rend it—it was his own flesh." Alluding to the conflict between Christian and Apollyon in the Valley of Humiliation, as narrated by John Bunyan in *The Pilgrim's Progress*, how could Taylor know the first thing about Jackson's prayers or their intensity? In adopting this kind of omniscient perspective, Taylor moved beyond the outskirts of military history into pure fiction.[41]

The fiction making extended to one of Taylor's signature allusions. One can look up Samuel Johnson, and one can look up Christian and Apollyon in the Valley of Humiliation, but one can wear out any number of reference books or keyboards and never find "the unhappy wretch from whose shoulders sprang the foul serpent." Not quite the same kind of original invention as Grant's self-reliant crow winging over the Shenandoah Valley, Taylor's nightmarish image was possibly an imperfectly remembered or garbled version of the punishment of Agnello Brunelleschi in the seventh ditch, reserved for thieves, in Malebolge, eighth circle of Dante's Inferno, here in the 1867 translation of Henry Wadsworth Longfellow:

> If thou art, Reader, slow now to believe
> What I shall say, it will no marvel be,
> For I who saw it hardly can admit it.
> As I was holding raised on them my brows,
> Behold! a serpent with six feet darts forth
> In front of one, and fastens wholly on him.
> With middle feet it bound him round the paunch,
> And with the forward ones his arms it seized;
> Then thrust its teeth through one cheek and the other;
> The hindermost it stretched upon his thighs,
> And put its tail through in between the two,
> And up behind along the reins outspread it.
> Ivy was never fastened by its barbs
> Unto a tree so, as this horrible reptile
> Upon the other's limbs entwined its own.
> Then they stuck close, as if of heated wax
> They had been made, and intermixed their colour;
> Nor one nor other seemed now what he was. (25.46–63)[42]

Even if Longfellow's recent translation of Dante did provide Taylor with raw material, the finished product was his own literary creation. Whereas the serpent who merges with Brunelleschi is initially separate from him (and actually another Florentine thief, Cianfa Donati, who has been transformed), Taylor recast the reptile as already a part of "the unhappy wretch." Appearing in print about eight years before the young Sigmund Freud began writing notes on Jean-Martin Charcot's lectures on male hysteria, Taylor's spurious allusion gave his readers a graphic image, every bit as potent as Freud's Oedipus, of a self in ceaseless combat with itself. Intended as an image of Stonewall Jackson's inner struggles with ambition, it quickly ramifies in many directions. After all, in Jackson's case "ambition" in the Shenandoah Valley would be a synonym for destruction of the U.S. armies there. Taylor's own language confirmed that Jackson's was not merely the ambition to win fame in the form of adulatory newspaper headlines; it was, like Oliver Cromwell's, "merciless." Taylor did not elaborate on Cromwell's mercilessness, but that quality was nowhere more evident than in his conquest of Ireland (1649–53), where he is still more widely and deeply hated than Sheridan is in the Shenandoah Valley. If we follow out the implications of Taylor's depiction of Jackson, we soon see that it anticipated by more than a hundred years Charles Royster's characterization of him in *The Destructive War* (1991): "Jackson did not go through the Civil War's often-described transition from notions of chivalric gallantry to brutal attrition. For him the war was always earnest, massed, and lethal." In other words, the hard truth that Richard Taylor had to face when observing Stonewall Jackson, from the retrospective vantage point of 1877, was that Philip Sheridan was not an exceptional monster; for him, as for Jackson, "war was always earnest, massed, and lethal," as it was for Cromwell and other military leaders of seventeenth-century Europe, as it always has been, as it always will be.[43]

"He loathed it, perhaps feared it; but he could not escape it—it was himself—nor rend it—it was his own flesh." If we reread this nervously self-interrupting, dash-broken sentence, this time substituting "Richard Taylor" for "he" and "the truth that war was always earnest, massed, and lethal" for "it," we get to the heart of the matter in "The Valley Campaign" and *Destruction and Reconstruction.* Taylor used his remarks about Jackson to describe himself, knowingly or not. Grandson of one soldier, son of another, effective combat leader in his own right, and lifelong student of military history, Richard Taylor loathed, perhaps feared, but could not escape the truth that religion, education, science, and art—especially education, on which he prided himself so highly—have not lessened human brutality, nor have they narrowed it to the anomalous actions of a few exceptional Yankee brutes such as Philip Sheridan. Viewed from this perspective, all war is dark war, and to label the Civil War the Dark War is tautological at best and, at worst, no more than historical narcissism, as we insist on seeing our twenty-first-century selves in it, as in a glass darkly. To see this way is to risk being out of harmony with the practices of the past, which is no less dangerous than to be out of harmony with the practices of one's own time or, for that matter, to be out of harmony with oneself, like Taylor's unhappy wretch with the foul serpent growing out of him. The threat or discomfort of this inner disharmony returns us to allusion and the role it plays in both "The Valley Campaign" in particular and in *Destruction and Reconstruction* in general.

Allusion and Reconstruction

There are many reasons to allude. Allusion can increase the sonority and resonance of a given passage, as though one were pressing on the sustain pedal while playing the piano. Allusion can show off and intimidate in order to consolidate and maintain one's authority or the appearance of it. Through allusion one can hide or conceal something by indirection. A given instance of allusion in Taylor's book may reflect one or more of these effects or intentions. But through allusion one can also project and construct one's ideal readership, creating a community of shared values, in Richard Taylor's case values of education, taste, cultivation, and refinement. Through allusion one can acknowledge that war is inescapably destructive but also affirm that its destructiveness is not the whole story, that it is only a part of human history and civilization. To put it another way, allusion was not simply a characteristic of Richard Taylor's writing; it was a deliberate mode and rhetorical strategy. It was, in short, his method of reconstruction. Although many readers may take the second term of his title as referring to nothing more than the period in the United States from 1865 to 1877, the year in which Taylor began to write, in fact reconstruction can also point to the second definition of "reconstruct" in the *Oxford English Dictionary*, a definition that dates from 1862: "To construct anew in the mind; to restore (something past) mentally." We use the word in this sense when we speak of reconstructing events for the purpose of analyzing or interpreting them, as in a court of law.

In two of his chapter titles, "Reconstruction under Johnson" and "Reconstruction under Grant," Richard Taylor clearly used "reconstruction" in its specific historical sense, although one suspects that he may have wanted to place the term in quotation marks to ironize it throughout, though he only does so once, holding it at arm's length this way: "General Grant yet appeared to agree with me about 'reconstruction,' as it was called; and I was anxious to preserve good feeling on his part toward the President." But the shape of his two-part title, *Destruction and Reconstruction*, symmetrically balanced across the fulcrum "and," suggests that he may also have had a more general sense of reconstruction in mind. Yes, in war destruction is a given, but it is not the end of the story, at least not for Taylor, because for every destruction there was, or could be, a balancing, compensatory reconstruction, whether that reconstruction took place in his own book or in something larger he called, in the lyrical final paragraph of his conclusion, "tradition": "Traditions are mighty influences in restraining peoples. The light that reaches us from above takes countless ages to traverse the awful chasm separating us from its parent star; yet it comes straight and true to our eyes, because each tender wavelet is linked to the other, receiving and transmitting the luminous ray. Once break the continuity of the stream, and men will deny its heavenly origin, and seek its source in the feeble glimmer of earthly corruption."[44]

In Richard Taylor's hands allusion was the engine of reconstruction, the preserver of unbroken continuity, the guarantor of tradition, as he thought of tradition from his particular geographical, social, and political vantage points. Many readers may agree with the final sentences of Jubal A. Early's unpublished review of *Destruction and Reconstruction*, which runs thirty-nine pages in manuscript: "There is often too great a straining after effect, and too great a propensity for pedantic display for history. It will be much read, and will perhaps call forth some sharp replies. Whoever undertakes to read it had better have an unabridged dictionary and an encyclopedia of biography at hand." Others, perhaps a small minority, will find themselves closer to agreement with Douglas Southall Freeman's affirmative assessment. Either way, they will discover that in closing "The Valley Campaign" Taylor extended the *North American Review* article and did not give the last word to Stonewall Jackson, who, "fortunate in his death, . . . fell at the summit of glory, before the sun of the Confederacy had set, ere defeat, and suffering, and selfishness could turn their fangs upon him." Instead, he closed the chapter by reconstructing a memorable breakfast, not long after the Battle of Port Republic, in Orange County, Virginia, "at the barbarous hour of sunrise," the only time Taylor, on the march toward the Seven Days' Battles, could spare his host:

> That night we camped between Charlottesville and Gordonsville, in Orange County, the birthplace of my father. A distant kinsman, whom I had never met, came to invite me to his house in the neighborhood. . . . It was a fine old mansion, surrounded by well-kept grounds. This immediate region had not yet been touched by war. Flowering plants and rose trees, in full bloom, attested the glorious wealth of June. On the broad portico, to welcome us, stood the host, with his fresh, charming wife, and, a little retired, a white-headed butler. Greetings over with host and lady, this delightful creature, with ebon face beaming hospitality, advanced, holding a salver, on which rested a huge silver goblet filled with Virginia's nectar, mint julep. Quantities of cracked ice rattled refreshingly in the goblet; sprigs of frag[r]ant mint peered above its broad rim; a mass of white sugar, too sweetly indolent to melt, rested on the mint;

> and, like rose buds on a snow bank, luscious strawberries crowned the sugar. Ah! that julep! Mars ne'er received such tipple from the hands of Ganymede. Breakfast was announced, and what a breakfast! A beautiful service, snowy table cloth, damask napkins, long unknown; above all, a lovely woman in crisp gown, with more and handsomer roses on her cheek than in her garden. 'Twas an idyl in the midst of the stern realities of war! The table groaned beneath its viands. Sable servitors brought in, hot and hot from the kitchen, cakes of wondrous forms, inventions of the tropical imagination of Africa, inflamed by Virginian hospitality.[45]

For the second time in "The Valley Campaign"—the first came in the digression on Tom Strother—Taylor turned to "my father" when depicting a phase of southern life built on slavery and now passed away. In closing the best chapter of *Destruction and Reconstruction*, he elected to give the last word to "an idyl in the midst of the stern realities of war," to a valedictory image of something other than total war, hard war, dark war. The archaic "'Tis" of the didactic "'Tis dangerous to be out of harmony with practices of one's own time" here changes to the past tense of "'Twas an idyl," the verb tense of mental reconstruction.

The coexistence or palimpsest of past and present, of Shenandoah Valley of 1862 and Shenandoah Valley of 1864, of delightful excitement and brutality of man, of reconstruction of a phase of aristocratic white southern life now passed away and Reconstruction of the postwar United States, of idyl and stern reality, was and is what makes "The Valley Campaign" unique among the chapters of *Destruction and Reconstruction* and *Destruction and Reconstruction* unique among Confederate generals' memoirs. It enabled Richard Taylor to harmonize, at least momentarily, the many disharmonies around and within him. But the harmony did not last, not in his book, not in the life that ended with its publication, not in the June 1862 breakfast somewhere in Orange County, Virginia. That the harmony was necessarily precarious and temporary does not mean that it was not fundamental to what Taylor called in his preface "an interior view." All harmonies are precarious and temporary, whether in lives or in histories, and yet few stories would have value without reference to them. As one of the final sentences of "The Valley Campaign" put it, "Duty dragged us from this Eden." Few will have to look up this allusion; we know the plot too well.[46]

4

ULYSSES S. GRANT AND THE ACHIEVEMENT OF SIMPLICITY

ALTHOUGH HE NEVER published his review of Richard Taylor's imaginative reconstruction of the Civil War, Jubal A. Early had audience expectations in mind when he wrote that review. "Whoever undertakes to read it had better have an unabridged dictionary and an encyclopedia of biography at hand." A few years after the publication of Taylor's allusive, erudite book, Mark Twain's Charles L. Webster and Company brought out the two posthumous volumes of Ulysses S. Grant's *Personal Memoirs*, the first at the end of 1885, the second at the beginning of 1886. Grant's reconstruction of the war met audience expectations in a wholly different way. Accessibility was Grant's hallmark, unpretentiousness his chosen mode. From 1885 down to the present day, many of Grant's readers have assumed his prose and the arrangement of his reconstruction somehow inevitable, the inescapable by-product of his integrity and humility. But such assumptions need further examination. Ulysses S. Grant did not begin by writing in the style of his memoirs; he had to learn it. Even more, as he learned the style, he learned about what to include and what to leave out. This learning would shape how he reconstructed what he remembered. The apparent simplicity of Grant's reconstruction raises larger questions about simplicity in general. Whenever simplicity in reconstructing the past becomes simplification of the past, simplicity requires a closer look. This statement goes for reconstructions of the Civil War in the nineteenth century or the twenty-first. Reading Grant illuminates the latter as well as the former.

How Simple Is Simplicity?

When Mark Twain published Grant's *Personal Memoirs*, reviewer consensus was that in addition to the interest inherent in recollection by the preeminent soldier on the victorious side, the literary achievement of Grant's work was superlative. What made it superlative, most agreed, was the simplicity of its style. Here is a sentence—unlike any of Grant's own—from the most prestigious review of the day, that of William Dean Howells in his regular column "Editor's Study" in *Harper's New Monthly Magazine*: "But these *Personal Memoirs of U. S. Grant*, written as simply and straightforwardly as his battles were fought, couched in the most unpretentious phrase, with never a touch of grandiosity or attitudinizing, familiar, common, even homely in style, is a great piece of literature, because great literature is nothing more nor less than the clear expression of minds that have something great in them, whether religion, or beauty, or deep experience."[1]

A close friend of Mark Twain, William Dean Howells may not have had a grip on military tactics and strategy firm enough to earn the pronouncement that Grant's battles were fought simply and straightforwardly—there is nothing simple or straightforward about the Vicksburg Campaign, Chattanooga, the Wilderness, Spotsylvania, or the Battle of the Crater—but in 1886 his literary judgment was authoritative. Writing privately to Twain in December 1885, Howells anticipated his review in *Harper's*, though he spoke in this instance not of Grant's simplicity but of his naturalness, a quality implicitly synonymous: "I'm reading Grant's book with a delight I've failed to find in novels. I hope you are still as much aglow over him as you were when I saw you last. I think he is one of the most natural—that is, *best*—writers I ever read. The book merits its enormous success, simply as literature. It is very handsome, too." Twain liked Howells's assessment enough to copy the first, third, and fourth sentences into his notebook.[2]

Twain's notebooks also contain the name of another important reviewer of Grant's memoirs, Thomas Wentworth Higginson. Colonel of the First South Carolina Volunteers, Higginson is known to Civil War readers as the author of *Army Life in a Black Regiment* (copyrighted 1869, published 1870) and to poetry readers as the correspondent and editor of Emily Dickinson. Reviewing the first volume of Grant's memoirs in the *Atlantic Monthly*, Higginson sounded the same note as Howells while adding touches of his own: "These memoirs . . . have the first and highest quality both of literature and manhood, simplicity. Without a trace of attitudinizing or a suspicion of special pleading, written in a style so plain and terse that it suggests the reluctant conversation of a naturally reticent man, they would have a charm if the author had never emerged from obscurity except to write them." In a subsequent review of the second volume, Higginson singled out Grant's undramatic treatment of an especially dramatic moment: "When he describes that famous interview between himself and General Lee, in which was settled the permanent destiny of the American nation, the tale is told far more quietly than the ordinary reporter would describe the negotiations for a college rowing match."[3]

When Higginson merged his two reviews into a single essay, published in 1900, he closed it with the original ending of the March 1886 review: "In writing his own memoirs he was simple as regards himself, candid toward opponents, and thus bequeathed to the world a book better worth reading than any military autobiography since Caesar's Commentaries." In a section of his autobiography dictated Friday, June 1, 1906, Mark Twain concurred: "By chance, I had been comparing the Memoirs with Caesar's 'Commentaries' and was qualified to deliver judgment. I was able to say, in all sincerity, that the same high merits distinguished both books—clarity of statement, directness, simplicity, unpretentiousness, manifest truthfulness, fairness and justice toward friend and foe alike, soldierly candor and frankness, and soldierly avoidance of flowery speech." Twenty years before he dictated this appraisal, Twain had written in his notebook, in early June 1885, "Caesar's Commentaries (on the Gallic & the Civil War) are the only books that rank with this [Grant's memoirs]. Like this, it is noted for its 'simplicity, naturalness & purity' of style."[4]

Twain's comments included a note about something that impressed him as an example of Grant's simplicity, naturalness, and purity of style: "'Mexicans not so discriminating—sometimes picked off his Juniors.[']" This was Twain's shorthand version of three sentences from Grant's twelfth chapter, in which he narrated his promotion to first lieutenant during the Mexican War, along with the capture of Mexico City. The original sentences run this way: "My regiment lost four commissioned officers, all senior to me, by steamboat explosions during the Mexican war. The Mexicans were not so discriminating. They sometimes picked off my juniors."[5]

Those who have praised Ulysses S. Grant for his simple style probably would agree that these three short, simple sentences typify that style. Out of twenty-nine words, seventeen are monosyllables, and the two- and three-syllable words either have lowered their Latinate altitude by descent through Old French (and common military usage: regiment, commissioned, officers, explosions) or are Latinate words familiar to anyone who has attended high school (senior, juniors). There is a single exception, to which we shall return. For now we can say that there is little among Grant's three sentences that thirty years later would cause the young Ernest Hemingway, starting out as a reporter guided by the style sheet of the *Kansas City Star*, to stumble. "Use short sentences. Use short first paragraphs. Use vigorous English. Be positive, not negative," the *Star* style sheet taught him, adding, among other specifics, "Avoid the use of adjectives, especially such extravagant ones as splendid, gorgeous, grand, magnificent, etc." Grant's short, vigorous sentences—the only static verb of being is a single "were," while "picked off" leavens the whole with a gritty, vernacular quality—contain no extravagant adjectives. For another *Star* dictum, "Eliminate every superfluous word," Grant's sentences are a paradigm.[6]

So simplicity seems simple; yet to call Grant's style simple is to oversimplify. In a notebook entry of July 1866, Twain explicitly noted and praised the simplicity of Grant's message to Confederate Brigadier General Simon Buckner at Fort Donelson, Tennessee, in February 1862: "No terms except an unconditional and immediate surrender can be accepted. I propose to move immediately upon your works." What could be clearer? Nineteen years later Twain was still admiring Grant's style, and the publisher of Grant's memoirs singled out the moment about exploding steamboats as an example. To say that either of these examples, one from Fort Donelson, one from Mexico, can serve as a model of simplicity is not provocative or controversial. But if we look and listen more closely, we realize that their simplicity is not the same simplicity.[7]

The history of the word "simple" shows that it meant "one-fold," as opposed to manifold. "Simple" and "single" come from the same root. When statements are simple, they mean a single thing. When Simon Buckner read Grant's demand for the surrender of Fort Donelson, "No terms except an unconditional and immediate surrender can be accepted," he knew what the message meant and not because West Point had taught him to understand the five-syllable word "unconditional." But when Grant wrote, "The Mexicans were not so discriminating," his lone five-syllable, Latinate adjective set in motion more than one meaning. It set in motion more than one tone, and it unleashed the suggestiveness of connotation. A steamboat cannot discriminate among casualties when it explodes, and the personifying juxtaposition of discriminating steamboats with less discriminating enemy soldiers in combat is inventive, quirky, tongue-in-cheek, even playful. There is wit here, as though Grant the narrator were giving his readers the sly, invisible wink of a wry humorist, wavering and dissembling between or among two or more meanings. Saying one thing while meaning other things points to duplicity, which means "twofold," and in many cases it produces irony. In other cases it produces metaphor, or figurativeness in general; in these cases Robert Frost called the duplicity poetry. Whatever we call it, Grant used it often, and Caesar, solemnly summarizing his own speeches through a remote, third-person point of view, did not.

Grant a humorist? William Dean Howells's short review of the memoirs never refers to Grant's wit or irony. Thomas Wentworth Higginson's longer essay does refer to his humor, but only once. Beginning with Grant's statement that Mexican soldiers often "stood up as well as any troops ever did"—again from Grant's twelfth chapter—Higginson continued, "He adds, with some humor, 'The trouble seemed to be the lack of experience among the officers, which led them, after a certain period, to simply quit without being whipped, but because they had fought enough.'" It is a slight but telling instance, one seasoned with the slangy assonance of "quit without being whipped." In a dry deadpan Grant commented on the lack of training and discipline among the Mexican soldiers he opposed. He did so, however, by slipping from a West Point professional's authority into the point of view of the undisciplined Mexican soldiers, courageous and capable but oblivious to the imperative that real soldiers do not stop fighting the moment they have had their fill of combat.

Higginson leaves the matter of Grant's humor there, passing on to a comparison with William T. Sherman: "This phlegmatic habit made General Grant in some respects uninteresting, as compared, for instance, with the impulsive and exuberant Sherman." From this judgment, which one could contest, Higginson moved on to another comparison: "Lincoln impresses one as representing, on the whole, a higher type of character than Grant—more sympathetic, more sensitive, more poetic." These judgments may say more about Thomas Wentworth Higginson than they do about Grant, Sherman, or Lincoln. One wonders, for example, how Lincoln's memoirs might compare with Grant's or Sherman's had he lived and had he chosen to write them. Lincoln's eloquent simplicity in a letter or speech or pungent story can be impressively memorable, but it is not the same thing as eloquent simplicity sustained through twelve hundred pages of historical narrative.[8]

If occasional duplicity, which says one thing and means another, complicates the plain terseness of Grant's memoirs, where did that duplicity come from? And the humor, what was its provenance? In September 1839, seventeen years old and at West Point since May, Grant wrote his cousin, McKinstry Griffith, the earliest of his letters that has survived. The letter is open, chatty, badly spelled, poorly punctuated, and neither phlegmatic nor uninteresting. The young man who wrote it had no fear of expressing his feelings frankly: "I do love the *place*. it seems as though I could live here ferever if my friends would only come too. You might search the wide world over and then not find a better." The new cadet had a lively sense of fun, too, and was quick to employ it at his own expense, making colorful and original comparisons. "My pants sit as tight to my skin as the bark to a tree and if I do not walk *military*. that is if I bend over quickly or run. they are apt to crack with a report as loud as a pistol. my coat must always be buttoned up tight to the chin. . . . it makes me look very singulir." Grant's willingness to poke fun at himself would show up more than forty-five years later, when he was concluding the first chapter of his *Personal Memoirs* with the anecdote about his youthful approach to horse trading. Having been sent by his father to bargain with the owner of a colt, the boy opens negotiations with utter guilelessness: "'Papa says I may offer you twenty dollars for the colt, but if you won't take that, I am to offer twenty-two and a half, and if you won't take that, to give you twenty-five.'" The droll commentary by Grant the narrator presages some of what will follow: "It would not require a Connecticut man to guess the price finally agreed upon." Winning as his youthfully naive self-portrait may be, only an instinctive storyteller, with some of a Connecticut Yankee's shrewdness, could intuit the effectiveness of contrasting for his reader the inexperienced boy with the celebrated man looking back at him.[9]

First Teacher

Willingness to poke fun at himself was not what shaped the sentence about the exploding steamboat, however. Developing that kind of humor required other models. As it happened, Ulysses S. Grant had two of the best. The first was Abraham Lincoln. In chapter 46 of his memoirs, which covers the first months of 1864, when Grant received orders to travel to Washington and receive the new rank of lieutenant general, he meets Lincoln for the first time. "I knew him, however, very well and favorably from accounts given by officers under me at the West who had known him all their lives." But Grant did not know Lincoln only from secondhand accounts. "I had also read the remarkable series of debates between Lincoln and Douglas a few years before, when they were rival candidates for the United States Senate." The adjective "remarkable" is not so extravagant that an editor for the *Kansas City Star* would have to strike it from a Hemingway article; yet it is one of a small handful of adjectives in the paragraph, and the others—few, rival, great—are not as remarkable as the hard-earned "remarkable" was for Grant. This was no empty, formulaic, overblown effusion; it meant that the seven Lincoln-Douglas debates of August, September, and October 1858 left an impression deep enough to warrant a rare descriptor reserved by Grant for something uncommon. What makes their effect on Grant even more important is that his appraisal of their quality—Lincoln's side of them in particular—did not come from uncritical partisanship. "I was then a resident of Missouri, and by no means 'a Lincoln man' in the contest; but I recognized then his great ability."[10]

A man floundering in his midthirties, having resigned from the army and returned to civilian farming life in Missouri as a father with a young family, could have absorbed much from reading Lincoln closely. He could have absorbed a great deal about how to argue and produce evidence and rebut, and this learning would not go to waste in the later composition of, for example, his demonstration in chapter 16 that "secession was illogical." He could follow how Lincoln adapted his approach for different audiences, not necessarily changing the basic message in going from an audience of perhaps fifteen thousand in Freeport to one of fifteen hundred in Jonesboro, but skillfully redistributing emphasis. And he could have learned how small moments of humor could help buttress larger, more precarious constructions. In the first debate at Ottawa on August 21, 1858, for example, and in the midst of fraught and dangerous argument about the distinction between restricting the spread of slavery into the territories, on the one hand, and, on the other, advocating racial equality, Lincoln made this canny, deflecting move: "Now gentlemen, I don't want to read at any greater length, but this is the true complexion of all I have ever said in regard to the institution of slavery and the black race. This is the whole of it, and anything that argues me into his idea of perfect social and political equality with the negro, is but a specious and fantastic arrangement of words, by which a man can prove a horse chestnut to be a chestnut horse."[11]

A newspaper transcript of the debate recorded that Lincoln got a laugh here, and reading it on Hardscrabble Farm, Grant may have chuckled, too. But there was nothing funny about what was at stake, and the recourse to folksy flippancy was a move as deftly evasive as it was daring. Something of the same thing is going on with Grant's discriminatingly explosive steamboat in the Mexican War; he is joshing his reader in the context of a war he himself called "unholy" nine chapters earlier. "For myself, I was bitterly opposed to the measure [the annexation of Texas], and to this day regard the war, which resulted, as one of the most unjust ever waged by a stronger against a weaker nation," Grant vented in his third chapter, adding this peremptory judgment to clinch the moment: "The Southern rebellion was largely the outgrowth of the Mexican war. Nations, like individuals are punished for their transgressions. We got our punishment in the most sanguinary and expensive war of modern times." Unholy, unjust, transgressive, the Mexican War had nothing risible about it from Grant's perspective, and yet there were his personified steamboats, those discriminating assassins.[12]

Grant read Lincoln four and a half years before he met him. After he met him, he became more than his reader; he became both his regular visitor and his frequent correspondent. "While my headquarters were at Culpeper, from the 26th of March to the 4th of May [1864], I generally visited Washington once a week to confer with the Secretary of War and President." At this rate Grant would have visited Lincoln half a dozen times before he opened the Overland Campaign with his move into the Wilderness. In his memoirs he particularized only one of these meetings, that of April 20, 1864, his "last interview with the President before reaching the James River." Grant recorded that on this occasion, "I explained to him that it was necessary to have a great number of troops to guard and hold the territory we had captured, and to prevent incursions into the Northern States." Whether or not Grant used the Latinate phrase "prevent incursions" in face-to-face conversation, this sentence reflects the basic principles of simplicity, and its unadorned lucidity continues in the next sentence as well: "These troops could perform this service just as well by advancing as by remaining still; and by advancing they would compel the enemy to keep detachments to hold them back, or else lay his own territory open to invasion." Straightforward and practical as his explanation to Lincoln was, it had gone on for the better part of the paragraph, when suddenly, with a comic storyteller's sense of timing, Grant juxtaposed the tone and length of his own remarks with the flavor and brevity of Lincoln's, about a third as long: "[Lincoln's] answer was: 'Oh, yes! I see that. As we say out West, if a man can't skin he must hold a leg while somebody else does.'"[13]

Grant left the remark, which casts him in the role of straight man, without comment. But the message of the moment is clear: Lincoln had a way with words that impressed him, that he knew would impress his reader, and that he sensed would enhance the personal story he had to tell. The moment has another element as well, as though Grant meant it to double as a parable about his book and his own use of language. In the second part of the 1886 review Grant never saw, Thomas Wentworth Higginson introduced his comparison of Grant and Lincoln with the formulation, "There is no more curious and inexplicable characteristic than the use of language." The Grant who narrates *Personal Memoirs* never says such a thing and never would. But his story about Lincoln's answer on April 20, 1864, shows that he understood the truth of what Higginson was saying. Grant was a westerner, too, every bit as much as Lincoln, who unlike his lieutenant general never saw the Pacific Coast, and such language as that in Grant's early West Point letter has as much western tang about it as anything Lincoln said. In his depiction of the moment with Lincoln in 1864, Grant was showing his reader that when it came to what

Higginson called the "curious and inexplicable characteristic" use of language, Grant was deliberately choosing to play the man who can't skin with language and must hold a leg while Lincoln did the verbal skinning.

Sixteen chapters later Grant held on once more and let Lincoln do the skinning, this time in an anecdote from "the occasion of his visit to me just after he had talked with the peace commissioners at Hampton Roads" in early February 1865. "After a little conversation, he asked me if I had seen that overcoat of [Alexander] Stephens's." Again, Grant cast himself as the straight man in the routine: "I replied that I had." Back to Lincoln: "'Well,' said he, 'did you see him take it off?'" The narrator continues to play it straight, setting up the punch line: "I said yes." And then Lincoln takes it the rest of the way: "'Well,' said he, 'didn't you think it was the biggest shuck and the littlest ear that you ever did see?'" In this case Grant did not leave the moment without comment. "Long afterwards I told this story to the Confederate General J. B. Gordon, at the time a member of the Senate. He repeated it to Stephens, and, as I heard afterwards, Stephens laughed immoderately at the simile of Mr. Lincoln." Sticklers might insist that Lincoln's was a metaphor, not a simile, but the quibble does not diminish the good humor of the moment, with Grant depicting himself as the admiring and appreciative purveyor of Lincoln's memorable one-liners. Once again, however, the moment is more complex. Why did Grant say nothing about Lincoln's earlier hold-and-skin remark but feel it necessary to comment here?

When Grant introduced Lincoln's remarks in face-to-face conversation, he usually did so to illustrate Lincoln's love of indirectness, especially indirectness packaged in a figurative image, such as skinning an animal or shucking corn, or in a parable-like story. Lincoln's indirectness served him in many ways throughout his presidency, but the passage about Alexander Stephens's oversized coat served Grant in a very particular way in this instance. One of the great omissions in his *Personal Memoirs* is Grant's own two-term presidency. The antepenultimate paragraph of the book gives it a slight nod, as the dying man alluded to his 1868 campaign slogan: "The universally kind feeling expressed for me at a time when it was supposed that each day would prove my last, seemed to me the beginning of the answer to 'Let us have peace.'" Otherwise, a reader of *Personal Memoirs* could finish the book without knowing that Grant had served as chief executive for eight years. In commenting on the comic afterlife of Lincoln's metaphor for Stephens's coat, Grant, by cagey indirection, pointed to the outward reconciliation with former high-ranking Confederates during his presidency. Former Confederate major general John

Brown Gordon was elected to the U.S. Senate in 1873, former Confederate vice president Alexander Stephens to the U.S. House of Representatives in the same year, the first of Grant's second term. As recounted by Grant, the laughter they shared, courtesy of Abraham Lincoln, hinted at more than the savoring of a good joke; it gestured toward the difficult politics of Reconstruction with an affability that may have been more hoped for than actual.[14]

When Lincoln makes his final appearance in Grant's memoirs, his indirectness takes the form of a story. "I remember one little incident which I will relate as an anecdote characteristic of Mr. Lincoln." Grant continued that the incident "occurred a day after I reached Washington, and about the time General Meade reached Burkesville with the army." If Grant's memory was correct, then the incident took place very close to the assassination of Lincoln, as the army began arriving in Burkesville on April 12, 1865. The anecdote does not make the connection between the events, however. Instead, it focuses on the request of Virginia governor William "Extra Billy" Smith that he and "a few others" be permitted "to leave the country and go abroad without interference," in the event that he should not be "allowed to perform the duties of his office" in the temporary state capital at Danville. When Grant repeated the contents of Governor Smith's letter to him, "Mr. Lincoln, supposing I was asking for instructions, said . . . that his position was like that of a certain Irishman (giving the name) he knew in Springfield." The anecdote then zeroes in on this Irishman "of considerable promise and very much liked": "Unfortunately he had acquired the habit of drinking, and his friends could see that the habit was growing on him."

At this moment, before the punch line, what was Grant thinking as he listened to Lincoln? For that matter, what was Lincoln thinking as he told the story to Grant? Lincoln knew the stories about Grant's drinking, and he supported him in spite of them. When telling the story about the Springfield Irishman, he must have known Grant knew he knew. It is hard and moving to try to fathom how many levels of unspoken understanding connected the two men at this moment. The punch line of the story has its obvious import. The Irishman takes a pledge to abstain; after a few days he tires of the pledge, which "began to grow distasteful to him"; and so, "holding the glass [of water] behind him, he said: 'Doctor, couldn't you drop a bit of brandy in that unbeknownst to myself.'" Implication of the anecdote? If Grant were to let Governor Smith and a few others go abroad without Lincoln's knowing, the scenario would suit the president. But the anecdote may have contained something personal for Grant, too; it may have contained both the generosity of acceptance and a lesson in using indirectness to signal it. Too much sobriety can grow distasteful, and a drop of "unbeknownst" brandy now and then can work wonders. Grant put this lesson to good use in the writing of his book.[15]

Second Teacher

Ulysses S. Grant's second model was Mark Twain, whom he addressed in private correspondence as S. L. Clemens. Unlike Lincoln's name, neither Mark Twain's nor Samuel Clemens's appears in the *Personal Memoirs*. If Abraham Lincoln offered Grant examples of strategic indirection and occasional drops of humorous brandy in a predominantly sober narrative, the man with the most famous pseudonym in the literary history of the United States offered him something else: a lesson in how to fashion a written mask.[16]

Simple, plain, clear, direct, terse, unpretentious, candid, truthful, fair, never posing or attitudinizing, the modern Caesar avoiding flowery speech as a soldier should: how natural. The consensus emerged early and, for the most part, has remained unchallenged. But Grant's narrative sobriety is not natural; it is artful and often dissembling. One person who saw through Grant's mask was Gertrude Stein. Stein's essay "Grant" opens her book *Four in America* (1947) with a demonstration of how complex simplicity can be: "I like this about West Point. Grant did. Not that he liked it but he did. He knew the difference between quiet and waiting and he knew there was no such thing as waiting." In her dizzying, oblique way Stein was approaching the contradictions of Grant as man and writer, contradictions behind the first words of Grant's title. Narrated from a first-person point of view, his books was personal in some ways. But in others it succeeded in hiding the personal.[17]

Mark Twain understood this truth only after Grant's death. Between his first meeting with Grant on January 15, 1868, when the two men shook hands at a reception hosted by the general, and July 23, 1885, when Grant died at Mount McGregor in Moreau, New York, Twain did not attempt to peek behind the mask, at least according to the documents we have. This is not to say he only tiptoed around Grant in hushed, deferential reverence; when it came to the business of selling Grant's book, Twain was not starry-eyed. He knew he had a commodity to move, and he moved it. But as he wrote Henry Ward Beecher, it was not until the day of Grant's funeral that he sat "an hour over a single drink & several cigars with [Stewart] Van Vliet & Sherman & Senator Sherman; & among other things Gen. Sherman said with impatient scorn," and here Twain turned his letter over to his rendition of Sherman's unmistakable voice: "'The idea of all this nonsense about Grant not being able to stand rude language & indelicate stories! Why Grant was *full* of humor, & full of the appreciation of it. . . . It makes me sick—that newspaper nonsense. Grant was no namby-pamby fool, he was a *man*—all over—rounded & complete.'" Sherman's remarks had the force of revelation for Twain, as he continued to Beecher, "I wish I had thought of it! I would have said to General Grant: 'Put the drunkenness in the Memoirs—& the repentance & reform. Trust the people.'" As Twain then acknowledged, "But I will wager there is not a hint in the book. He was sore, there. As much of the book as I have read gives no hint, as far as I recollect."[18]

Grant was a *man*. To Sherman, at least in this context, Grant's manhood meant that he relished humor without squeamishness. As Twain marveled to Henry Ward Beecher, "Sherman & Van Vliet know *everything* concerning Grant; & if you tell them how you want to use the facts, both of them will testify." Then, as if explaining to himself as much as to Beecher, he continued, "Regular army men have no concealments about each other; & yet they make their awful statements without shade or color of malice—with frankness & a child-like naivety, indeed, which is enchanting—& stupefying." The man who wore the Mark Twain mask would seem not to be someone easily stupefied by awful statements about someone's private past. But that Sherman could talk about Grant, or what he knew about Grant, in ways both enchanting and scandalous to Twain amounts to another kind of fraud. Or it amounts to a peek behind the Twain mask at someone who concealed sensitivity to indelicate stories when they came from professional soldiers more candid than he was.[19]

While he got many things right about the author of *Personal Memoirs*, Thomas Wentworth Higginson got wrong the side of Grant that Sherman and others claimed to know. "Lincoln would tell an indelicate story with the zest of a bar-room lounger," Higginson commented, "while Grant, by the general testimony of his staff officers, disliked and discouraged everything of the kind." That Higginson could have seen Grant this way does not mean merely that Grant acted one way with his subordinates and another with his West Point peers, although undoubtedly he did; it means that the way Grant acted with his subordinates is also the way he acted with his readers. Of the six times Grant refers to "the reader" of his book, the fifth is the most interesting. "It would prolong this work to give a detailed account of all that took place from day to day around Petersburg and at other parts of my command," he asserted near the end of chapter 58, adding, "and it would not interest the general reader if given." So close to the end of his book, and the difficult end of his extraordinary life, prolonging his work was not what he wanted. The debilitating conditions under which he wrote during his terminal illness are well known, thanks to Grant's many biographers. But the moment stands out as Grant's only explicit acknowledgment that he was withholding information from someone he envisioned as a general reader. In fact, many general readers of Grant's memoirs would be intensely interested in "all that took place from day to day around Petersburg," especially from Grant's point of view and in Grant's words. If a reader had already signed on for twelve hundred pages in the first edition, what difference would fifty more make? General readers opening Grant's memoirs in 1886 no doubt differed from general readers now; most of the latter need some interest in the American Civil War to fuel them, whereas the former needed only an interest in a celebrity of their time. But the point has been made. Grant the truthful, Grant the candid, Grant the natural had a reader in mind for the material he was shaping, and that reader was not William T. Sherman or anyone who knew him well at West Point.[20]

That reader was more like Mark Twain. Here the story takes a not-so-simple turn. Twain had been admiring Grant's way with words since his message to Simon Buckner at Fort Donelson in February 1862, and Grant knew that Twain had read his article "The Battle of Shiloh" in the February 1885 issue of *Century Magazine*. He also knew that Twain was reading the galley proofs of his memoirs as each chapter appeared. But the reading and admiration did not run in only one direction. Grant was also a reader of Mark Twain. Although Grant's son Fred was reading *The Adventures of Huckleberry Finn* in February 1885, the month Grant contracted to publish *Personal Memoirs* with Webster, and although Charles Webster told Twain that he had sent Grant a copy of the book, there is no firm evidence that Grant himself read the novel, though he would have seen at least a portion of it; the same issue of *Century* that printed his article "The Battle of Shiloh" also printed a long excerpt from *Huckleberry Finn*. What we do know is that Grant attended a performance of Mark Twain's *Colonel Sellers* (1874), a play based on *The Gilded Age: A Tale of To-Day*, the 1873 novel by Twain and Charles Dudley Warner about, among other things, corruption in Congress during Grant's first term. We know that Grant heard Mark Twain give speeches in 1879 ("The Babies" speech), 1880, and 1882. We know that when Grant traveled to the Holy Land during his world tour of 1877–79, he took with him three books, the Bible, a guidebook, and Mark Twain's *Innocents Abroad*. And we know that Grant read an early draft of Twain's "Private History of a Campaign That Failed."[21]

"He was sore, there." What Twain wrote of Grant's silence in the memoirs about his drinking goes for "The Private History of a Campaign That Failed," Twain's comic treatment of the brief service during June 1861 by twenty-six-year-old Clemens as a second lieutenant in the Marion County Rangers, an irregular outfit under the command of Missouri State Guard Brigadier General Thomas Alexander Harris. "The Private History" did not appear in *Century* until December 1885, the same month as publication of the first volume of Grant's *Personal Memoirs*. But in a marginal notation beside an entry of May 26, 1885, Twain recorded, "General said he read my article first & all the family afterward," suggesting that Grant had been looking at an early draft of "The Private History" two months before he died.[22]

"The Private History of a Campaign That Failed" has generated disagreement among its readers, past and present, with some condemning Twain—at the time a very young Samuel Clemens—for desertion and cowardice while others see him as a combination of conscientious objector and nonconforming skeptic, a rebel's rebel who repaid secession in kind by seceding from the seceders. Albert Bigelow Paine, Mark Twain's friend, biographer, and editor, made an early attempt to explain away the disagreement by noting, "Convictions were likely to be rather infirm during those early days of the war, and subject to change without notice. Especially was this so in a border State." In context Albert Bigelow Paine meant that infirm convictions about disunion were not uncommon in Missouri, or by extension in Kentucky, Maryland, Delaware, and what in 1863 became West Virginia. But his statement is true in a larger, figurative way that he perhaps did not intend.[23]

"The Private History of a Campaign That Failed," like much of Mark Twain's work, maps a border state, an uncertain, ambivalent region between or among shifting affiliations, emotions, and identities. Whether geographical entities that remained in the Union after Confederate secession or mental zones that change their boundaries and inclinations, border states are not simple or single; they are by nature twofold. *Personal Memoirs of U. S. Grant* makes perfectly plain that when it came to Grant's convictions as a loyal citizen and a professional soldier, there was nothing infirm about them. But there are aspects of *Personal Memoirs*—both large ones, such as the silence about drinking, and small ones, such as local anecdotes and comments—that suggest Grant may have learned something about twofold border states from Mark Twain before he read "The Private History of a Campaign That Failed." To take one example, the general's bracing verdict that the Civil War was the punishment visited on the United States for the transgression of the Mexican War might have fallen on some Manifest Destiny ears as disloyal, unpatriotic, and even heretical. It also sounds uncharacteristically biblical and apocalyptic for a sensibility otherwise inclined toward temperate agnosticism.

When he set out to write his memoirs, Grant certainly would have had a sense of the unstable borders between sentimentality and satire, romanticism and realism. Knowing that Grant had with him Twain's *Innocents Abroad* in the Holy Land makes reading chapter 11 of John Russell Young's two-volume *Around the World with General Grant* (1879) an exercise in border-state double vision. When Young reported on their 1878 pilgrimage to the Garden of Gethsemane, for instance, he surrendered to the full grip of nineteenth-century American biblical romanticism: "And if one could know the hearts of those who were about the tree, who stood around in silence, I have no doubt that he would know of many a silent prayer breathed to Heaven that in the hour of extremity the grace there implored for sinning souls might be our portion."[24]

Julia Grant's version of the moment echoes Young's. As the group wandered from one old tree to another, "wondering under which one Christ had knelt," Mrs. Grant was suddenly "seized with a violent shivering and felt deep emotion." She claimed she "knew now" that "this was the tree under which our Saviour knelt!" By stark contrast, in a letter of February 22, 1878, Grant gave Adam Badeau a less romantic version of events, reporting laconically, "Our visit to Jerusalem was a very unpleasant one." To this bare summary he added one more sentence of description: "The roads are bad and it rained, blew and snowed all the time." The same day, in a letter to Elizabeth King, he reeled off the places he had visited, which included "Jerusalem; the garden of Bethsemane; the Mount of Olives."[25]

Grant may have crossed Bethlehem, which he spelled correctly in the same letter, with Gethsemane. Or perhaps he never had a firm grip on the name at all. But if Gethsemane had meant to him what it apparently meant to his wife, chances are that he would have gotten the name right. John Russell Young's hyperventilating rendition pants with the same tone as the one pervading William C. Prime's 1857 *Tent Life in the Holy Land*. When he made his own trip to the Holy Land in 1867, Mark Twain lampooned this book, and the sensibility of its author, without mercy. Twain's mordant burlesque of Prime's sentimental romanticism must have helped ease the unpleasantness of Grant's experience.[26]

In Lincoln's stories and images Grant found models for indirectness. In the writings of Mark Twain he found abundant models for detachment, circumspection, and manipulation of perspective, most often away from exaggeration, sentimentality, and romanticism. Where melodrama, sentimentality, and romanticism crop up in Twain's writings, they usually do so as objects of parody. Grant's writing avoids them altogether, preferring instead to gesture toward a large context by focusing on a small detail, particularly one framed by a negative. In his account of the second day of Shiloh, for instance, Grant repeats a favorite move of Twain's. Finding himself suddenly fired on by "a battery with musketry . . . from the edge of the woods," Grant and two companions galloped away. "In the sudden start we made, Major [John] Hawkins lost his hat." Then comes the Twain touch: "He did not stop to pick it up." It is the same move as the earlier comment, "It would not require a Connecticut man to guess the price finally agreed upon." As Twain so often did, Grant insinuated by negation, rather than offering a fuller description of the fix in which he found himself.[27]

Ulysses S. Grant did not follow the example of Samuel Clemens in adopting a pen name. Why would he, when it was his name that helped make his memoirs a best seller? But he did follow Mark Twain's prescription when it came to the style of his writing. Twain's prescription appears in the chapter "Enchantments and Enchanters," the forty-sixth of *Life on the Mississippi*, published in 1883, the year before the Wall Street Panic and the swindling of Grant by Ferdinand Ward. Twain inscribed a copy of *Life on the Mississippi* "To / U. S. Grant, Jr / from the Author," and dated the inscription 1885. Known as Buck, Ulysses Jr. had entered into partnership with Ward in 1880. Whether he read *Life on the Mississippi* and shared the book with his father, we do not know, and Grant may have received a copy already.[28]

In the end it does not matter whether Grant read *Life on the Mississippi*. Nor does it matter that Mark Twain's distinction between southern and northern literary styles appeared a year before Grant began writing and two years before he was finishing. What matters is that Twain's descriptions of the two styles show that he and Grant tuned to the same scale. In Twain's view, Sir Walter Scott's "pernicious" *Ivanhoe* (dated 1820; released in late 1819) "restored" the silliness of medieval chivalry, and according to Twain, all but a few southern writers still suffered from the Sir Walter disease. In becoming Mark Twain, Samuel Clemens had his own tussles with the disease, and his relationship to Scott is complex and ambivalent. By comparison any case Grant had was mild and brief. The Sir Walter symptoms include "wordy, windy, flowery 'eloquence,' romanticism, sentimentality." But "whereas the southern writer still clings to it—clings to it and has restricted market for his wares, as a consequence," according to Twain, "the North has thrown out that old inflated style." Ulysses S. Grant had thrown out "that old inflated style" when he came to write his memoirs. In some ways Abraham Lincoln helped the purge, in some ways Mark Twain did. There was also one other simplifying influence.

Telegraph as Tutor

"I spent something over a day in N. Orleans, and its being a tolerably large place, and my Bump of Acquisitiveness prompting me on to see as much of the place as possible, the result was that I went over the town just fast enough to see nothing as I went, stoped long enough at a time to find out nothing atall and at the end found . . . myself perfectly tired out." Spelling and proofreading aside, this well-balanced, well-coordinated sentence sounds as though it came straight out of Mark Twain's *Life on the Mississippi.* It did not; Samuel Clemens was eight and a half when it appeared. Or it could have come from the pen of Charles Dickens, whose North American tour of 1842 resulted in the publication of *American Notes for General Circulation*, which reached the United States in November of that year and was widely excerpted in newspapers. But Dickens did not visit New Orleans on this trip; Richmond, Virginia, was the farthest south he traveled in the east and Cairo, Illinois, in the west. The writer who visited New Orleans, with his Bump of Acquisitiveness, one of the zones mapped on phrenological charts, adopted the witty, chatty, urbane irony of much travel literature, whether by Dickens or his predecessors.[29]

Whatever his preparatory reading, the author of this sentence was twenty-two-year-old Ulysses S. Grant, brevet second lieutenant in the Fourth Infantry Regiment. The date was June 4, 1844; the place of writing Camp Salubrity, three miles from Natchitoches, Louisiana; and the recipient of the sentence eighteen-year-old Julia Boggs Dent of White Haven Plantation, near St. Louis. In her memoirs, which include remarks on "the comforts of slavery" that "passed away forever" with the Rebellion, Julia noted that she did not see her young suitor again until 1848, "when the army returned from Mexico." "In the meantime," she continued, "I received by every mail long letters from him, many written on the field after he went to Mexico." The letter of June 4, 1844, is the earliest of these.[30]

Letters between lovers belong to a genre of their own. There is no reason someone proficient in that genre as a young man should not also master the memoir genre as an older one. Proficiency in one does not preclude proficiency in the other. What the 1844 sentence shows is that there was nothing naturally or inevitably plain, simple, or terse about the writing of Ulysses S. Grant. Whether or not he understood phrenology in 1844—context suggests that he may have confused acquisitiveness with inquisitiveness—by 1885 he certainly knew how to write in more than one mode. Between 1844 and the composition of his memoirs, Grant learned to master another genre, one brand-new to the world, and the rhetorical mode that went with it. That genre was the telegram, which he began writing in May 1861, and the rhetorical mode was the telegraphic, characterized by the conciseness omnipresent in his memoirs. Grant appears to have been slow in coming to the telegraph. In a letter of April 27, 1849, penned to Julia from Detroit, the new husband wrote his bride of eight months, "I received your Telagraphic dispatch yesterday morning from which I see that you are on the way to St. Louis." The misspelling here suggests more than a lapse in orthography; it suggests the novelty of the technology itself, at least to Lieutenant Grant.[31]

Twelve years after his wife, Ulysses S. Grant began composing telegraphic messages, sending his first on May 17, 1861, to John B. Wyman of the Illinois Adjutant General's Office. In July and August, Grant sent half a dozen telegrams, most of them to John Pope, then in command of northern Missouri. With September 1861 Grant's use of the telegraph increased significantly. That month he sent more than forty telegrams to Department of the West commander John C. Frémont alone, sometimes at the rate of two or three a day.

The telegrams Ulysses S. Grant sent to Frémont during the three weeks between September 2 and September 23, 1861, show him adapting to the new genre. His first telegram, of September 2, still retained the epistolary conventions of his letters. Grant opened with a salutation, a simple "SIR" on the first line, and he closed with the full signature, "Respectfully / Your obt Servt / U. S. GRANT / Brig Genl Comdg." Between the salutation and the signature, the telegram occupies thirteen lines of printed type. In recounting to Frémont a disagreement with Virginia-born Benjamin Prentiss about who outranked whom, Grant employed the continuous syntax and diction of a letter. "Genl Prentiss raised the question of rank and finally refused my orders," he explained, continuing, "Last night he tendered his resignation after being refused a leave of absence, but said he would command as directed untill your deciseon." The vestiges of epistolary style continue with the telltale adverb in Grant's next sentence: "To day he positively refused and reported himself in arrest." In this early telegram Grant preserved the connective tissue of events in a sequence, arranging his narrative with the temporal markers "finally," "Last night," "after being refused," and "To day." He also retained the coordinating conjunction "but" to signal the antithesis between one part of his statement and another.[32]

Three weeks later Grant's telegraphic language had stripped down to new austerity. On September 22, when he telegraphed Frémont from Cairo, the opening salutation had shifted to an unceremonious "MAJ. GEN. FREMONT" and the signature to "U.S. GRANT, Brig. Gen." The telegram between them read, in its entirety, "Your telegraph rec'd, will send the guns to Genl. Smith at once, Noble's Cavalry here." The following day, with salutation and signature the same, Grant's next telegram to his commander began, "Information from Columbus indicate the rebels are crossing to Belmont, taking away two gun boats." The editors of this document note that the punctuation, added later, was not Grant's. As the telegram continues, the original absence of punctuation suggests not a grammatical slovenliness but the speed of composition in a rush of events. "The third [gun boat] is laid up & weakening my force as has been done may force me to abandon Norfolk & Fort Jefferson." Gone now is the connective "but," which, in the epistolary mode, could have introduced the next sentence: "I will hold on to them as long as it is prudent." What rhetoricians call parataxis, or the side-by-side placement of independent phrases or clauses without conjunctions, became Grant's mode in this telegram, which ends, "Our pickets had a passage at arms last night one & half miles below Hunters, three men & horses missing."[33]

Although the evidence is clear that during September 1861 Ulysses S. Grant developed a new way of writing sentences and fragments of sentences as he learned his way around telegraphic technology, it is important not to oversimplify that evidence or overstate its significance. Grant did not suddenly abandon the conventions of letter writing in favor of the telegraphic mode. On September 22, 1861, the same day he wrote Frémont a fifteen-word telegram, he wrote his commander a four-paragraph letter with punctuation and complete sentences and a full signature. Even so, purged from the letter are the unnecessary adverbs of the communication about Benjamin Prentiss, written three weeks earlier. It is as though the mental activity that adverbs reflect has disappeared or gone quiet. Grant's need to modify, qualify, inflect, or editorialize seems to have diminished. Facts, events, and circumstances fend for themselves; they are sufficient without nuance or embroidery.[34]

Much has been written about the telegraph and its effects on communication, commerce, diplomacy, empire building, news reporting, perceptions of time and space, and certain features of many people's ordinary lives, such as observing the Sabbath. Formulations about how technology has shaped the kinds of communications we send and receive are familiar to citizens of the digital age. What makes the telegraphic writing of Ulysses S. Grant different from the writing of a twenty-first-century digital native, who also writes short sentences or sentence fragments that dispense with older conventions of letter writing, is that for Grant the telegraphic was one among many modes he could adopt. Grant's development as a writer took him from pretelegraphic plenitude through telegraphic paring down and on to the composite mode of *Personal Memoirs.*

Common sense warns against reductive arguments that our technological tools necessarily determine all aspects of our communications. Even through the new telegraphic medium, characteristic uses of language still come through. The telegrams of Abraham Lincoln still sound like Abraham Lincoln. In chapter 57 of his memoirs, Grant quoted in full a deciphered telegram from Lincoln, sent from Washington on August 3, 1864. Grant called this particular telegram a "very characteristic dispatch." Responding to a telegram from Grant, who wanted "Sheridan put in command of all troops in the field, with instructions to put himself south of the enemy, and follow him to the death," Lincoln composed an answer that ended with his unmistakable combination of rhythmic sonority and stern resolve: "I repeat to you it will neither be done nor attempted unless you watch it every day, and hour, and force it." As he did with Lincoln's anecdote about one person holding a leg while another skins, Grant singled out this communication to stand for others in the president's particular telegraphic mode.[35]

To illustrate Lincoln's telegraphic mode by quoting a "very characteristic dispatch," Grant could have chosen another Lincoln telegram, however, one in which the language is also characteristic and the resolve also unfaltering. But Grant did not choose the later telegram, and his decision to leave it out points to another omission from his memoirs and another kind of masking. Sent in cipher, the telegram began, "Happy Moses Marshall Elizabeth For Magic Tulip." With "Magic" serving as one of Grant's code names, the decrypted first line reads, "Washington August 17 10:30 A.M. For U. S. Grant Period." From this point on, Lincoln's imagery is so vivid not even Anson Stager's unbreakable, route-cipher encryption can defang and declaw the commander in chief's animal metaphor: "I have seen your dis patch express sing your unwilling ness to break your Produce where you are yacht neither am I willing yard Produce on with a bull dog grip and chew & choke as much as possible yawl Balfour good." Code-named Balfour, Lincoln composed this telegram six days before his so-called Blind Memorandum of August 23, in which the incumbent president anticipated his defeat by challenger George B. McClellan in the upcoming November election, along with the negative implications of that defeat for preservation of the Union. In Lincoln's *Collected Works*, the earlier telegram of August 17, 1864, composed two months into Grant's nine-month siege at Petersburg, closes with a sentence technology can neither enhance nor attenuate: "Hold on with a bull-dog gripe [*sic*], and chew & choke, as much as possible."[36]

Grant's omission of this telegram from his memoirs may have resulted from a decision not to confront his post-Reconstruction readers with Lincoln's unblinking version of hard war. Hold, chew, and choke? Where was the Abraham Lincoln whom Thomas Wentworth Higginson described as "a higher type of character than Grant—more sympathetic, more sensitive, more poetic"? Trust the people, Mark Twain wished he had said to Grant about putting the drinking in his memoirs. The memoirs show that Grant did not trust the people in that context, and he appears not to have trusted them in this one. During the initial term of Grover Cleveland, first Democrat elected since the war, how well would Lincoln's hold-chew-and-choke imperative sit alongside Grant's own presidential motto, Let us have peace?

The telegraphic mode of Ulysses S. Grant entailed deliberate omission. As he did in his written orders for battle, he tended to omit anything suggesting the shiftiness of twofold connotation, as opposed to simple, single-ply denotation. Whereas for Abraham Lincoln, the telegraphic mode did not necessarily rule out the suggestive play of connotation, for Grant it usually did. For him the telegraph meant speed, brevity, expediency. It also meant a good excuse for keeping things simple, and keeping things simple meant leaving things out. Grant's memoirs moved toward greater narrative and descriptive fullness than his telegrams, but even in his memoirs he retained the right to withhold. He withheld his drinking, his presidency, the importance of his marriage to Julia. But there is another withholding that drove Grant's *Personal Memoirs* toward their final form. Unlike the drinking, this withholding was not a total one. It permitted hints and partial glimpses but allowed nothing like full disclosure. The few carefully managed, partial disclosures cannot help but complicate the picture of Ulysses S. Grant as nothing but a truthful, simple, natural writer who never poses. In this context his memoirs amounted to a telegram writ large.

Matters Treated Of

Personal Memoirs of U. S. Grant is about the author's Civil War. As Grant put it in the penultimate sentence of the preface he dated July 1, 1885, three weeks before he died, "The comments are my own, and show how I saw the matters treated of whether others saw them in the same light or not." What Grant lumped under "the matters treated of" covers a vast canvas of people and events, causes and effects. In shuttling between or among large vistas and small details, he is agile, and although it would be wrong to credit the agility solely to his early reading, it would be equally wrong to dismiss that early reading entirely. "Much of the time, I am sorry to say, was devoted to novels," Grant admitted in his chapter on West Point, but he quickly explained, "but not those of a trashy sort." The list he gave in the next sentence is revealing: Edward George Earle Lytton Bulwer-Lytton, Frederick Marryat, Walter Scott, Washington Irving, and Charles Lever: all men, either British or American; all born within thirty-five years of each other; all publishing what for Grant would have been recent fiction of the early nineteenth century; and all working, at some point, with historical fiction or fiction about the army or navy.[37]

Despite a tendency to treat "fiction" as a synonym for "lie" or "falsehood," originally the word referred to that which is shaped or fashioned or manipulated by the fingers, as clay is. Part of the shaping Grant did in his memoirs, and the greatest part of what he withheld from the general reader he envisioned, had to do with what Walt Whitman called the horrors of fratricidal war and what others have referred to as the Dark War. This last phrase is not new; it appeared in a contemporary review of Frank Wilkeson's *Recollections of a Private Soldier in the Army of the Potomac* (1887), which called the book "a contribution to the history of the darker side of army life." By contrast, Grant did not set out in his memoirs to make a large contribution to the history of the darker side, and not because he did not see it; his high rank did not insulate him from the horrors of war, as some too willingly believe and cite as a reason for preferring accounts by people who were not general officers. Grant did see the darker side and, with a few telling exceptions, chose to withhold it or to treat it with a brevity and meagerness reminiscent of his telegraphic mode. A few examples will suffice—they must because he gave only a few—and they will serve more effectively to illustrate the point if we consider them against a statement by William T. Sherman about conditions at Vicksburg.[38]

In a letter of February 1887 to Colonel John E. Tourtellotte, Sherman tore into Henry Boynton, who had published "Grant's Liquor Drinking" the month before, and into another correspondent, Murat Halstead of the *Cincinnati Commercial*. Newspaper correspondents were particular targets of Sherman's scorn and vituperation, but his dislike of reporters by itself cannot account for the voltage running through the letter. Continuing his blast that Lincoln "had more sense than a thousand Boyntons," he inveighed against "Halsteds [*sic*]

&c who from their safe places in the rear knew how to fight battles, and to hold Generals responsible, for high water crowded camps and the consequent pestilence which we tried to hide from the Country, and even from the men." Tried to hide from the country? At issue here is not an ethical question about whether Grant, Sherman, and other high-ranking U.S. officers should have tried to hide anything from the civilian population "and even from the men" during the Vicksburg Campaign; at issue here is our recognition that there were details of waging war Grant withheld from others. "I well remember," Sherman continued, plunging right into these details, "when the high water of the Mississippi drove us to the Levees which were the only burial places, when the living & the dead lay with but a foot of damp earth between, when Grant & his army demonstrated the largest measure of patience and Courage and perseverance." Grant maintained his patience, courage, and perseverance, Sherman concluded, "whilst Halsted [*sic*] in Cincinnati . . . was trying to create panic, mistrust and failure."[39]

Part of Ulysses S. Grant's courage as a writer was the courage to withhold. Sherman did not say so explicitly, but his strong defense of Grant points toward this conclusion. In reconstructing his version of the Civil War, Grant had in mind a general reader on whose behalf he excluded some material. Whereas another writer who worked to render the darker side of war, such as Ambrose Bierce, might have served up sensory details, in the case of shallow burials in a Mississippi levee, with graphic ghastliness bordering on the pornographic, Grant did not. His strategic omissions suggest a larger parable about any reconstruction of the Civil War. Any reconstruction is necessarily selective, and selection necessarily means exclusion. Motives for selecting one detail while excluding another are many. A given writer might select or exclude because of defensive self-interest or because of a specific political bias or out of deference to prevailing tastes or in compliance with the wishes of an editor or a publisher with an eye on book sales. In any reconstruction something is missing, and identifying what is missing is the key to evaluating the reconstruction. When one reconstruction selects what another excludes, friction becomes inevitable.

Personal Memoirs of U. S. Grant offers readers an apparently simple, straightforward reconstruction of the Civil War ostensibly closer to disinterested truthfulness than most of its contemporaries. But William T. Sherman knew its author better than most people did. A few sentences later in the February 1887 letter he touched the truth about his friend and comrade: "Grants whole character was a mystery even to himself—a combination of strength and weakness not paralleled by any of whom I have read in Ancient or Modern History."

Sherman read widely throughout his life, and if the third-person remoteness of Julius Caesar had hinted at any mystery in him, Sherman would have found it. By the time he made this February 1887 statement to Tourtellotte, Sherman had read Grant's memoirs, too. Sherman's insight into the mystery of Ulysses S. Grant, into Grant's singular combination of strength and weakness, does more to account for the composite mode of *Personal Memoirs of U. S. Grant* than any simple statements about simplicity. It also illuminates why Grant drew on many modes—epistolary, novelistic, telegraphic, Lincolnian, and Twainian—to help manage the mystery while treating wartime matters for a general reader.

Take the mystery of Grant's thirteenth chapter. "Every Sunday there was a bull fight for the amusement of those who would pay the fifty cents." This lean sentence appears midway through the opening paragraph. The time is late winter of 1848, when Grant was among those waiting for the Senate to ratify the Treaty of Guadalupe Hidalgo so they could go home. During the delay "officers and men . . . contented themselves as best they could." "Not wishing to leave the country without having witnessed the national sport," Grant elected to attend a bullfight, but "just one," he was careful to add. His response to the spectacle would not have gratified Ernest Hemingway, who otherwise admired Grant: "The sight to me was sickening." This from the man whom newspapers of spring 1864, during the forty days of the Overland Campaign, called the Butcher? The next sentence, last of the paragraph, is indeed personal and shows how Grant saw matters he was treating: "I could not see how human beings could enjoy the suffering of beasts, and often of men, as they seemed to do on these occasions." Fair enough. That is all he needed to say on the subject.[40]

But he continued. The next two paragraphs describe in detail what he saw, and these paragraphs could be grafted into Hemingway's *Death in the Afternoon* (1937) without standing out as anomalies. Why did Grant go on with a detailed picture of proceedings that sickened him, describing the "uncontrollable frenzy" of the bull about to be killed by matadors with long, sharp blades and noting that "matadors" means "literally murderers"? Was this digression intended to regale his general reader? Why include it if the point of the Mexico chapters was for Grant to show how "My experience of the Mexican war was of great advantage to me afterwards." How is feeling sickened by a bullfight an important part of Grant's experience of the Mexican War? How would it have been of great advantage to him in the Civil War? The bullfight material is something he could have withheld. No, we need it to get to know Grant better, some might say. Perhaps, but what does it tell us that we need to know?

Whether his sickened feeling reveals a strength or a weakness depends on a particular reader's sensibility. What does not depend on a particular sensibility is the incongruity between Grant's picture of himself sickened by a single bullfight and the historically informed reader's association of Grant with the subsequent suffering of tens of thousands of beasts and men, not to mention women and children linked to those men or caught in the path of Grant's armies. Does the bullfight material present a straightforward, simple, truthful picture of Grant as a young officer, one intended to personalize him for his reader? Or does it telegraph another message, an encrypted one about the later suffering to be withheld from the reader by the same person who directed much of the violence that intensified the suffering?

If we recognize this last possibility, a pattern emerges in *Personal Memoirs of U. S. Grant*. Again and again in his book Grant approached instances of violence and suffering indirectly, withholding much and providing only spare, telegraphic renderings. In his account of the Battle of Shiloh, for example, his narrative reaches the night of April 6–7, 1862, a night of drenching rain and pain resulting from a fall Grant took from his horse. "Some time after midnight, growing restive under the storm and continuous pain, I moved back to the log-house under the bank." The log house had become a hospital, "and all night wounded men were being brought in, their wounds dressed, a leg or an arm amputated." Wounds are the wages of war, Grant could have said. Or he could have remarked on witnessing at close range the results of his decisions and commands. What he offered instead was a single sentence that could have been written by Frank Wilkeson or any private soldier, one who bore no responsibility for what he was seeing: "The sight was more unendurable than encountering the enemy's fire, and I returned to my tree in the rain." One does not have to be a pacifist to wonder how the commanding general can justify turning from the harvest he had helped to sow. No doubt several of the surgeons and orderlies would have liked to turn away, too. What did he want his reader to learn from the vulnerability he revealed? Why not omit the sentence altogether?[41]

The pattern continues in chapter 33 with the Mississippi battle of Grand Gulf on April 29, 1863. Having quoted the orders he sent John A. McClernand, Grant turned in the next paragraph to the ineffective bombardment of the Confederate position and his subsequent boarding of the *Benton*, Admiral David D. Porter's flagship, hit by a shell "which penetrated the ship's side and exploded between decks where the men were working their guns." In language recalling the bullfight, Grant again focused on his own response, omitting any larger commentary about his connection to events or any expression of concern or compassion for the people involved: "The sight of the mangled and dying men which met my eyes as I boarded the ship was sickening." The combination of sensitivity and detachment is odd or, in Sherman's language, mysterious. In this case, the connection between Grant's orders and the casualties that followed them is more explicit than in the Shiloh chapter, if only because Grant placed the reprinted orders and the references to casualties side by side. But why tell us he is sickened? Why place his own suffering at the center? Is his psychic distress more important for a reader than the physical ordeal of the mangled and dying men? Or is he implying that you, too, general reader, would have felt the same way if you had been there, and so let us say no more about it?[42]

A variation in the pattern closes chapter 35, which culminates in the Battle of Champion's Hill, fought east of Vicksburg on May 16, 1863. "While a battle is raging one can see his enemy mowed down by the thousand or the ten thousand, with great composure," Grant began the final sentence of the chapter. He then supplied what some might have missed in earlier accounts of Shiloh and Grand Gulf: "but after the battle these scenes are distressing, and one is naturally disposed to do as much to alleviate the suffering of an enemy as a friend." At this moment, halfway through his book, Grant balanced composure with compassion, fulfilling a popular image of him: he did not shy from violence he believed necessary, but after violence subsided, he worked for healing and reconciliation. One might even suspect that Grant-the-reader-of-novels shaped his memoirs with a subplot to put this enlargement of his sensibilities on record shortly before the end of volume 1. If he did so, the book becomes in part about his own development, not only as a military leader but as a human being. This reading is attractive but not adequate because it does not account for the phrase "these scenes are distressing." Omit this phrase, with the "and" that follows, and the ideal of Grant as compassionate warrior shines more brightly. Retain the phrase, and Grant's own psychic distress is still part of the picture. Not only is it part of the picture; it appears to be what prompted his efforts to ease suffering. What if he felt no distress about his enemy's suffering? He would not be the only one among general officers, U.S. or Confederate. Few people associate Nathan Bedford Forrest with such distress, for example.[43]

Volume 2 of *Personal Memoirs of U. S. Grant* contains fewer expressions of Grant's distress at the sight of wounded and dying men. Some may argue that a reader cannot expect of volume 2 the level of crafting in volume 1 because of Grant's final illness, but this argument is not necessarily sound. Grant's final illness did keep him from including material he might have added if had lived longer. He might have spent more time, for example, on details of the Petersburg Campaign he claimed would not interest a general reader. His illness also meant he had to depend on his sons, particularly Fred, "to verify from the records every statement of fact given," as he stated in the preface. But the intensity of his own suffering, and the brevity of time he had remaining, may have helped focus Grant's writing. There was no room for a digression into bullfighting. And with his own sickness bearing down on him, telling his reader how battle casualties sickened him may have seemed beside the point. Whatever the truth, the writing of volume 2, particularly as it moves toward Appomattox, gathers a focused momentum fully appropriate to the matters it treats and the imperatives of satisfying closure. There is, however, one large exception to this statement: Cold Harbor.

When he first picked up pen or pencil to fulfill the contract he made with Mark Twain, Ulysses S. Grant knew he had an appointment with June 3, 1864. His own commitment to honesty might have served him as a sufficient prompt, but if it did not, he also had the knowledge that any member of his audience with a memory of the Overland Campaign would be expecting some explanation of that day. Even with U.S. victory, two terms as president, and a world tour as the most famous American alive all behind him, Grant had to face the assault he ordered for 4:30 a.m. that Friday at Cold Harbor; he had to face it knowing it contributed to public images of him as a butcher. In confronting Cold Harbor, Grant had to write about the magnitude of his responsibility for suffering caused by violence he ordered. To make matters more difficult and complex, he had to write about his responsibility for violence and suffering that were unnecessary. He faced this task with his mysterious combination of strength and weakness. "I have always regretted that the last assault at Cold Harbor was ever made." If he had been telegraphing, he might have pared down to "Always regretted last assault at Cold Harbor," but the version in the memoirs, hardly inflated, augments its force with the phrase "was ever made," which gives Grant's regret an echoing resonance through time, both the subsequent time of his life and that of Civil War history as it has been written from 1864 to the present.[44]

Grant's admission of regret took strength. But the weakness shows up in his rendering of what happened at Cold Harbor. Commenting sparely, telegraphically, "This assault cost us heavily and probably without benefit to compensate," he went on to print four pages of documents—an uncharacteristically large number for him to include in the body of his text—beginning with a message to George G. Meade and then following with four messages to Robert E. Lee, sent from June 5 through June 7, 1864. Writing retrospectively twenty years later, Grant let his 1864 messages to Lee express his concern for "wounded men, probably of both armies, now lying exposed and suffering between the lines." In the next sentence he put on record his appeal to a larger principle of civilized warfare: "Humanity would dictate that some provision should be made to provide against such hardships." Nowhere in the four messages did he speak explicitly of his own distress, and nowhere did he let Lee, who did not need to be told what humanity would dictate, speak for himself. Grant was managing the story carefully for his readers. He briefly summarized Lee's responses and interpolated these summaries between his own messages. The closest Grant came to expressing his distress came in a refrain running through his final message, sent at 10:30 a.m. on Tuesday, June 7, four days after the cessation of fighting, by which time many of the wounded had died. "I regret," Grant began, referring to the late arrival of Lee's last message. He then expressed regret that "two officers and six men of the 8th and 25th North Carolina Regts.," who were out searching for bodies from their respective regiments, were captured "owing to this want of understanding." And he expressed regret a third time in the closing sentence of the message: "Regretting that all my efforts for alleviating the sufferings of wounded men left upon the battle-field have been rendered nugatory, I remain, & c."[45]

The regretful refrain continues in the next paragraph with "I have always regretted the last assault at Cold Harbor." Regret, regret, regret, regret. A reader could move through these pages and think, How open Grant was about his regret, and how humane, working hard to alleviate suffering—the same phrase he used when describing the aftermath of Champion's Hill—also regretting when his efforts proved "nugatory," an unusual word for Grant, a rarely used Latinate one meaning inconsequential, vain, or trifling (from *nugae*, meaning "trifles"). Closing the subject, Grant waved away Cold Harbor in the final sentence of the paragraph: "When we reached the James River, however, all effects of the battle of Cold Harbor seemed to have disappeared." In his memoirs, then, Grant made Cold Harbor unfortunate but of no lasting significance.

This dismissal of Cold Harbor did not end the chapter, however. Grant spent one more long paragraph justifying an assault he "might say the same thing of," the assault of May 22, 1863, at Vicksburg, in which U.S. casualties exceeded three thousand. Unlike the assault at Cold Harbor, however, "there was more justification for the assault at Vicksburg," and the justification continued for almost four hundred words more, about twice the length of Grant's commentary on Cold Harbor after the four messages to Lee. If the subject of the paragraph about the May 22 assault at Vicksburg were really that assault, then the corresponding paragraph belonged at the end of chapter 36, where Grant actually said much "the same thing" he said later of Cold Harbor: "This last attack only served to increase our casualties without giving any benefit whatever." But that is not the real subject of the final paragraph of the Cold Harbor chapter; the real subject was the inevitable fallibility of Grant's judgment and how haunting and costly his mistakes could be.[46]

He withheld that subject, perhaps for him the most distressing of all, and the way he manipulated the omission becomes clear when we compare the four letters he sent Robert E. Lee with Lee's responses. Lee's responses to Grant's messages reveal that the Confederate leader was working just as hard as Grant to alleviate suffering, but Lee wanted to stick to the established practice of displaying a white flag wherever there were wounded or dead to recover. Delays in communication exacerbated the difference in approaches, and ineffectiveness followed. Grant's memoirs make it seem that Lee frustrated his efforts and humane intentions. But the correspondence between Grant and Lee did not end with the four messages printed in the memoirs. At 2:00 p.m. on June 7, Lee acknowledged receipt of Grant's 10:30 a.m. message and continued, "I am willing, if you desire it, to devote the hours between 6 and 8 this afternoon to accomplish that object upon the same terms as set forth in my letter of 7 p.m. yesterday." "If this will answer your purpose and you will send parties from your lines at the hour designated, with white flags," Lee added, "I will direct that they be recognized, and be permitted to collect the dead and the wounded." Grant endorsed this letter, which he referred to Meade, with the notation "I will notify Gen. Lee that hostilities will cease from 6 to 8 for the purposes mentioned." But then at 5:30 p.m. Grant wrote Lee, "It will be impossible for me to communicate the fact of the truce by the hour named by you, (6 p.m.) but I will avail myself of your offer at the earliest possible moment which I hope will not be much after that hour."[47]

Including these last communications would end the Cold Harbor chapter more truthfully, but doing so would not present Grant the same way or meet audience expectations the same way. The version in the memoirs downplays Grant's costly mistake at Cold Harbor by overemphasizing a carefully shaped account of his correspondence with Lee and by shifting away from Cold Harbor to the misplaced digression about May 22, 1863, at Vicksburg. Even the grammar of his confession muffles his role in events. He did not say, "I have always regretted I ordered the last assault at Cold Harbor"; he muted the admission with the passive construction of his regret that "the last assault . . . was ever made." It is possible to point out these strategies without condemning Grant, however. If he chose to omit his drinking from his book, that was his choice and his business; if he could admit regret about the assault at Cold Harbor but could not quite bring himself to probe the depth of that regret and the causes of it more fully, he was showing the mysterious combination of strength and weakness William T. Sherman knew well.

When *Personal Memoirs of U. S. Grant* next treats correspondence with Robert E. Lee, ten months have passed in the war, and ten chapters in the book. Arriving at April 1865, Grant did not summarize Lee's letters this time; he let Lee speak for himself. He also included a detail that recalled the sickening bullfight and other references to his distress. Having quoted communications on April 7 with the Confederate leader about the surrender of his army, Grant turned to April 8, which found him in Curdsville, Virginia, feeling unwell. "I was suffering very severely with a sick headache, and stopped at a farmhouse on the road some distance in the rear of the main body of the army." If a bullfight could sicken Grant in a single afternoon, and brief glimpses of the wounded at Shiloh and Grand Gulf do the same, what effect would eleven months of fighting the Army of Northern Virginia have on him? This time, however, Grant did not make explicit the link between his distress and what was going on around him. He lingered instead on details of a nineteenth-century remedy for a migraine. "I spent the night in bathing my feet in hot water and mustard, and putting mustard plasters on my wrists and the back part of my neck, hoping to be cured by morning." Coming across this sentence in isolation, one might fail to guess that its source was *Personal Memoirs of U. S. Grant*. The scene is homely, prosaic, unmilitary, unheroic. It hardly suggests material for a book with a general's four gold stars stamped on his cover. But the scene is personal, as personal as anything in *Personal Memoirs*, and it provided exactly the right detail, worthy of novelists he admired, for Grant to show—not tell—what the war was doing to him. Waking on Palm Sunday, April 9, he "was still suffering with the sick headache." But when he "saw the contents" of Lee's note requesting "an interview in accordance with the offer contained in your letter of yesterday"—Grant actually received duplicate copies sent by Lee—he made three small words do the telegraphic work of hundreds: "I was cured."[48]

News of Robert E. Lee's willingness to surrender the Army of Northern Virginia could not help but have a salutary effect of Ulysses S. Grant, but Grant's management of this scene—the details, the pacing, the tone—suggests a miracle story as dramatic and sudden as anything in the Bible or the writings of other religions. Manuscript evidence shows he made one small but significant change to it. In its earlier form the relevant sentence reads, "I stopped night of 8th at farm house suffering very much from nervous headache." If not cured by miracle, any headache cured so suddenly would suggest one with psychosomatic origins. Along with its other meanings, the word "nervous" has described a disorder or dysfunction of the nerves since the fifteenth century. It is certainly the right word in this context, and yet Grant changed it. Why? The word "nervous" appears only twice in *Personal Memoirs*, and each time it describes someone Grant did not admire: General William J. Worth, in Mexico ("He was nervous, impatient and restless on the march") and Secretary of War Edwin M. Stanton ("Finding that I was out he became nervous and excited"). Although there is plenty of evidence to suggest that Ulysses S. Grant battled with his nerves, "nervous" carried connotations he apparently preferred to do without, opting instead for the plain, four-letter Germanic word "sick," which appears frequently in the memoirs and which he had used before to describe his response to wounds and suffering. Revising a nervous headache into a sick one is not the same as omitting drinking or withholding sickening specifics of war, but it suggests that Grant's phrase "the matters treated of" points not only to the matters themselves but to the treatment of those matters, the way they are managed and handled by someone keenly aware of how he is conducting himself in writing. With the nervous headache revised to a sick one, and the sick one cured by a note, Grant had prepared his reader for his treatment of the one scene without which there would be no memoirs.[49]

Full Circle

"When I put my pen to the paper I did not know the first word that I should make use of in writing the terms." So Grant resumed his story after quoting in full the terms of surrender he wrote out for Robert E. Lee and the Army of Northern Virginia in the parlor of Wilmer McLean's house. But earlier surrenders in Tennessee and Mississippi, as well as correspondence with Lee over the last two days, would suggest Grant could not have entered the McLean house with his mind a blank slate. If his statement meant he was improvising wholly from scratch, it is a bit of a stretcher, as Mark Twain would say. If his statement meant only that he did not bring with him a rough draft of the surrender terms written out in advance, it is more credible and still impressive. What makes the statement more noteworthy, especially for someone admired for his humility, is that it smacks a little of bragging. The story does not require it.

By this point in *Personal Memoirs*, we have seen many important documents written by Grant, and he has never told us about their genesis or the process of their composition before. In a letter written to Julia from City Point, Virginia, dated August 1, 1864, we get a vivid glimpse of his wartime writing routine. "Love to all and kisses for you and the children. I write, as usual, after every body else is in bed, and with full twelve hours constant wrighting to do, which I must do, before me." Somewhere along the way during four years of war, with so much writing to do and after he mastered the art of composing telegrams, Grant learned to write according to the principle he laid out in the next sentence: "I only knew what was in my mind, and I wished to express it clearly, so that there could be no mistaking it." This principle shaped the message he sent Simon Buckner at Fort Donelson in February 1862, and it continued to shape letters, reports, and telegrams he wrote afterward. But the document he penned in Wilmer McLean's parlor was different, and Grant obviously knew it. Its significance in April 1865 was large enough; it directly affected prospects for the cessation of hostilities in Virginia and in other theaters, where hostilities could have continued in the form of guerrilla war. Between 1865 and 1885 its significance only increased, as it directly affected Grant's postwar relations with former Confederate leaders, his acceptability as a presidential candidate, and the course of Reconstruction during his term in office. That anyone could compose such an important document in one draft, needing only two minor cancellations and three small insertions, certified the writer as one of uncommon ability.[50]

The principle also shaped how Ulysses S. Grant wrote his memoirs. Or that is the implication behind his rendering of the scene in McLean's parlor: This is the unpremeditated way I wrote out the surrender terms at Appomattox Court House, and it is the same unpremeditated way I have been writing out the big, two-volume book before you, general reader. "I only knew what was in my mind, and I wished to express it clearly." William Dean Howells and Thomas Wentworth Higginson, along with many others, did not question then, and have not questioned since, Grant's artless transparency. For these readers what Grant had in his mind is what he gave us, clearly and unmistakably. Higginson's comment about Grant's rendering of the Appomattox scene is worth recalling here: "When he describes that famous interview between himself and General Lee, in which was settled the permanent destiny of the American nation, the tale is told far more quietly than the ordinary reporter would describe the negotiations for a college rowing match." Quietly? Gertrude Stein should put us on our guard against that word. What Grant had in his mind, in 1885 when he told his tale, may not have been quite so simple.

Consider, for example, Grant's often-repeated contrast between Robert E. Lee's uniform and his own: "In my rough, traveling suit, the uniform of a private with the straps of a lieutenant-general, I must have contrasted very strangely with a man so handsomely dressed, six feet high and of faultless form." One can read this sentence as Grant's self-effacing acknowledgment that during the muddy, rushing, head-aching finale of the Appomattox Campaign he inadvertently underdressed for the occasion. One can also read it as a parable about the triumph of democratic average, as Walt Whitman called it, over aristocratic privilege. The uniform of a private with the straps of a lieutenant general offers an apt metaphor for the ideal of U.S. citizenship. "I once had a sparrow alight upon my shoulder for a moment while I was hoeing in a village garden," Henry David Thoreau wrote in *Walden* (1854), a book celebrating this ideal, "and I felt that I was more distinguished by that circumstance than I should have been by any epaulet I could have worn." When it came time to publish Grant's book, after the general had added a fourth star to his straps, Samuel Clemens the businessman and Mark Twain the fiction maker knew the symbolic power of what the son of an Ohio tanner wore on his shoulders, and the publisher made sure to stamp its likeness on the cover of Grant's book.

What else was in Grant's mind as he sat in Mount McGregor and drew the contrast between himself and Lee? Manuscript evidence gives no help here; one of the unsolved mysteries in Grant scholarship is the whereabouts of the draft pages about the surrender scene at Appomattox. They do not reside with the drafts of *Personal Memoirs of U. S. Grant* at the Library of Congress. In his manuscript account the last pages describe only Grant's headache on April 8 and his approach to Appomattox Court House on April 9. Then they switch abruptly away to William T. Sherman's progress in North Carolina. We cannot mull over the drafts to see what the author had in mind. But we can look a little more closely at the relevant passages in the memoirs.

In the paragraph immediately preceding the one contrasting his appearance with Lee's, Grant made a foray into his own interior. "What General Lee's feelings were I do not know," he admitted. "Whatever his feelings, they were entirely concealed from my observation." This is the language of trustworthy witness; it does not presume to project itself beyond what the senses make available. But the same trustworthy witness, without appearing to violate his own objectivity, could open for his reader a glimpse into the personal: "but my own feelings, which had been quite jubilant on the receipt of his letter, were sad and depressed." No general reader, whether from the nineteenth century or the twenty-first, could ask for more artless transparency than that. The transparency is all the more remarkable coming from someone who often looked inscrutable to others, as, for that matter, he may well have looked to Robert E. Lee. A glimpse of personal feelings at this moment should come as no surprise to a reader who has watched Grant in Mexico in 1848 at the bullfight or in Missouri in 1861 at the abandoned Confederate camp of Thomas A. Harris, where the newly commissioned colonel of the Twenty-First Illinois learned a valuable lesson on discovering that "Harris had been as much afraid of me as I had been of him." What may come as a surprise is the quick transition in the Appomattox scene from Grant's personal feelings to his politics: "I felt like anything rather than rejoicing at the downfall of a foe who had fought so long and valiantly, and had suffered so much for a cause," he continued, expressing sentiments wholly compatible with reconciliation between white citizens of the warring sections. But then came the pivot: "though that cause was, I believe, one of the worst for which a people ever fought, and one for which there was the least excuse." Grant's turn in this sentence, which leaves unclear whether he was talking about slavery or secession, reverses the structure of a moment in Abraham Lincoln's Second Inaugural Address. Whereas Grant began with a gesture of acceptance and then moved toward judgment, Lincoln did the opposite: "It may seem strange that any men should dare to ask a just God's assistance in wringing their bread from the sweat of other men's faces; but let us judge not that we be not judged." Though built differently, each man's sentence performed the same feat, accepting and judging at the same time.[51]

From the interior Grant moved nimbly to the exterior and the contrast between his appearance and Lee's, a contrast now invested with larger implications from the previous paragraph. Having said how "very strangely" he must have looked next to Lee, Grant finished with this addendum: "But this was not a matter that I thought of until afterwards." Asserting the absence of self-consciousness at Appomattox, on the one hand, this statement admits, on the other, the onset of self-consciousness later. The difference between the original absence of self-consciousness and its subsequent presence complicates any notion of what Grant had in his mind and was trying to express clearly and unmistakably. For one thing, his appearance at Appomattox was not as casual, or apparently inadvertent, as he suggested. It was modeled closely on the appearance of Zachary Taylor in Mexico. "General Taylor never made any great show or parade, either of uniform or retinue," Grant observed with implicit admiration in chapter 7, the first about the war in Mexico. "In dress he was possibly too plain, rarely wearing anything in the field to indicate his rank, or even that he was an officer." At Appomattox Grant did not follow Taylor in being "possibly too plain," but he did make certain to avoid anything like what he described as the two "unfortunate" occasions on which Taylor appeared in full uniform in Mexico. Although Grant may not have thought about the contrast between Lee and himself until afterward, he had clearly thought about the example set by Zachary Taylor before the meeting at Appomattox. The straps of a lieutenant general do not just appear on the uniform of a private. That contrast takes some forethought, and it is not artless. It says, I am like Zachary Taylor in one way, but I am not too plain, as he was.

Then there is the matter of the Robert E. Lee with whom Grant contrasted himself, "six feet high and of faultless form." From the perspective of Grant's five feet, eight inches, Lee certainly looked taller, but Grant's account magnified the Confederate leader. At the end of March 1863, Lee was "aged fifty-six, florid, about 5 feet 10 ½ inches in height, and weighed about 165 pounds," according to Douglas Southall Freeman. That month he was diagnosed with "inflammation of the heart-sac." Although by April 1865 Lee may have recovered from attacks of sciatica, lumbago, or rheumatism (October 1863) or ten days of debilitating diarrhea (May–June 1864), he still would not have reached six feet in height, and after the rigors of the Appomattox Campaign it is doubtful he could have been "of faultless form." True, according to Freeman, Robert E. Lee had good teeth, whereas we know from a letter to Julia that Grant had dentures. But good teeth do not make a six-footer of faultless form. For that image one would need the popular tradition of Jesus as the only human being exactly six feet tall. Whether or not Grant had this ideal anywhere in his mind, front or back, when describing Lee, his description of his adversary was not as artless as Thomas Wentworth Higginson believed.[52]

In rendering Lee as a six-foot man of faultless form, Grant was playing with what he himself called a few paragraphs later "the purest romance." He used this phrase in dismissing the story that Lee had handed over his sword, only to have Grant hand it back. By 1885 Grant had to contend with the purest romance in many forms, with myths and legends that had arisen in the twenty years since the surrender, as in the case of "the famous apple tree," under which the surrender was supposed to have taken place. "Like many other stories, it would be very good if it was only true," Grant quipped with the dry humor of Abraham Lincoln and Mark Twain. But the humor had a serious side. In the following chapter, Grant turned the same deflating scrutiny on the mythology of the Lost Cause or, in the phrasing of the chapter title, on "Relative Conditions of the North and South." "I have often heard gentlemen, who were thoroughly loyal to the Union, speak of what a splendid fight the South had made and successfully continued for four years before yielding, with their twelve million of people against our twenty, and of the twelve four being colored slaves, non-combatants." Then for the next few pages Grant rebutted, with the rigorous precision of Lincoln in his debates against Stephen A. Douglas, various claims that the North enjoyed all the advantages during the war.[53]

As for the purest romance about Robert E. Lee's sword, it brought Grant back to his composition of the surrender document. "The word sword or side arms was not mentioned by either of us until I wrote it in the terms," Grant explained. What came next restated the earlier claim about how he wrote at Appomattox: "There was no premeditation, and it did not occur to me until the moment I wrote it down." Where did the sudden prompting come from? Grant mentioned the Bible exactly once in *Personal Memoirs*, in chapter 2 during remarks about the "line between the Rebel and Union element in Georgetown . . . so marked that it led to divisions even in the churches." But the son of Jesse and Hannah Grant, who helped found the Methodist church in Georgetown, Ohio, knew his Bible and in describing how he wrote at Appomattox, he was echoing, consciously or not, a well-known verse from Matthew: "Take no thought how or what ye shall speak: for it shall be given you in that same hour what ye shall speak" (10:19). Even without the biblical precedent, Grant's portrait of himself as spontaneous writer aligned him with the mysterious energies of special inspiration, classical or romantic, divine or secular.

Mark Twain left no evidence that he doubted the tale Grant told, whether about how he wrote the surrender terms at Appomattox or about anything else. But over the twenty years since he praised Grant's simple message to Simon Buckner at Fort Donelson, Samuel Clemens had learned much as Mark Twain about good stories, how to make them better, and how to sell them. In the case of *Personal Memoirs of U. S. Grant*, Twain knew he had twelve hundred pages of good stories and more. He also knew that Ulysses S. Grant had developed unusual powers as a writer, and when it came to producing and marketing the book Grant left behind, he knew how to call public attention to those powers, even if doing so meant contributing to romance. Between pages 496 and 497 of volume 2, Charles L. Webster and Company inserted a "fac-simile of the terms of Lee's surrender . . . copied from the original document furnished the publishers through the courtesy of General Ely S. Parker, Military Secretary on General Grant's staff at the time of the surrender." Printed on yellow paper, "the color of the paper of the original document," the foldout insertion measures about fourteen inches by ten inches when opened and carries the 1885 copyright of Charles L. Webster and Company at the bottom. With the insertion open, readers of the first edition could see "all interlineations and erasures" while pondering the feat of Grant's unpremeditated composition. Readers of modern paperback editions, even those that reprint the document on regular-sized black-and-white pages, do not have the same experience.

The first edition of *Personal Memoirs of U. S. Grant* contained one other foldout insertion, which modern paperback editions do not include. This one also showed readers an original document written by Grant, and when opened out from between pages 312 and 313 of volume 1, the facsimile measures about twenty inches, extending roughly fifteen beyond the edge of the right-hand page. It appears on white paper, and no long footnote from the publisher accompanies it. The facsimile consists of a triptych of letters, one by Ulysses S. Grant filling the middle space. The other two letters, flanking Grant's, reproduce those written to him by Simon Buckner at Fort Donelson in February 1862. The central letter is the one mentioned in Mark Twain's journal in July 1866. Twain may have gotten the idea for inserting a facsimile of it after reading Lew Wallace's article "The Capture of Fort Donelson" in the December 1884 issue of *Century*, which also included an excerpt from *The Adventures of Huckleberry Finn*. *Century* devoted a full page of Wallace's article to a facsimile of Grant's "Unconditional Surrender" dispatch. Whether or not the inspiration for going *Century* one better, with the larger foldout, was Twain's own, the insertion paid homage, once again, to the eloquent simplicity of Ulysses S. Grant. The younger Samuel Clemens recognized it, and the older Mark Twain published it. Without that eloquent simplicity Twain might not have done so. If he had not done so, he would have had no reason to try to follow up Grant's successful reconstruction with others designed to gratify audience expectations, too.

5

GEORGE B. McCLELLAN'S MANY TURNINGS

George Brinton McClellan died in October 1885, three months after Ulysses S. Grant did and a little more than a year before Mark Twain's Webster and Company published *McClellan's Own Story: The War for the Union, the Soldiers Who Fought It, the Civilians Who Directed It, and His Relations to It*, copyrighted 1886 with an 1887 date on its title page. When it came to meeting audience expectations, Webster and Company faced a new situation with McClellan's book. Although it was published posthumously, as Grant's was, McClellan's book also was assembled posthumously, as Grant's was not. Missing from publication of *McClellan's Own Story* was the author's dramatic race against terminal illness to complete his book the month he died, a contest widely covered by the press. Public attitudes toward McClellan also varied more widely than did attitudes toward Grant. Grant certainly had his admirers and his detractors, but McClellan inspired both more intense affection among some and more intense disgust among others. Mark Twain himself belonged to the second group, but he set aside his distaste in order to cash in on Little Mac's popularity. As he wrote his wife in July 1887, after a train trip during which he read part of *Memoirs of Prince Metternich* (1880–82), "Metternich's book removes the obloquy from his name, but McClellan's deepens that upon *his*, & justifies it." Despite Twain's reservations, McClellan's book turned a profit, and profit is what mattered to the man in charge of Webster and Company.[1]

Over the nearly 150 years since publication of his book, views of McClellan's role in the military and political drama of the Civil War remain divided. The aim here is to set aside for a moment both censure and praise in order to examine an understudied event in the military-literary history of the Civil War, the publication of McClellan's reconstructed war. This event repays dispassionate scrutiny apart from the controversies in which it originated and which it in turn has helped to perpetuate. *McClellan's Own Story* offers an instructive example of how the Civil War memory market depends on division to sell its products, which in turn perpetuate division. Good as truth and reconciliation may be for social and political healing, they are not so good for the Civil War memory business. Whereas Twain's competitors profited from division by publishing books from North and South, Twain attempted to profit from it by publishing books on either side of a northern divide, Grant's and McClellan's.

Soldiers' Love versus His Dark Side

In the small public park bounded by California Street, Columbia Road, and Connecticut Avenue in northwest Washington, D.C., stands an equestrian statue of George B. McClellan. One of nine equestrian statues of U.S. Civil War generals in the District, that of McClellan, perhaps on Dan Webster, the horse he called most trustworthy, is the work of Frederick William MacMonnies, graduate of the École des Beaux-Arts and choice of a commission advised by fellow artists Daniel Chester French, Augustus Saint-Gaudens, and Charles Follen McKim. At the unveiling on Thursday, May 2, 1907, not quite twenty-two years after McClellan's heart failed him at age fifty-eight, President Theodore Roosevelt gave the address to a crowd that included Mrs. George B. McClellan, called Nelly by her husband, and their son, George B. McClellan Jr., known to his family as Max, then serving his second term as mayor of New York. As was his wont, Roosevelt exhorted his audience to live active lives of strenuous effort and endeavor in the performance of challenging duty. This particular chapter in the muscular and masculine gospel according to Theodore Roosevelt moved beyond the equestrian statue before him into panoramic national vision: "America will stand for much provided only that it treats material comfort, material luxury, and the means for acquiring such, as the foundation on which to build the real life, the life of spiritual and moral effort and achievement."[2]

Roosevelt's speech runs about ten pages in published form. Of those ten pages George McClellan himself received exactly one paragraph:

> To General McClellan it was given to command in some of the hardest fought battles and most important campaigns of the great war of this hemisphere, so that his name will be forever linked with the mighty memories that arise when we speak of Antietam and South Mountain, Fair Oaks and Malvern; so that we never can speak of the great Army

> of the Potomac, without having rise before us the figure of General McClellan, the man who organized and first led it. There was also given to him the peculiar gift, one that is possessed by but very few men, to combine the qualities that won him the enthusiastic love and admiration of the soldiers who fought under him, and the qualities that in civil life endeared him peculiarly to all who came in contact with him.[3]

Many things stand out here, among them one of Roosevelt's favorite adjectives, "mighty," which appears two other times in the same address; the selective listing of McClellan victories out of chronological order, as they also appear on the plinth of his statue; and the familiar description of McClellan as an excellent organizer much loved by the rank and file he organized. By the time of Roosevelt's speech, this description had established itself as orthodoxy in public memory of the Civil War, even among McClellan's critics. With the appearance in 1901 of Peter S. Michie's biography *General McClellan* in the Great Commanders series, published in New York by D. Appleton and Company, the orthodoxy became available to Roosevelt, sworn in after the assassination of William McKinley that year, in this neatly compressed, one-sentence form: "But whatever may be the judgment that history will ultimately formulate with regard to McClellan's qualifications in the domain of strategy and tactics, there will be no divided opinion with respect to his talents and attainments for the organization of armies, and the wonderful power that he possessed of implanting in the hearts of his soldiers a personal affection and devotion that has never been excelled."[4]

Abridged as it may be, Roosevelt's affirmative summary of McClellan's career scrupulously avoided negative, hyperbolic caricatures of him in wide circulation, beginning with wartime newspapers and political cartoons, continuing in recent memory with Ken Burns's documentary *The Civil War* (1990), and still flourishing today. In March 1862 Nathaniel Hawthorne, along with publisher William D. Ticknor, traveled from Massachusetts to Washington "to look a little more closely at matters" there and subsequently published his account of the trip as the controversial essay "Chiefly about War-Matters," printed in the July 1862 *Atlantic Monthly*, where the author signed himself "A Peaceable Man." In this essay, which some read partly as a tongue-in-cheek hoax, especially in its fictional footnotes, Hawthorne noted meeting McClellan against the backdrop of "a most fierce and bitter outcry, and detraction loud and low, against [him], accusing him of sloth, imbecility, cowardice, treasonable purposes, and, in short, utterly denying his ability as a soldier, and questioning his integrity as a man." In contrast, Hawthorne offered his own more favorable endorsement, taking his cue from the cheers of McClellan's soldiers as the general rode past them: "If he is a coward, or a traitor, or a humbug, or anything less than a brave, true, and able man, that mass of intelligent soldiers, whose lives and honor he had in charge, were utterly deceived, and so was this present writer; for they believed in him, and so did I; and had I stood in the ranks, I should have shouted with the lustiest of them."[5]

Since Hawthorne put the dark side of McClellan's reputation on public record in 1862, it has remained alive and well, despite formulaic, often token homages to his ability to organize soldiers who loved him. Deriving their authority from the ascendancy and prestige of psychoanalysis, McClellan's harshest critics have attempted to account for his negative reputation by subjecting McClellan himself to unsparing, if not anachronistic, psychiatric examination. In his judiciously balanced study *George B. McClellan and Civil War History* (1998), Thomas J. Rowland efficiently summarized the various pseudoclinical damnations of McClellan that had accumulated by the close of the twentieth century, compiling a formidable train of terms and descriptors for McClellan's innate psychological defects: manic depression, arrogant confidence, wretched self-abasement, vanity, instability, inherent lack of discipline, pathological lying, unrestrained ego, delusions of grandeur, possession by demons, psychosis, morose view of life, dark fatalism, martinet tendencies, innate querulousness, persecution complex, messianic complex, paranoid personality disorder, and, finally, in a quaint nod to the pre-psychoanalytic worldview of Aristotle's *Poetics*, tragic flaw. Having taken his grim inventory, Rowland moved to refute the thinking behind it: "A specious line of reasoning underlies these conclusions." He countered that historians of McClellan "have acted upon their own prejudices and invoked a form of inductive reasoning to ferret out evidence for preordained conclusions," in particular the conclusion that McClellan was a failure whose failure can only be explained by employment—Rowland's word is "exploitation"—of psychological reasons "for the a priori condition of McClellan's failure."[6]

A little garden-variety skepticism and homegrown critical thinking should lead the student of George McClellan to keep in mind a few basic considerations. For one, it is not a self-evident truth that he was a failure. Whether we call the Battle of Sharpsburg-Antietam a draw or a U.S. victory, McClellan's achievement there had large consequences, national and international, for the development and advancement of northern war aims, especially with respect to the timing of Abraham Lincoln's Emancipation Proclamation and its preempting of British intervention. After McClellan was relieved of command in November 1862, the army he built and trained managed to survive disasters under Ambrose E. Burnside and Joseph Hooker, remaining intact until the appointment of George G. Meade before Gettysburg and the advent of Ulysses S. Grant before the Overland Campaign. None of these commanders had to build an army from scratch, and every one of them owed something to McClellan's exhaustive work during the latter part of 1861 and the first part of 1862.

Then there is the question of exactly who failed at what before and during the Peninsula Campaign. Until January 14, 1862, George McClellan's boss was Lincoln's first secretary of war, Simon Cameron, and no one has argued that he was a success in this position. Nor has anyone argued the Cameron's successor, Edwin Stanton, set new standards for transparency, truthfulness, plain dealing, and mental health. Just as important, the U.S. commander in chief, newly elected, raw, untested Abraham Lincoln, was not yet the noninterfering, deferentially supportive war president he would become by the time he brought Grant east as general-in-chief in March 1864. All these men, along with their Confederate counterparts, began 1862 with naive assumptions about the nature of the war they had started, about its intensity and its duration. They did not and could not imagine that by the cessation of fighting in 1865 they would have assisted in transforming war into something for which the terms "home front," "shell shock," "refugee crisis," "war crime," "weapons of mass destruction," "collateral damage," and "posttraumatic stress disorder" had not yet been invented but soon would need to be. In this sense, they were all failures, at least as of early 1862. There are other considerations, too. Was the collapse of the Peninsula Campaign wholly due to McClellan's failure, or did any of it have to do with Robert E. Lee's success? The wound that disabled Joseph E. Johnston at the Battle of Seven Pines brought to Confederate command someone who by the end of the war had a solid record of defeating, or at least checking, the numerically superior Army of the Potomac, and there is no reason to assume that Lee's success against McClellan was either anomalous or entirely a matter of McClellan's weakness. Finally, the supposed failure of McClellan's retreat to Harrison's Landing, Virginia, from which he wrote his superiors recommending it for future operations, looks less delusional or self-serving when one considers that three years later, in the final phase of the war, Ulysses S. Grant also would make the same stretch of the James River his base of operations, though on the opposite shore.[7]

Against the backdrop of controversy, George McClellan's posthumous memoir was largely the work of his literary executor, Democratic newspaper editor William Cowper Prime, whose popular 1857 travel book *Tent Life in the Holy Land* was lampooned by Mark Twain in *The Innocents Abroad* (1869), in which Twain interspersed quotations from William C. "Grimes" with disparaging comments about him. Any twenty-first-century reader of *McClellan's Own Story* interested in Prime's role in its formation owes a large debt to Stephen W. Sears for his thorough detective work into the provenance, editing, and reception of the book. Sears's biography *George B. McClellan: The Young Napoleon* (1988) closed with a brief epilogue summarizing this research and culminating in the conclusion, "Historians have been grateful enough to Prime, certainly, but if his wish [that McClellan would have approved of his editing] was ever granted, it required truly saintly forgiveness on McClellan's part."[8]

From Sears we learn that McClellan began his narrative in the summer of 1865 in Switzerland, where he was living in self-imposed exile after his defeat in the 1864 election. He worked on it until 1868, when he returned to the United States, and resumed it in the mid-1870s, when memoirs by Joseph E. Johnston and William T. Sherman appeared. McClellan completed his narrative in 1881, after his term as governor of New Jersey, and then traveled to Europe for six months, only to return in October 1881 to news that the warehouse in which he had stored the manuscript had burned. Having recovered gamely from discouragement, McClellan set about rewriting his story and was still working on it as late as February 1884, but by the time he died at the end of October 1885, he had completed only 166 manuscript pages, which brought the Army of the Potomac to the Battle of Hanover Court House, May 27, 1862. William Prime then took up the task of filling out a book of nearly seven hundred pages, a task he discharged by assembling a pastiche of McClellan's second manuscript, his 1864 *Report on the Organization and Campaigns of the Army of the Potomac*, dispatches or letters to and from various soldiers and civilians, and, most controversially from Sears's point of view, eleven chapters of excerpts from McClellan's letters to Nelly.[9]

Sears's appraisal of *McClellan's Own Story* was understandably mixed. On the one hand, he endorsed the assertion of *Atlantic Monthly* reviewer John C. Ropes that he "was not moved by the arguments McClellan raised on his own behalf and had little sympathy for him"; Mark Twain himself shared with his wife a similar opinion. No doubt there are fair-minded readers, among the few who still look into *McClellan's Own Story*, who will concur in this judgment, and it is improbable that historians, academic or not, who are already convinced of the dark side of McClellan's psyche will find enough in the book to budge them. On the contrary, it is this very book that has provided them with abundant grist for their psychoanalytic grinding. On the other hand, Sears conceded that "no other major Civil War figure disclosed so much of himself" as McClellan did in what Prime chose to include, and, in the words of a formulation echoed at the end of his biography, "certainly history is grateful to have General McClellan so revealed."[10]

Can one have it both ways? Can one damn, censure, and repudiate the "bastardized" product of William Prime's "protective editing" and still gobble up, with a good, hearty appetite, the fruits of Prime's labor? If integrity and fairness are to be the measures of our endeavors, especially when it comes to the research and writing of history, then why not disregard improperly presented evidence, as a judge would instruct members of a jury to do? At this point one can imagine Mark Twain hearing out Sears's case against Prime and then asking Sears, with a barely suppressed smile, So what? When it came to the business of making and selling books, Twain was no neophyte, and he knew what he was about. In a letter of February 3, 1875, he wrote his friend P. T. Barnum a sentence that could serve as the invisible, understood epigraph for any book he authored or helped to publish. Two weeks before, Barnum had sent Twain passes to the "Greatest Show on Earth," along with a request that the author of *The Innocents Abroad* and *Roughing It* (1872) write something to help boost publicity. In his reply Twain declined, explaining that he had been ill and adding, "I couldn't write the article, anyway, for any price, because it is out of my line; & you know, better than any other man, that success in life depends strictly upon one's sticking to his line."[11]

When it came to Charles L. Webster and Company, and to the publishing of the so-called Shoulder Strap series of memoirs by U.S. generals, Twain's line was getting marketable books out of people who were not professional writers and whose deadline was often death itself, as in the cases of Grant, Sheridan, and Sherman, each of whom died just before or soon after Webster published his book. In the cases of Winfield Scott Hancock and George Armstrong Custer, that mortal deadline had passed, and there could be no question about whose pen produced the book. The title page of *Reminiscences of Winfield Scott Hancock* (1887) states that the book is "By His Wife," Almira, not identified until a picture facing the copyright page, and the title page of *Tenting on the Plains, or General Custer in Kansas and Texas* (1887) reads quite clearly, "By Elizabeth B. Custer / Author of 'Boots and Saddles.'" Samuel Crawford was the lone Shoulder Strap author who outlived his book, *The Genesis of the Civil War* (1887), by several years.

It is only in the case of *McClellan's Own Story* that there could be any ambiguity or room for controversy. The title page reads "By George B. McClellan / Late Major-General Commanding the Armies," while the name William C. Prime does not appear until page xiii, which introduces the "Biographical Sketch / of / George B. McClellan / by / W. C. Prime, LL.D." In the final pages of his biographical sketch, Prime offered a plain statement of his editorial procedure and his editorial aspirations: "In editing this volume for the press I have tried to do that which my friend would approve. The discretion he gave me was ample. I have exercised it by omissions, not by changes." As for his use of McClellan's letters to Nelly, Prime was also direct: "I confess that I hesitated very much about giving any part of these letters, written in the most sacred confidence of life, to the public eye. Others advised that, as he belonged to his country, and innumerable citizens and soldiers loved him with devout affection, they could well be allowed, had indeed a right, to read portions of these letters which reveal McClellan the man, as his narrative shows McClellan the soldier."[12]

Having quoted both these passages, Stephen Sears dismissed them, in the first case pronouncing that Prime's "judgment failed his good intentions." Sears may think so, condemning Prime for his omissions, but in a statement dated November 8, 1881, placed before the first chapter of *McClellan's Own Story,* McClellan anticipated and authorized the "judicious pruning to fit [his account] for public use," claiming that he had "no present intention of publishing anything" during his lifetime. If this statement was true, then McClellan never intended to see his story through publication. He knew any publication would have to be posthumous, and he knew that "judicious pruning" had to be a part of the process. In the case of the second quotation, Sears commented that "it is difficult to understand why Prime believed publishing these letters would enhance his friend's memory." Nevertheless, if Prime believed that publishing McClellan's letters would enhance his friend's memory, he was not necessarily alone. The exact parts played by McClellan's wife and daughter, Nelly and May, remain unclear, but Sears's assertion that there "is no indication that Ellen McClellan had any role in the preparation of her husband's memoirs" cannot satisfy. As Candace Shy Hooper has pointed out, it was Nelly who preserved McClellan's letters, so they did not go up in smoke with his original manuscript in the burning warehouse. More important, Nelly was the general's legal executrix, and it is hardly credible that while living under the same roof with her mother, May could or would have copied out excerpts for Prime without her mother's knowledge and cooperation, or at least her acquiescence.[13]

It is at this point that literary history and military history need to talk. Just as no thorough military historian of Grant's Overland Campaign could tell the whole story of its progress without factoring in the parts played by Quartermaster General Montgomery C. Meigs or Chief Quartermaster Rufus Ingalls, so no thorough historian of *McClellan's Own Story*, military or literary, can tell the whole story without reference to Charles Webster, Mark Twain, and what William Prime called "the money question." Logistics count for much in the military and in publication (as book-publishing historians know perfectly well with respect to their own careers), and historians who approach McClellan's book for the sole purpose of psychoanalyzing him, without reference to how the logistics of publication shaped what they are analyzing, risk doing so naively and through a glass darkly, or at least through a one-way mirror. If Civil War historians read *McClellan's Own Story* in order to damn either McClellan or his editor or both, there is no law prohibiting them from doing so. But one hopes they would acknowledge that damning the former would be more difficult without the work of the latter, and the work of the latter did not emerge in a social or economic vacuum.

To expect the posthumous editing of William Prime to result in something like the memoirs of Sherman, Grant, and Sheridan is to make a mistake of generic classification. If we imagine a spectrum, with an ideal of pure written transcription of Civil War events at one end and an ideal of pure literary invention at the other, then it should be obvious that *The War of the Rebellion: A Compilation of the Official Records of the Union and Confederate Armies* (1880–1901) would be closer to the first end and Stephen Crane's *Red Badge of Courage* (1895) would be closer to the other. Among other differences between them, the Government Printing Office did not publish the *Official Records* with any thought of their strength as literary legal-tender, whereas D. Appleton and Company published *Red Badge of Courage* with that thought uppermost. Memoirs of Sherman, Grant, and Sheridan would fall somewhere between these extremes, as would memoirs written by their Confederate counterparts and published by powerful New York firms, memoirs of Joseph E. Johnston and Richard Taylor, for example. All these memoirs pay homage to standards of factual accuracy as embodied in a written record while bowing to pressures of the literary marketplace. Inevitably the results were hybrids, grafting rhetorical skill and readable presentation for the sake of contemporary sales onto material mined by future historians for documentary evidence in campaign narratives or biographies.

The genre of *McClellan's Own Story* differed from that of books by Sherman,

Grant, and Sheridan only in comprising not a memoir authored by the principal but something closer to an anthology of his writings assembled by an editor. In this way it was more like *Recollections and Letters of General Robert E. Lee*, assembled by Robert E. Lee Jr. and published in New York by Doubleday, Page, and Company in 1904. During the Civil War centennial Edmund Wilson wrote of this last work, "We can only come at all close to Lee through the volume of personal documents compiled by his son, Captain Robert E. Lee." But how close was that? *Recollections and Letters* was, in the phrasing of Gary W. Gallagher, the first book about Lee Sr. "to explore the private man," but the explorations carried out by Robert E. Lee Jr. could not have been less protective of his father than William Prime was of George McClellan. In the cases of both *McClellan's Own Story* and *Recollections and Letters of General Robert E. Lee*, the twenty-first-century reader must work to recover the implied understanding among editor, publisher, and a particular general readership of more than a century ago.[14]

If we think of *McClellan's Own Story* as an anthology of McClellan's writings in different genres rather than the unified narrative he might have written had he survived long enough, and if we consider that Prime's presentation of McClellan was not necessarily more selective or protective than Sherman's or Grant's or Sheridan's presentation of himself, we stand a much better chance of appreciating the readable revelations of George McClellan that William Prime aimed, with Mark Twain's benediction, at a book-buying audience. That audience included, at least hypothetically, veterans of the Army of the Potomac who, in Prime's words, "loved him with devout affection." It also included more than 1.8 million citizens who voted for McClellan in the 1864 election, as well as those living in the South, or sympathetic to it, who valued the prospects of McClellan's election for negotiating their independence.

What shape did the story in *McClellan's Own Story* take for the 1887 readership of the book, and what shape can it take for us now? Privately tutored in Greek and Latin, the young McClellan may not have progressed far enough to read Homer in the original language, but his early exposure to the classics must have included an encounter with some English version of the first line of the *Odyssey*: "Tell me, Muse, about the man of many turns." Among numerous English translations made since the early seventeenth century, this one by Albert Cook comes closest to a literal rendering of Homer's adjective for his eponymous hero, πολύτροπον or *polytropon*, which means "much turned," as in much traveled or much wandering. The George McClellan revealed by William Prime in *McClellan's Own Story* was likewise a man of many turns, some of them whiplashingly sharp. True, the same could be said of hosts of people who led twisting, turning lives much less publicly than McClellan. In McClellan's case, though, the many turnings often caused or accompanied major turnings in the Civil War during the span of his service from April 1861 to November 1862, which is also the narrative span of the book. In rebuttal one could argue that William T. Sherman, Ulysses S. Grant, and Philip H. Sheridan were men of many turnings, too. True again, but Sherman's and Grant's narratives of the war itself showed them turning upward once, from respective nadirs before and after the Battle of Shiloh in 1862, and never looking back as they moved toward victory, while Sheridan's wartime turnings, at least as he wrote about them, included none that led downward.[15]

McClellan's story, by contrast, was one of drastic ups and downs. The first editor of his Mexican War diary, William Starr Myers, a professor of history and politics at Princeton and the colleague there of George B. McClellan Jr., appointed professor of economic history in 1912, put it this way: "His life covered barely fifty-nine years, his services of national prominence only eighteen months, but during this time he experienced such extremes of good and ill fortune, of success and of failure, as seldom have fallen to the lot of one man." Unusual extremes of fortune compressed into unusually short periods of time are the stuff of good stories and have been since the beginning of storytelling, as the tale of Job, which may have originated in ancient Near Eastern folk tradition, makes clear. Some of these extremes had their origins in McClellan's life before the opening of *McClellan's Own Story* in 1861 but had important consequences for his wartime career. One, from the Mexican War, was malaria, which he called his "Mexican disease" and which came back to afflict him in August 1861 and during the Peninsula Campaign. Nor was this the only illness that adversely affected his career. In December 1861, having been called as the first witness to appear before the Joint Committee on the Conduct of the War, McClellan fell seriously ill with typhoid fever and could not appear to defend himself against or influence the terms of debate from the outset. Then there was McClellan's European tour, from April 1855 to April 1856, with a military commission authorized by Franklin Pierce and sent by Secretary of War Jefferson Davis to study the major armies of Europe and observe the war in the Crimea. The report McClellan prepared in Philadelphia during the spring of 1856, published by Congress in 1857, established his authority on matters of military organization. The experience and knowledge behind the report provided the foundation for the later organization of the Army of the Potomac and for McClellan's subsequent legacy in this context.[16]

As for the many turnings of April 1861 to November 1862, a significant portion of 1887 readers already would have known that McClellan's story began with minor successes of the West Virginia campaign, followed by the summons to Washington because of them. Then came the fortification of the capital and the beginnings of army organization. After the lapse at Ball's Bluff, there was the appointment to general-in-chief and Joseph E. Johnston's evacuation of Manassas. The organization of army corps, the removal from his position as general-in-chief, and the opening of the Peninsula Campaign continued the narrative, leading to the Peninsula Campaign, during which McClellan fought the Battle of Williamsburg, described by him as "one of the most brilliant engagements of the war." But a long stretch of dismal, rainy weather that swelled the creeks and rivers followed, as did the wrangling over assignment of Irvin McDowell's corps to service in the Shenandoah Valley. Then came the Seven Days' Battles, the retreat to Harrison's Landing—"cleverly executed," in the words of Robert E. Lee's nephew Fitzhugh—and the controversial letter written there to Abraham Lincoln, along with the withdrawal from the Peninsula and transfer to Washington. The familiar plot turned next to the reassignment of a large portion of the army to John Pope before Second Manassas–Bull Run, the restoration to command, and the move into Maryland. Next the story advanced to the serendipitous recovery of lost Special Order 191, the Battle of Sharpsburg-Antietam, and Burnside's poor performance. Finally, McClellan's decision not to pursue Lee across the Potomac after the battle brought relief from command and the farewell to the army with which *McClellan's Own Story* concludes.[17]

Among Civil War generals who produced books after the war, or who had books associated with them, the career of McClellan's friend Joseph E. Johnston came closest to approximating the dramatic ups and downs of McClellan's, though Johnston's drama unfolded over all four years of war, which brought him to the age of fifty-eight, whereas McClellan's was compressed into a year and a half, which brought him not quite to thirty-six. The more familiar of McClellan's many twists and turns have generated copious commentary, beginning with coverage in wartime periodicals and continuing into the twenty-first century with Ethan S. Rafuse's *McClellan's War* (2005), John C. Waugh's *Lincoln and McClellan* (2010), and Chester G. Hearn, *Lincoln and McClellan at War* (2012). This vast body of commentary could not help but influence general readers. But *McClellan's Own Story* also has striking features that have escaped much or most commentary, features that could help to shape the way the book has been read by many. Here we will consider three.[18]

McClellan and the Almighty

The first feature is God. Another of McClellan's prewar turnings was that of his conversion—or in the words of Stephen Sears his "evangelical religious regeneration"—toward the Presbyterianism, or "rigid Calvinism," of Nelly's family during the seven months of their engagement from October 1859 to May 1860. In his 1901 biography Peter Michie gave a single sentence to this moment in McClellan's life and then said no more about the marriage, Christianity, or their effects on McClellan: "It proved to be a union of two minds that were counterparts of each other, and of two souls whose mutual love was continually strengthened by the powerful influence of a Christian faith." In his introduction to the 1917 edition of McClellan's Mexican War diary, in which the word "God" appears only once, William Starr Myers was similarly succinct: "In after years he became extremely serious, deeply and sincerely religious, sometimes oppressed by a sense of duty." True as these statements may be, the truth behind them has not had a large effect on popular memory of the Civil War, in which the temperate Episcopalian Robert E. Lee and the zealous Presbyterian Stonewall Jackson are prominent fixtures. After them Leonidas Polk, William S. Rosecrans, and Oliver Otis Howard might come to mind. But few twenty-first-century students of the Civil War think first of Christianity when they think of George McClellan, and few popular images of him suggest the connection. There is nothing about it, for example, in Theodore Roosevelt's 1907 speech or Ken Burns's documentary.[19]

Without looking into *McClellan's Own Story*, one would have no reason to distinguish McClellan in this context from the more secular-sounding William T. Sherman, Ulysses S. Grant, and Philip H. Sheridan. In Sherman's memoir "God" appears twenty-five times, either in quotation from someone else (for example, in John Bell Hood's side of the correspondence about treatment of the civilians of Atlanta), in the legal phrase "act of God," or in interjections such as "for God's sake" or "Great God!" In Grant's *Personal Memoirs* "God" appears only six times, always in quotation, direct or indirect from someone else. In Sheridan's memoir it appears four times, twice in quotations and twice in an oath prescribed in the text of the 1867 act "to provide for the more efficient government of the rebel States." Even Joseph E. Johnston, baptized by Leonidas Polk during Sherman's Atlanta Campaign, used "God" only three times in his *Narrative of Military Operations*, once in quotation of Jefferson Davis, once in quotation of Braxton Bragg, and once on his own behalf in closing a letter to the Confederate president, "But the hand of Almighty God has delivered us in times of great danger!"[20]

Readers of *McClellan's Own Story* will find the word "God" appearing ninety-two times, seven in Prime's biographical sketch and eighty-five in the rest of the book, most often in excerpts from letters to Nelly. Some might say that this high number reveals the editorial hand of William Prime, whom Mark Twain called "the gushing pietist." Following the lead of Stephen Sears, others might say that here is incontrovertible evidence of McClellan's messianic complex. Meanwhile, Thomas Rowland and Ethan Rafuse have provided more balanced readings of McClellan's religious sensibility and its social background. Rowland has argued that to "the predominantly secular society of today" McClellan's "stark expression of Calvinist theology and highly stylized piety reverberates discordantly," whereas he was not out of line with the millennialist spirit that characterized "the religious mainstream of his day," and Rafuse has maintained that there was nothing about McClellan's new Presbyterianism incompatible with the Philadelphia Episcopalianism of his upbringing, his inclination toward Whig politics, and a "worldly ambition" that promoted self-improvement, progress, social stability, and "the values of rationalism, moderation, and order."[21]

At least since the adoption of the first amendment to the Constitution, the United States has had a complex and ambivalent relationship to the use of religious language in public places. Add to this complex ambivalence the chasm that divides, on the one hand, relative comfort and familiarity with public language influenced by Judeo-Christianity in the nineteenth century from, on the other, often strong antipathy toward the same in the twenty-first, and many twenty-first-century readers of *McClellan's Own Story* stand little better chance of evaluating its frequent references to God than they do its occasional phrases in Latin. For many contemporary readers the use of religious rhetoric is toxic; there is no getting past it and no appraising its nuances. But religious rhetoric is like any other rhetoric; some people use it in more interesting, significant ways than others, and two skillful rhetoricians can use it in very different ways. Lincoln, for example, often wielded rhythms and images straight from the Bible, while remaining evasive about his religious convictions, whereas McClellan, outspoken about his religious convictions, did not echo or allude to the Bible, at least in the material that comprises *McClellan's Own Story*.

"McClellan could write." The truth of this three-word formulation by William Starr Myers does not rule out the truth of Myers's next sentence: "In fact his pen was too ready and in later years [after the Mexican War] it often led him into difficulties." McClellan's rhetorical readiness, along with the difficulties it sometimes caused him, cannot be separated wholly from his frequent references to God. Several examples from *McClellan's Own Story* illustrate the point, among them some passages sent privately to Nelly, one order issued publicly to the Army of the Potomac during the Peninsula Campaign, and one letter addressed to Abraham Lincoln but subsequently published to the world.[22]

Those who maintain that George McClellan's conversion brought him under the spell of a messiah complex either have to ignore some revealing moments in the correspondence excerpted in *McClellan's Own Story* or massage the word "messiah" to suit their own purposes. Nowhere in the New Testament does the Messiah—the Greek uses *Messias* only twice, both times in the gospel of John, otherwise rendering the Hebrew concept of the anointed one with some form of *Christos*—say anything that sounds like either of these vulnerable moments:

> I appreciate all the difficulties in my path: the impatience of the people, the venality and bad faith of the politicians, the gross neglect that has occurred in obtaining arms, clothing, etc.; and, above all, I feel in my inmost soul how small is my ability in comparison with the gigantic dimensions of the task, and that, even if I had the greatest intellect that was ever given to man, the result remains in the hands of God. (October 31, 1861)

> I hope and trust that God will watch over, guide, and protect me. I accept most resignedly all He has brought upon me. Perhaps I have really brought it on myself; for while striving conscientiously to do my best, it may well be that I have made great mistakes that my vanity does not permit me to perceive. When I see so much self-blindness around me I cannot arrogate to myself greater clearness of vision and self-examination. (July 17, 1862)

The first of these passages was written ten days after the fiasco at Ball's Bluff, the second six days after Henry W. Halleck was named to replace McClellan as general-in-chief. If he sounded like anyone in these passages, it was not Jesus, the anointed one, but Paul, apostle to the Gentiles, who called himself the worst of all sinners (1 Timothy 1:15–16) and spoke figuratively of having a thorn in his flesh that kept him from becoming conceited in the course of his missionary work around the eastern Mediterranean in the middle of the first century (2 Corinthians 12:7). The Messiah or Christ about whom he preached never refers in the gospels to his own small ability, his great mistakes, his vanity, or his blindness. In three of the gospels, Matthew, Mark, and Luke, Jesus prays in Gethsemane that the cup of death be removed from him, and in Luke only he quotes from the cross the opening of Psalm 22, "My God, my God, why hast thou forsaken me?" (King James Version). But these are very different utterances from Paul's or McClellan's, and they are conspicuously absent from John, the most Messianic or Christological of the gospels.[23]

Writing to Nelly in these moments, McClellan showed himself, in his midthirties, to be all too human and, to his credit, aware of it. Even his reference to the uselessness of having the greatest intellect that was ever given to man showed disarming self-awareness. In his biography of his uncle, Fitzhugh Lee stated in a footnote, "General Lee said, after the war, that he considered General McClellan the most intellectual of the Federal generals," but as both Lees learned after Grant assumed overall command in 1864, the most intellectual general and the most effective general are not necessarily the same. In context the footnote followed the statement that "General Lee . . . was sorry to part with McClellan" in November 1862. The cynical reading would be that Lee was sorry to part with someone he bested in the Peninsula Campaign, if not in the Maryland one. In fact Fitzhugh Lee took his uncle's reference to his adversary's intellectual superiority to mean "that as long as McClellan was in command everything would be conducted by the rules of civilized warfare." For his part, McClellan knew that his intellectual power often made him vain, arrogant, and, in the memorable formulation of William Starr Myers, "one of the worst subordinates and best superiors that ever lived." At least McClellan's frequent invocations of God included some that acknowledged this truth.[24]

It is not clear that readers in our own moment are equipped to appreciate the nuances of McClellan's references to God and the rhetoric of his faith. By contrast, many readers of 1887 would have been able to notice distinct features of those references, or more accurately, distinct absences from them. Nowhere in *McClellan's Own Story* did McClellan mention Jesus. He never used the word "Messiah" or "Christ" or "Savior." He never referred to the resurrection or, in a theological context, salvation. He never quoted or alluded to the Bible. He spoke of sin exactly twice, as in a letter to Nelly of August 8, 1862, when he referred to it in a context that would have gratified Robert E. Lee—that of taking "the highest Christian ground for the conduct of the war"—but not in the context of redemption from personal sins, such as sloth, lust, avarice, gluttony, pride, envy, or wrath: "I will not permit this army to degenerate into a mob of thieves, nor will I return these men of mine to their families as a set of wicked and demoralized robbers. I will never have that sin on my conscience."

People do not have to call themselves Christians to use the word in this familiar, idiomatic way.[25]

We can begin to appreciate the distinct quality of McClellan's Christian rhetoric when we contrast it with that of Robert E. Lee, also writing privately to his wife, Mary, in a letter of November 15, 1856, sent from Fort Brown, Texas:

> It was pleasant to join in the prayers again, & Mr P gave us a plain but good sermon. I see though he has brought to this wilderness the colouring of the high church which had much better be left behind. There is already enough of Romanism in this country inherited from Mexico, & there is more want of "the worship of spirit & of truth" in all the beauty of its sincerity & holiness. When I see its perversion by man from the purity preached by our Saviour, there is an inward rebellion over which I have no control, & I think it better for me to remain in the wilderness from whence I came & adore the Great God with all the power & all the strength he has given me free from the detraction, & disturbing forces around me.

Lee's distaste for Mexican Catholicism imprinted this letter, though during the Civil War many of his Baptist, Methodist, and Presbyterian soldiers no doubt associated his own Episcopalianism with "the colouring of the high church." Nevertheless, Lee's particular brand of rebellious Calvinist Protestantism came through loud and clear in this letter, with his insistence on "the purity preached by our Saviour"; the biblical allusion to the wilderness, here associated not with the Judean desert and Isaiah's image of a voice crying out there or the rebellious protest of John the Baptist but with sparsely populated Texas; and the imperfectly remembered quotation of John 4:24 in the King James Version: "God is Spirit: and they that worship him must worship him in spirit and in truth." These rhetorical features, along with Lee's references to divine spirit and private adoration of "the Great God," have no counterparts in McClellan's letters to Nelly.[26]

The religious faith of Robert E. Lee and his world figured indirectly in *McClellan's Own Story*, where it inspired homage. Chapter 22 of the book opens with McClellan's account of coming upon White House in mid-May 1862, "a very fine plantation belonging to Mrs. Gen. Lee" and "the residence of Mrs. Custis when she was married to Washington." Having visited Saint Peter's Church there, "a lonely old building beautifully placed on a command hill," McClellan gave his posthumous readers a small glimpse of his inmost religious impulses: "Finding one's self alone within that historic building, it was a natural impulse to invoke the aid of God to enable me to serve the country as unselfishly and truly as did the great man who had often worshipped there." In context McClellan meant Washington, but Lee, for whose ability McClellan said he had "the highest respect," must have worshiped in Saint Peter's too, and his presence hovers over the passage. The account of this solitary moment was significant enough to McClellan for him to refer to it both in a letter written to Nelly on May 16, 1862, and in the narrative he knew one day would be made public. In the letter he wrote that "I could not help kneeling at the chancel and praying that I might serve my country as truly as he did." Among guides to his spiritual interior, this one is more reliable than many, and what it suggests is that for McClellan God was primarily to be invoked or petitioned in the context of service, duty, and ethical conduct; God was not primarily to be praised and adored out of self-forgetting, worshipful love that had no practical or instrumental value.[27]

For readers of *McClellan's Own Story*, both now and in 1887, this aspect of McClellan's personal faith becomes or became especially significant against the background of public debate, beginning in 1862, about what it meant to wage Christian warfare. To testimony by Fitzhugh Lee we have already seen, we can add two sentences that appear early in *McClellan's Own Story*, the second of which displays the disciplined syntactic organization characteristic of the writer who built the Army of the Potomac: "Since the war I have met many of my late antagonists, and have found none who entertained any personal enmity against me. While acknowledging, with Lee and other of their generals, that they feared me more than any of the Northern generals, and that I had struck them harder blows when in the full prime of their strength, they have all said that I fought them like a gentleman, and in an honorable way, and that they felt nothing but respect for me." As with his ready pen he so often did, in this passage McClellan mixed boastfulness and self-justification with pathos and some important truth. It is easy to think about Ulysses S. Grant's relentless Overland Campaign and scoff at McClellan's implicit pride in being most feared, but the qualification "when in the full prime of their strength" should give the scoffer pause. Although he himself labored under delusions about the strength of his enemy, not all of which were his fault, during the Seven Days' Battles the Army of Northern Virginia, with somewhere around ninety thousand soldiers, bristled with its greatest wartime strength. At the beginning of the Overland Campaign two years later, with about the same number of troops McClellan had on the Peninsula, Grant faced approximately two-thirds of this number. More to the point at hand are the words, "I fought them like a gentleman, and in an honorable way."[28]

One might prefer not to have McClellan testifying so baldly in his own behalf, but Fitzhugh Lee seconded the statement, and he added the relevant term: "McClellan was always and everywhere a gentleman, who believed in conducting war in a Christian and humane manner." For all the boastfulness and self-justification so off-putting to McClellan's critics, past and present, the pathos and the truth of his many wartime turnings are that his turnings coincided exactly with a seismic shift in U.S. strategy during the Civil War. The shift meant discarding an ineffectual ideal of fighting in the respectful, conciliatory manner of a humane, Christian gentleman and adopting a newer, more expedient ideal of making war as humane as possible by making it as brief as possible, while making it as brief as possible by making it as hard as possible. The most famous apostles of this new creed were Grant, Sherman, and Sheridan, and at least from the point of view of the loyal states, their success confirmed the new reasoning.

To twenty-first-century readers of *McClellan's Own Story*, some of whom may recollect that the same reasoning preceded the atomic bombing of Japan, the 1862 turning point in American military history may not feel comfortable, but from the perspective of today it cannot help but look inevitable. To readers of 1887, however, with the Spanish-American War still a decade away and the wars of the twentieth century inconceivable, the turning point was recent enough, and postwar reconciliation difficult enough, thanks in part to hard-war policies, that some could still think of McClellan as the champion of another kind of lost cause.[29]

Take for example McClellan's General Orders No. 7, on the subject of the Sabbath, issued in Washington on September 6, 1861, when he was still thirty-four years old:

> The major-general commanding desires and requests that in future there may be a more perfect respect for the Sabbath on the part of his command.
>
> We are fighting in a holy cause, and should endeavor to deserve the benign favor of the Creator.
>
> Unless in the case of an attack by the enemy, or some other extreme military necessity, it is commended to commanding officers that all work shall be suspended on the Sabbath; that no unnecessary movements shall be made on that day; that the men shall, as far as possible, be permitted to rest from their labors; that they shall attend divine service after the customary Sunday morning inspection, and that officers and men shall alike use their influence to insure the utmost decorum and quiet on that day. The general commanding regards this as no idle form; one day's rest

in seven is necessary to men and animals; more than this, the observance of the holy day of the God of Mercy and of Battles is our sacred duty.

The word "holy" appears in *McClellan's Own Story* three times, once in an ironic reference to the South declaring its peculiar institution "a holy ordinance" and twice in these orders. Whereas Lee wrote to Mary of holiness in the context of private adoration and worship, McClellan referred to public observance of the fourth commandment, as numbered by Presbyterians, Episcopalians, and denominations that follow Calvin: "Remember the sabbath day, to keep it holy" (Exodus 20:8 KJV). His emphasis fell on duty, described as "sacred"; on form, insisting that it not be "idle"; and on outward decorum and quiet. That Jesus had pointed out in the Sermon on the Mount (Matthew 5) how one could keep the letter of the commandments outwardly and still violate their spirit inwardly does not seem to have concerned McClellan, whose legalistic focus on Sabbath-keeping resembled that of the scribes and Pharisees more than that of the upstart Galilean they sought to kill for Sabbath-breaking.[30]

"I will not fight on Sunday if I can help it." Ken Burns's documentary helped to link such a statement to popular memory of Stonewell Jackson, who nevertheless fought on Sundays at First Manassas–Bull Run, First Winchester, Cross Keys, and Savage's Station. Had he not been mortally wounded the night before, he would have fought on Sunday at Chancellorsville as well. But in fact this statement was made by McClellan to Nelly in a letter of May 23, 1862, written before he did have to fight on Sundays at Seven Pines and Savage's Station. That statement was not a casual or an idle one; McClellan's wish to observe the Sabbath was real, even anxious. But with the first major battle of the war having been fought on a Sunday, with the second day of Shiloh having fallen on a Sunday, and with all the battles still to occur on or include Sundays—Resaca, Spotsylvania, Trevilian Station, Second Kernstown, Fort Fisher, Hatcher's Run, Bentonville, and the final capture of Confederate works at Petersburg—his dutiful fidelity to the Sabbath and his desire to impose its weekly rhythm on fighting that could not be constrained by it reflects a larger disjunction between his ideas of waging Christian warfare and the new kind of warfare erupting before him. To his critics this disjunction could point toward a kind of reactionary nostalgia for the theocratic order of Moses leading the Israelites through the wilderness. To more sympathetic readers it could suggest the pathos of a prophet crying out in the wilderness to an unheeding host of straying apostates.[31]

Nowhere did the mismatch between McClellan's idea of waging Christian warfare and the new exigencies of the Civil War that would emerge after the turning points of the Seven Days and the subsequent withdrawal of the Army of the Potomac to Harrison's Landing, also called Harrison's Bar, appear more sharply than in McClellan's 850-word letter to Lincoln of July 7, 1862. In light of what followed, many have come to view the Harrison's Landing letter as not merely one more distasteful instance of McClellan's arrogance but as damning evidence of his gross insubordination. In undertaking to lecture Lincoln that the "time has come when the government must determine upon a civil and military policy covering the whole ground of our national trouble," McClellan overstepped his purely military authority in ways that anticipated William T. Sherman's exceeding of his authority in drafting the initial surrender agreement with Joseph E. Johnston on April 17, 1865, in North Carolina.[32]

The composition and delivery of the Harrison's Landing letter was surely a turning point for McClellan himself. Having read the letter in McClellan's presence, Lincoln did not respond at length, and the letter did not find its way into public circulation until McClellan submitted his official report on the Peninsula Campaign, dated August 4, 1863. But in the meantime Lincoln did show the letter to members of his cabinet, and it helped to turn opinion against McClellan. Within two weeks, for example, Salmon P. Chase was urging the president to remove his general. Beyond its immediate implications for his career, however, McClellan's letter captured in microcosm a major turning point of the war itself. Invoking "the highest principles known to Christian civilization" and "the influences of Christianity and freedom," McClellan positioned these Christian principles and influences in opposition to the shifting policies emerging around him. Eleven days before the date of the Harrison's Landing letter, John Pope had been named commander of the new Army of Virginia, and within the next month Pope's infamous General Orders No. 5, 6, and 7 indicated that the treatment of white Virginia civilians would no longer correspond to McClellan's idea of conciliatory Christian warfare, the characteristics of which he spelled out explicitly for Lincoln in his letter:

> It should not be a war looking to the subjugation of the people of any State in any event. It should not be at all a war upon population, but against armed forces and political organizations. . . . In prosecuting the war all private property and unarmed persons should be strictly protected, subject only to the necessity of military operations. All private property taken for military use should be paid or receipted for; pillage

> and waste should be treated as high crimes; all unnecessary trespass sternly prohibited, and offensive demeanor by the military towards citizens promptly rebuked.

Within a year Ulysses S. Grant and William T. Sherman would be prosecuting a different brand of warfare in Mississippi, and by the end of the war Sherman's campaigns through Georgia and South Carolina and Sheridan's treatment of the Shenandoah Valley, all endorsed or ordered by Grant, would mark how sharp the turn after the Peninsula Campaign had been.[33]

The Harrison's Landing letter, and the particular vision of Christian warfare it encapsulated, also pointed to another turn, one that had been under way since Confederate victory at First Manassas–Bull Run and would accelerate ten days after McClellan handed his letter to Lincoln beside the James River. Staunchly maintaining that the "Constitution and the Union must be preserved," McClellan was equally unequivocal in exhorting Lincoln not to tamper with slavery: "Neither confiscation of property, political executions of persons, territorial organization of States, or forcible abolition of slavery should be contemplated for a moment. . . . A declaration of radical views, especially upon slavery, will rapidly disintegrate our present armies." Behind these sentences hovered debate and passage of the First and Second Confiscation Acts, signed into law on August 6, 1861, and July 17, 1862, respectively. One could argue that the unfavorable results of McClellan's Peninsula Campaign pushed Congress to reach a compromise on passing the Second Confiscation Act, as one could argue that the results of the Peninsula Campaign advanced the progress of the Emancipation Proclamation. But the turn toward policy aimed at the disruption of slavery had begun weeks before McClellan took command of the Army of the Potomac in August 1861. Although the vicissitudes of his tenure as commanding general may have helped to shape the timetable of emancipation policy, they did not initiate the disruption of slavery. If readers of 1887 came to *McClellan's Own Story* with open-mindedness, they would have found in William Prime's presentation of the relevant documents, especially those pertaining to McClellan's vision of Christian warfare and its implications for the treatment of white southern civilians, abundant food for thought.[34]

McClellan and What-If?

The second feature of *McClellan's Own Story* that has escaped much notice or commentary, one especially relevant to many ongoing debates about the Civil War, consists of the what-ifs or counterfactuals. Their distinct rhetorical flavor arises from heavy seasoning with the grammatical mood we call the subjunctive: What if Joseph E. Johnston or Pierre G. T. Beauregard had pursued routed U.S. soldiers back to Washington after First Manassas–Bull Run and captured the capital? What if Stonewall Jackson had not been mortally wounded at Chancellorsville? What if William F. "Baldy" Smith and Winfield Scott Hancock had cooperated to move more quickly and efficiently into Petersburg in mid-June 1864? What if John Frederick Parker had stayed at his post at the entrance to Lincoln's box at Ford's Theatre, instead of adjourning to a nearby tavern? Skeptical pragmatists might dismiss such speculations as trivial indulgences in thought experimentation, but they are not; they are an inevitable part of the process of reconstructing the welter of converging contingencies into historical narratives. What events or developments really do make major differences? When it came to composing his own narrative, or the different narratives William Prime pieced together to make *McClellan's Own Story*, no one resorted to subjunctive counterfactuals more often than McClellan himself. Here is one example from relatively early in the book: "In the light of the experience of the twenty-two years which have elapsed since this Memorandum was so hastily prepared, and after full consideration of all the events of the long and bloody war which followed it, I still hold to the soundness of the views it expressed. Had the measures recommended been carried into effect the war would have been closed in less than one-half the time and with infinite saving of blood and treasure."[35]

The memorandum to which McClellan referred here was a lengthy one of August 2, 1861, "submitted to the President at his request" and later included in *McClellan's Own Story*. The memorandum outlined McClellan's grand strategy for prosecuting the war on all fronts, not only in Virginia, and it offered his alternative to Winfield Scott's Anaconda Plan, which relied heavily on naval blockading of southern ports and on the eventual workings of Unionist sentiment in the Confederate states. By contrast McClellan's memorandum did not mention blockading at all; it focused on Virginia, Missouri, Kentucky, and eastern Tennessee. It advocated "a strong movement to be made on the Mississippi." It recognized the construction of railroads as having "introduced a new and very important element into war." It ventured "to suggest the policy of an ultimate alliance and cordial understanding with Mexico," and for "the main army of operations" it estimated a total force of 273,000 men. Most important for the discussion here is that unlike several of McClellan's other counterfactuals, some of which appeared in documents composed in the heat of the moment, the subjunctive formulation, "Had the measures recommended been carried into effect the war would have been closed in less than one-half the time and with infinite saving of blood and treasure," was one to which he still held in the full hindsight of rewriting the manuscript lost in the warehouse fire.[36]

Not all McClellan's counterfactuals were created equal. To be sure, there are many among his subjunctive had-x-happened statements that smack of sour grapes to set the teeth of McClellan critics on edge, such as this one: "Had Gen. McDowell joined me by water I could have approached Richmond by the James, and thus have avoided the delays and losses incurred in bridging the Chickahominy, and could have had the army united in one body instead of being necessarily divided by that stream." This sentence commented on a letter from Stanton dated May 18, 1862, in which the secretary of war informed McClellan that McDowell's force would be needed to defend against movements by Stonewall Jackson in the Shenandoah Valley and could not reinforce him. In itself it is not particularly objectionable, but when read in light of a sentence nine lines above, it becomes harder to accept: "Herein lay the failure of the campaign." Although McDowell's arrival by water could have made unnecessary the laborious bridging of the rain-swollen Chickahominy, it did not necessarily follow that the entire Peninsula Campaign had to fail because he did not join McClellan in May 1862.[37]

The problem for discerning readers is that McClellan's habitual resistance to accepting blame—and he was not unique among Civil War generals in this respect—inevitably led him to make frequent use of self-justifying counterfactuals, and it can become too easy to dismiss those counterfactuals as all of a piece and all reminiscent of the boy who cried "Wolf" once too often. But the power of Aesop's original fable is that eventually the real wolf does attack. That McClellan defaulted to counterfactual statements too often in his own defense does not mean that he never had grounds for self-defense. His counterfactual subjunctives about Ambrose Burnside's poor performance at Sharpsburg-Antietam, for example, have something to them:

> If this important movement had been consummated two hours earlier, a position would have been secured upon the heights from which our batteries might have enfiladed the greater part of the enemy's line, and turned their right and rear. Our victory might thus have been much more decisive. . . . I have only adverted to the very pernicious effects of Burnside's inexcusable delay in attacking the bridge and the heights in rear. What is certain is that if Porter or Hancock had been in his place the town of Sharpsburg would have been ours, Hill would have been thrown

> back into the Potomac, and the battle of Antietam would have been very decisive in its results.[38]

"Nothing is certain in war." McClellan had written this sentence to Edwin Stanton in a letter of February 3, 1862, which appeared in *McClellan's Own Story*, as it had in the 1864 *Report on the Organization and Campaigns of the Army of the Potomac.* One does not have to be a Presbyterian Calvinist to embrace such a sentiment, and in light of McClellan's frequent statements about bowing to the will of God, it is odd that in this particular counterfactual of Burnside's lapses at Sharpsburg-Antietam he could have asserted any alternative human scenario as "certain." Nevertheless, McClellan had a point: Had someone more aggressive been in command at Burnside's bridge, the Battle of Sharpsburg-Antietam might well "have been very decisive in its results." Had the battle been very decisive in its results, Lincoln's frustration with what he saw as McClellan's failure to pursue Lee to the Potomac might not have arisen. Had Lincoln's frustration not arisen, Ambrose Burnside might not have been in command at Fredericksburg. Had Burnside not been in command at Fredericksburg . . . and so on.[39]

What is particularly compelling about the use of counterfactuals is that they are, among other things, clear signs that no matter how often we intone the apparent truth that nothing is certain, in fact most of us find it nearly impossible to live amid complete uncertainty. In the language of the English Romantic poet John Keats, very few of us are equipped to demonstrate "*Negative Capability*, that is, when a man is capable of being in uncertainties, mysteries, doubts, without any irritable reaching after fact and reason." Certainly, few historians are so equipped, as the writing of history consists of nothing so much as the reaching after facts and reasons operating behind events; nor was George McClellan, for all his professed submission to the will of God. It is all very well, and all too easy, to censure McClellan for his often irritable reaching after fact and reason in his own defense. But the complicated pathos of McClellan's Civil War service was and is that he has been the object of tremendous criticism leveled at him by people who are no more capable of living in uncertainty than he was. This statement is especially true in the realm of popular memory, which rarely shows affection for uncertain complexity. Familiar images of McClellan as an overcautious whiner always crying out for reinforcements exhibit their own reductive counterfactuality: Had McClellan shown a "little of the nerve . . . which the Romans displayed during the campaign against Hannibal," he "would have settled the fate of Richmond in very few weeks."[40]

In fact, these words were McClellan's own, and he used them to criticize his civilian superiors for the failure of the Peninsula Campaign: "A little of the nerve *at Washington* which the Romans displayed during the campaign against Hannibal would have settled the fate of Richmond in very few weeks" (emphasis added). Although mutual recrimination is rarely edifying, once again McClellan had a point, which can get lost in the general disparagement of his memory: not all the loss of nerve was his. Many people in Washington were uncertain about what was true in the spring of 1862, and they displayed their uncertainty with their own versions of caution, not infrequently at McClellan's expense. For many readers of 1887, what-if counterfactuals, whether they emanated from McClellan or from Washington, were not merely hypothetical thought experiments, as they are today. They bore directly on the lives of numerous late nineteenth-century readers. The final counterfactual of *McClellan's Own Story* underscores the point:

> Late on the night of the 7th [November 1862] I received an order relieving me from the command of the Army of the Potomac, and directing me to turn it over to Gen. Burnside, which I at once did. . . .
>
> Had I remained in command I should have made the attempt to divide the enemy, as before suggested; and could he have been brought to a battle within reach of my supplies, I cannot doubt that the result would have been a brilliant victory for our army.[41]

Before writing off this moment as yet one more instance of arrogance blended with sour grapes, one would do well to consider that although there is no convincing proof for McClellan's bold claim, neither is there any sure proof for its converse. For all we know, he might have been able to achieve a brilliant victory sometime after November 7, 1862; he was learning, too, along with the Lincoln administration, and we cannot know what might have happened. He managed the Maryland Campaign better than he had managed the Peninsula one, and it is difficult to believe that his next performance would have been worse than Burnside's at Fredericksburg or Joseph Hooker's at Chancellorsville. What matters more, at least when it comes to accounting for Mark Twain's winning bet on the success of *McClellan's Own Story*, is the effect that such a statement could have had on a reader in 1887, someone for whom a brilliant victory by McClellan in 1862 might have meant that the losses of 1863, 1864, and 1865 were in some way diminished. Even the hypothetical fantasy of such a victory, with the mitigation of loss that might have followed, could have had compelling power. If some large, personal bereavement had followed

November 7, 1862—and hundreds of thousands of them did—then this particular counterfactual, and the light in which it cast the turning point of McClellan's relief from command, could have haunted with unavoidable force. McClellan's earlier counterfactual about his memorandum of August 1861, "Had the measures recommended been carried into effect the war would have been closed in less than one-half the time and with infinite saving of blood and treasure," may sound like so much bloviating windbaggery nearly a century and a half later, but to someone who suffered loss of blood or treasure, directly or indirectly, in the immediate wake of McClellan's relief from command, the specter of what-if could have been hard to shake off.

McClellan's Heart

A third and final feature of *McClellan's Own Story* important to readers Mark Twain envisioned in 1887 remains important to readers today. It is the power of empathy and emotional connection, and it returns us to one of the familiar orthodoxies about McClellan that appeared in Peter Michie's 1901 biography, later echoed in Theodore Roosevelt's 1907 dedication speech at the equestrian statue in Washington: McClellan possessed "the wonderful power . . . of implanting in the hearts of his soldiers a personal affection and devotion that has never been excelled." Nearly a hundred years after the publication of *McClellan's Own Story* Michael Shaara drew on this particular aspect of McClellan iconography in the early Joshua Lawrence Chamberlain chapters of his Pulitzer Prize–winning novel *The Killer Angels*, which had sold approximately 3.5 million copies as of 2013. That many of the soldiers who served under George McClellan had deep affection for him has not been news since Nathaniel Hawthorne published his account of his 1862 visit to Washington. What may be news, and what emerged in William Prime's editing, are the many instances in *McClellan's Own Story* showing how fully McClellan returned his soldiers' affection and devotion. One can argue that if he had been able to detach himself from his affections, he might have been a more aggressive and effective combat leader. One can also argue that some of the expressions of McClellan's affections in *McClellan's Own Story* border on sentimentality, which can be the kiss of death for a twenty-first-century reader. But nineteenth-century readers differed in this respect, as Mark Twain knew very well, and William Prime could deliver in this area, as Twain also knew.[42]

By the 1950s the phrase "bleeding heart" had become a pejorative term, especially in the adjectival form "bleeding-heart liberal," but when George

McClellan wrote to Nelly in the aftermath of the debacle at Second Manassas–Bull Run, on the day Lincoln instructed him to reassume command after the Confederate invasion of Maryland, such language had no such negative connotations for him:

> Sept. 5, [1862,] 4 P.M.— . . . It makes my heart bleed to see the poor, shattered remnants of my noble Army of the Potomac, poor fellows! and to see how they love me even now. I hear them calling out to me as I ride among them, "George, don't leave us again!" "They sha'n't take you away from us again," etc., etc. I can hardly restrain myself when I see how fearfully they are reduced in numbers, and realize how many of them lie unburied on the field of battle, where their lives were uselessly sacrificed. It is the most terrible trial I ever experienced. Truly, God is trying me in the fire. . . .

Readers of 1887 could have known this passage only through the editorial offices of William Prime. It did not appear in McClellan's 1864 *Report*, and he had not reached September 1862 in his rewritten manuscript when he died. Confided to Nelly alone, this passage, with ellipses identical to those of the version in Stephen Sears's 1989 edition of McClellan's Civil War papers, revealed the young commander in the grip of overwhelming emotion, hardly able to restrain himself, presumably from some outward display, such as weeping or howling or cursing or all of them at once. That a psychoanalyzing critic looking over his shoulder 150 years later might take exception to his focus on himself ("the most terrible trial I ever experienced," "God is trying me in the fire") only confirms the unguardedness of his outpouring to the wife who shared his theological language. There is no passage about the love between commander and soldier as powerfully raw in the memoirs of Sherman, Grant, and Sheridan, although Sheridan did describe the emotional leave-taking from his soldiers when he was ordered east in 1864.[43]

But there is an analogous passage in *Recollections and Letters of General Robert E. Lee*, and the congruence is significant. Also writing to his wife, on Christmas Day 1862, in the wake of his victory at Fredericksburg and three months after McClellan's letter to Nelly, Lee spoke of his gratitude "to Almighty God for His unspeakable mercies" and then adopted a different tone: "But what a cruel thing is war; to separate and destroy families and friends, and mar the purest joys and happiness God has granted us in this world; to fill our hearts with hatred instead of love for our neighbors, and to devastate the fair face of this beautiful world! . . . My heart bleeds at the death of every one of our gallant men." Even permitting the anachronism, no one could rightly call Lee a bleeding heart, and the similarity between the confessions of the two generals to their wives makes all the more poignant and remarkable another moment that readers of 1887 could have known only because of Prime's inclusion of a letter to Nelly of July 22, 1862, written from Harrison's Landing:

> I am about doing a thing to-day which will, I suppose, cause the abolitionists and my other friends to drive the last nail in my official coffin. You know that our sick and wounded in Richmond are suffering terribly for want of proper food, medicines, and hospital supplies. I have ordered a boatload of all such things—lemons, tea, sugar, brandy, underclothing, lint, bandages, chloroform, quinine, ice, etc., etc.—to be sent up to Gen. Lee to-day, to be used at his discretion for the sick and wounded of both armies. I know he would not, and could not, receive them for our men alone, therefore I can only do it in the way I propose, and trust to his honor to apply them properly—half and half. I presume I will be accused now of double-dyed treason—giving aid and comfort to the enemy, etc. What do you think of it? Am I right or wrong?[44]

"Am I right or wrong?" McClellan's disarmingly vulnerable appeal to Nelly's judgment put before 1887 readers a McClellan unknown to most of us now. The Greek term for this conflict in the soul is *psychomachia* (spirit battle or mind combat), and there is no hint of it in the equestrian statue on Connecticut Avenue, nor is there much acknowledgment of it among the harshest critics of McClellan. And yet there it was on full display for the Shoulder Strap series readership, the tightly knotted entanglement of political awareness, principled commitment to waging Christian warfare, and harrowing compassion for his soldiers that characterized McClellan as much as arrogance or caution. Was he right or wrong? His 1887 editor believed him right, consensus now believes him largely wrong, and critical thinking should guard against any easy oversimplification or reduction. It should also ask McClellan's own question of the thousands of soldiers who loved him: Were they right or were they wrong? Was their devotion wholly misguided? Was it some kind of collective delusion? Did it signify nothing?

At the very least it suggests that George McClellan had some real gift, what Theodore Roosevelt called "the peculiar gift," one we associate with the word "charisma." Although used mostly in secular contexts now, this term has biblical connections as well, and those connections could not be wholly lost on biblically literate readers able to associate McClellan's visits to wounded soldiers in the hospitals with ministrations to the ailing and afflicted in first-century Palestine:

> This morning I visited the general hospital not far from here, and went through it all, finding the patients comfortable and all improving in health. They are nearly all in hospital-tents and are well provided for; in truth, they are about as well off as they could be away from home, and many of them doubtless better off than they would be there. I find the men more contented than the officers. I confess that the men enlist my sympathies much more warmly than the officers. They are so patient and devoted. They have generally entered the service, too, from higher and more unselfish motives. Poor fellows! I can never willingly break the link that unites me to them, and shall always be very proud of them and of their love for me, even if it is not decreed by Providence that I am to lead them to Richmond. (July 31, 1862)[45]

Readers of the Shoulder Strap series encountered nothing like this moment in the memoirs of Grant, Sherman, and Sheridan. We have other powerful images of hospital visits during the Civil War—Abraham Lincoln at City Point, Virginia, Walt Whitman and Louisa May Alcott in Washington, Phoebe Yates Pember in Richmond—but we do not have them in the memoirs of other Civil War generals. And they would not have reached the public when they did, if not for William Prime working in cooperation with Mark Twain. Was George McClellan telling the truth when he confided to his wife that he would remain very proud of his soldiers and of their love for him, "even if it is not decreed by Providence that I am to lead them to Richmond"? If so, then he could be rightfully proud for the remainder of his life. Were George McClellan's hospital visits or the devotion they signified enough to answer all the charges of all his critics, then or now? No, they are not. But they were and are a large part of McClellan's own story and its continuing power; to overlook them or to underestimate them is to slight history and bow to amnesia.

It is also to overlook or underestimate the power of emotional self-interest and the role it plays in driving the Civil War memory market. When readers feel their own emotions stirred or shared by a leading actor in historical events, those events take on a new aura for them. Much as historians and students of the Civil War may pride themselves on delving into records and archives, resolved to be objective, detached, and dispassionate, following the evidence wherever it leads, they share with their nineteenth-century precursors an inclination toward good stories. Many engines power good stories, among them suspense, intrigue, surprising plot twists, and humorous anecdotes, but emotional urgency has more horsepower than any of them. The twenty-first century may look dismissively on what it regards as nineteenth-century sentimentality, but though storytelling conventions have changed, the appetite for emotional connection has not. The phrase "human interest story" surged into common usage in the 1920s, and the phrase "soft news" has done likewise since the 1960s. The convention of opening a piece of journalism by focusing on a particular person's story before moving on to a more general topic has become naturalized into inevitability.[46]

A Civil War general's memoir might not be the first place many readers would think to look for emotional connection, but *McClellan's Own Story,* as William Prime reconstructed it and Mark Twain marketed it, shows that a general could deliver in this area, despite prevailing social codes of masculinity and military codes of conduct becoming an officer. Like the friendship between Joseph E. Johnston and William T. Sherman, the peculiar gift that made George B. McClellan loved by his soldiers persists in popular imagination of the Civil War today. It also shows how inextricable popular imagination of the war is from the human interest story. In its own day readers did not open *McClellan's Own Story* primarily for its value as a cautionary tale; yet twenty-first-century readers, awash in evidence of what can happen in popular imagination when human interest stories fray into division about which humans and whose interests, can do so in their own best interest. It is improbable that Civil War memory will shed all emotional charge; it would be a challenge to its market if it did. It is possible that deeper understanding of the charge, and more conversation about it, may make it less dangerous.

6

THE MERIT OF PHILIP H. SHERIDAN'S MEMOIR CAMPAIGN

PHILIP H. SHERIDAN'S *Personal Memoirs* was the last book published by the triumphant triumvirate of the U.S. Army high command, following William T. Sherman's in 1875 and Ulysses S. Grant's two volumes in 1885 and 1886. Of the three memoirs, Grant's sold best and continues to sell best, with Sherman's coming in second. Sheridan's memoirs have had a less radiant career. One can offer various explanations for this fact, both at the end of the nineteenth century and now, including the argument that Grant and Sherman were and are the more important historical figures or that their memoirs have more expressive quality. But despite the opening disclaimer of Sheridan's preface, "I make no pretension to literary merit," his memoirs offer readers many richly textured glimpses of moments and subjects that have no counterparts in Grant's and Sherman's accounts.[1]

Another explanation for Sheridan's third-place finish is that by 1888 his book would have to compete in a market quickly becoming saturated by Civil War memoirs, as Frederick J. Hall, assistant to Charles L. Webster and later one-third partner of the company, warned Mark Twain. Like Twain, Hall was aware of the potential benefits of giving Sheridan's book the same *Personal Memoirs* title as Grant's, thereby linking the two works in the minds of book buyers. But in a letter of May 19, 1887, written a few months after Webster and Company published *McClellan's Own Story*, he also conceded that "the way we handle [Sheridan's book] will either increase the good reputation made on the 'Grant Memoirs' or destroy it." Hall continued that "people are so tired of 'war-literature' that something extraordinary is required to command large sales," adding that "General Sheridan will probably take Grant's 'Memoirs' as the standard by which to judge of the success of his own." In a letter of October 15,

1888, Hall compounded this sour dose of the reality principle: "We have got to hustle everlastingly to get rid of 75,000 sets of Sheridan. I had set my mind on 100,000 sets but am forced to lessen this figure. There is not a man today who could write another book on the war and sell 5000 in the whole country."[2]

Saturation of the late nineteenth-century market for Civil War remembering has not diminished the twenty-first-century one. In addition to savoring his observations and his storytelling powers, contemporary readers of Sheridan can find in his memoirs a parable of Civil War memory and its market. In addition to other McClellan-style, counterfactual what-if questions, Sheridan's case poses these: If the war had turned out differently, who would have written memoirs and what readership would they have found? Despite the cliché that victors write the histories, Confederate memoirs have found readers all along. If Sherman had not taken Atlanta in September 1864, and Sheridan had not subdued the Shenandoah Valley in October 1864, and McClellan had defeated Lincoln in November 1864, what is now the United States might be two, three, or four sovereign states. Failure to triumph would not necessarily mean that northern generals did not write memoirs. Commander of U.S. forces in Vietnam from 1964 to 1968, William C. Westmoreland published his memoir *A Soldier Reports* in 1976. Ulysses S. Grant would still have needed money, Mark Twain would still have been a publishing entrepreneur, and *Personal Memoirs of U. S. Grant* might still be on many bookshelves, albeit in a different form.

What about Sheridan? His book offers readers an emotional connection, as McClellan's does, but not the same connection. Whereas McClellan's offers emotional connection despite negative aspects of his character and performance, Sheridan's offers emotional connection because negative aspects of his impulses and his gambles paid off, in the Appomattox Campaign, when it counted. His *Personal Memoirs* dramatize the role of contingency in what many choose to reconstruct as a morality play.

Mark Twain understood the role of contingency, especially when it came to book publishing. "Dear Sir: / I beg to introduce you to Mr. C. L. Webster, who may not succeed with the conspiracy which he has in mind, but I very much hope he *will*." Dated December 26, 1884, in Hartford, Connecticut, this brief letter from Twain to fifty-three-year-old Philip H. Sheridan apparently envisioned the writing of what would become the two-volume *Personal Memoirs of P. H. Sheridan*, published in New York by Charles L. Webster and Company in 1888, each spine bearing the general's four-star insignia, each cover stamped with a gilt image of hat-waving Sheridan on galloping Rienzi. Seventeen months before Twain penned this letter, the *North American Review* had published Sheridan's brief essay "The Last Days of the Rebellion," consisting of ten pages of text and a full-page map. Covering the six-day period from April 4 to April 9, 1865, Sheridan's essay—presumably among the promptings for Twain's query—formed the basis for the general's expanded narrative of the Appomattox Campaign in the second volume of his *Memoirs*, where it runs for about eighty pages, from the fifth through the eighth chapters. Sheridan's narrative of the Appomattox Campaign will occupy the second part of this chapter, but fuller understanding and appreciation of both that narrative and its narrator can begin with some remarks about Sheridan's first volume and the context in which he undertook, at Twain's instigation, to write it.[3]

Planning to court Sheridan with a special presentation copy of Grant's memoir, in a notebook entry of November 1885, Twain jotted, "Send full morocco to Sherman & Sheridan, with their names printed in gilt on them." In betting that Sheridan's memoirs would succeed in the same market as Grant's, Twain was not alone. The late 1880s appeared to be Sheridan's moment, as the "Publisher's Note" to *"Little Phil" and His Troopers: The Life of Gen. Philip H. Sheridan: Its Romance and Reality* (1888), written by Frank A. Burr and Richard J. Hinton, made clear: "The story of the life of General Sheridan seemed to the publishers of this volume a matter of public interest well worth recording. . . . At the time the work was first contemplated there was a possibility of his being the candidate of a great political party for President of the United States, if not in '88, perhaps in '92." But with the death of Sheridan on August 5, 1888, at the age of fifty-seven, the publishers "deemed it wise to delay the work," adding that they had "considered the life and services of General Sheridan, as they would those of Washington, Lincoln, or Grant, a matter of public record and of public interest."[4]

Sheridan is no longer grouped with Washington and Lincoln on anybody's list, but that he once was associated with these two presidents, and considered a possible successor to them, shows the risk of our twenty-first-century perspective contracting into myopia. Those tempted to dismiss Sheridan's memoirs as less important than Grant's or Sherman's might well heed the Gilded Age fatigue with books by Civil War generals. Then, as now, some will read the original length of Grant's twelve hundred pages with absorbed eagerness; some fewer will tackle eight hundred more by Sherman. But only a resilient remnant will then move on to another thousand by Sheridan, and they would have to be readers undeterred by the vilification of him in Richard Taylor's *Destruction and Reconstruction* or in the writings of other Lost Cause authors. In

A Memoir of the Last Year of the War for Independence (1866), Jubal A. Early opined, with respect to Sheridan's performance against him at the Battle of Winchester (September 1864), "I have always thought that instead of being promoted, Sheridan ought to have been cashiered for this battle," adding, "He seems to be a sort of pet of Grant's." In *The Lost Cause*, also published in 1866, Edward A. Pollard described Sheridan as "a man of a coarse, active nature, excessive animal spirits, and an intensely combative temperament—an antagonist not to be despised, although he had shown no distinct military genius, and was only remarkable in the war for the execution of single tasks indicated to him by his superiours." Mitigating these negative judgments of Sheridan would be nothing like the magnanimity Ulysses S. Grant showed Confederate soldiers at Appomattox or the postwar friendship William T. Sherman enjoyed with Joseph E. Johnston.[5]

The timing of Sheridan's death meant he did not live to see whether Fred Hall's pessimistic sales prophecies were fulfilled. Like Grant, Sheridan barely had time to finish his memoirs, sending them off to Webster on March 23, 1888, and suffering a severe heart attack, the first of many, two months later on May 22. He dated his preface a mere three days before his death. But Sheridan did fulfill Hall's prophecy that he would take Grant's *Personal Memoirs* as his standard, if not for judging the success of sales he did not see, then as a model for how to write his memoirs. True, he had other models available to him, but when Twain sent Sheridan the morocco-bound, gilt-stamped copy of Grant's book, he gave him a star by which to steer.[6]

Sheridan the Wordsmith

Sheridan the writer went about the business of writing in much the same way Sheridan the soldier went about the business of soldiering. In a letter of December 21, 1886, he acknowledged receipt of a contract for the memoirs and told Webster, "I am going right along with the book + will push it especially after the new year. I have a pretty good start on it now." This tone of confident competence echoed the can-do tone of the memoirs. By the time Sheridan's contemporary readers arrive at his narrative of the Appomattox Campaign, they will have seen instance after instance in which he found himself faced with a new challenge, developed a strategy or technique for meeting it, and implemented that strategy or technique effectively. Examples are legion, but some of the most intriguing involve—not surprisingly in the case of someone teaching himself how to tell his own story—successful uses of languages or methods of communication. While serving in Texas at Fort Duncan during 1854, for example, Sheridan's "constant association" with a Mexican guide enabled him "to pick up in a short time a smattering of the Spanish language, which was very useful to one serving on that frontier." Likewise, when in negotiations with hungry Coquille Indians living near Yaquina Bay, Oregon Territory, in the summer of 1856, Sheridan "talked in the Chinook language all the day long," having "learned at an early day to speak Chinook (the 'court language' among the coast tribes) almost as well as the Indians themselves."[7]

To put it another way, Sheridan was a man of many tongues. He could speak the language of humor, often self-deprecating, as in the two-page story of his astonishment ("a mild way of putting it") on learning that two women, disguised as soldiers, had been serving under him and were discovered only when "these Amazons . . . secured a supply of 'apple-jack' by some means, got very drunk, and on the return had fallen into Stone[s] River and been nearly drowned." He could also speak the lyrical language of aesthetic appreciation, as in his description of watching the Twenty-Sixth Ohio and Fifteenth Indiana moving at dusk during the Battle of Missionary Ridge, November 25, 1863: "Just as they reached the crest of the ridge the moon rose from behind, enlarged by the refraction of the atmosphere, and as the attacking column passed along the summit it crossed the moon's disk and disclosed to us below a most interesting panorama, every figure nearly being thrown out in full relief."[8]

An especially noteworthy instance of Sheridan's polyglot shape-shifting came with an anecdote that can serve as a larger parable for his various capabilities, verbal and otherwise, an anecdote of his working with oxen while engaged in the "tedious and laborious" toil of building a road—the double-adjective connected by "and" is a Sheridan signature—"across the coast mountains from King's Valley to the Siletz [River]" sometime after he was assigned to Fort Haskins, his consistent version of "Hoskins," in Oregon Territory in July 1856. The road freshly completed, Sheridan set out to "demonstrate its value practically" by starting "a Government wagon over it loaded with about fifteen hundred pounds of freight drawn by six yoke of oxen." After the wagon had gone about seven miles, the sergeant in charge reported to Sheridan that he could go no farther. "Taking up a whip myself, I directed the men to lay on their gads." This personal intervention had no effect on "the demoralized oxen." At this point Sheridan's narrative took an illuminating turn: "but following as a last resort an example I heard of on a former occasion, that brought into use the rough language of the country, I induced the oxen to move with alacrity, and the wagon and contents were speedily carried to the summit." The key, it turned out once again, was language: "The whole trouble was at once revealed: the oxen had been broken and trained by a man who, when they were in a pinch, had encouraged them by his frontier vocabulary, and they could not realize what was expected of them under extraordinary conditions until they heard familiar and possibly profanely urgent phrases."[9]

Creating a Protagonist

A signal achievement of Sheridan's *Personal Memoirs*, one of distinct literary merit, was the creation of its protagonist, Phil Sheridan. "Camerado, this is no book, / Who touches this touches a man." These lines come from Walt Whitman's 1860 poem "So Long!" but they could serve aptly as an epigraph for Sheridan's *Personal Memoirs*. Not only did he offer his readers many homely, personal, flesh-and-blood details, such as his enjoyment of a good night's sleep or a particular meal when keenly hungry; Sheridan could be boldly and disarmingly frank about himself, and with the anecdote of the demoralized oxen, he established his credentials as a speaker of—in addition to Spanish and Chinook—"possibly profanely urgent phrases" under "extraordinary conditions." The sly wink of nineteenth-century circumlocution still does its work effectively, and one has no trouble imagining that in high gear Sheridan could sear the auditory nerve, whereas one faces many obstacles in imagining, say, Joseph E. Johnston doing the same after a reading of his always decorous, tamped-down *Narrative of Military Operations*. Like a skilled novelist, once he had characterized his protagonist Phil Sheridan this way, Sheridan the writer could later call up plentiful resonance by lightly touching the same chord, as when, in volume 2, he described exchanging "hot words" with William W. Averell, commander of the Cavalry Second Division, whom Sheridan subsequently relieved because of Averell's apparent indifference to following up the victory at Fisher's Hill on September 22, 1864. Similarly, the anecdote of the oxen enhanced, by implication, the acoustics of Sheridan's "acrimonious interview" with George G. Meade in a "peppery temper" over the proper use of U.S. cavalry in the Overland Campaign that began in May 1864: "Meade was very much irritated, and I was none the less so. One word brought on another, until, finally, I told him that I could whip Stuart if he (Meade) would only let me."[10]

A familiar convention of Gilded Age memoirs by Civil War generals was self-justification, which came in various hues and intensities, and no memoir stayed wholly free of it, not even Grant's. But by comparison with Sherman or Johnston, for example, Sheridan served up refreshingly small helpings of self-justification, at least in the first volume. Much more likely to second-guess another officer, whether Union or Confederate, he did so frequently, with prominent examples from volume 1 including critiques of Henry Halleck for not ordering more vigorous pursuit of P. G. T. Beauregard in northern Mississippi during the spring of 1862; of Braxton Bragg's failure "to utilize the chances falling to him" during his advance into Kentucky in the fall of 1862; of Don Carlos Buell for his mismanagement of the Battle of Perryville, "an example of lost opportunities," on October 8, 1862; of "the enemy," presumably Jefferson Davis, for "the serious fault of detaching Longstreet's corps—sending it to aid in the siege of Knoxville in East Tennessee—an error which has no justification whatsoever" in the fall of 1863; and of J. E. B. Stuart for "his error" of concentrating his troops at Beaver Dam before the Battle of Yellow Tavern, where Stuart was mortally wounded by Sheridan's troops on May 11, 1864.[11]

Lest one think that Sheridan merely rerouted self-justification through criticism of others, it is only fair to note he also candidly censured himself, most often for his tendency toward stubborn willfulness, if not downright insubordination. Again, examples are bountiful, the first one coming a mere eleven pages into the first chapter, with the story of Sheridan's "quarrel of a belligerent character in September, 1851, with Cadet William R. Terrill" at West Point in the fall of his fourth year as a member of the class of 1852. A cadet sergeant, Terrill had given Sheridan an order in what he considered "an improper tone, to 'dress' in a certain direction, when I believed I was accurately dressed." Believing he had a grievance, Sheridan "made toward him with lowered bayonet, but my better judgment recalled me before actual contact could take place." This incident resulted in Sheridan's one-year suspension from West Point by the secretary of war and placed him with the class of 1853, which included James B. McPherson, John M. Schofield, and John B. Hood. In his summation Sheridan did not spare himself: "Though the mortification I then endured was deep and trying, I am convinced that it was hardly as much as I deserved for such an outrageous breach of discipline."[12]

This was no conversion story; Sheridan did not tell it in order to show he learned a hard lesson about a tendency he never again indulged. He told it as part of a pattern of other instances of his unruliness, among them disobedience of a direct order by Samuel R. Curtis, commander of the Army of Southwest Missouri, to which Sheridan had been assigned as chief commissary on December 26, 1861. Without full knowledge of the situation, Curtis had ordered Sheridan to make payments for stolen horses dishonestly proffered to the army for purchase, and Sheridan had refused point-blank, bringing on himself a court-martial. Relieved by Halleck at his request, and ordered to St. Louis, "forlorn and disheartened"—again, the double adjective—Sheridan avoided the court-martial.

Less spectacular than the incidents with Terrill and Curtis, though tending in the same direction of insisting on his own autonomy, were the "acrimonious interview" in May 1864 with Meade, his commanding officer, over the proper use of cavalry, and his earlier interview with Grant, in Corinth, Mississippi, in September 1862. Grant wanted Sheridan and his command to remain with him, but not surprisingly, Sheridan had his own ideas: "Since I was of the opinion that the chief field of usefulness and opportunity was opening up in Kentucky, I did not wish him to retain me, which he might have done, and I impressed him with my conviction, somewhat emphatically, I fear." Sheridan wrote this sentence after reading Grant's version of the same interview, and his closing admission "somewhat emphatically, I fear" tacitly acknowledged the irritation he had caused his future friend, who recalled in his own memoirs, "I felt a little nettled at his desire to get away and did not detain him."[13]

Like his fluency with profanity, his desire "to get away" and be his own boss had two sides, one that could produce unquestionably positive results and one that could get him into trouble, and Sheridan owned them both. What is more remarkable about these potentially volatile characteristics is that they throw into even sharper relief what made Sheridan such an effective leader. It was not simply that he could swear majestically, and it was not simply that he strongly preferred operating independently to being under anybody's thumb; it was that while exhibiting these high-tempered, hot-blooded characteristics, he demonstrated repeatedly his deep concern and solicitude for any person or animal he had in his charge.

At a moment in its social history when the twenty-first-century United States is flooded by the products of the leadership-training industry—schools, programs, courses, retreats, books, articles, online encapsulations of various kinds—Sheridan still embodies a natural, homegrown gift for, and a profoundly simple theory of, effective leadership. Throughout his *Personal Memoirs*, especially in volume 1, he articulated, directly and without fanfare, the principles and assumptions that made him the leader who would contribute so significantly to the Appomattox Campaign.[14]

Sheridan's first statement of his understanding of leadership appeared in his memoirs three pages before the anecdote of the demoralized oxen. In the summer of 1856 the men of Sheridan's small command were ordered elsewhere, while he himself was assigned to Fort Haskins. In recounting this separation,

Sheridan admitted, as he often did, his strong feeling on the occasion: "I regretted exceedingly to see them go, for their faithful work and gallant service had endeared every man to me by the strongest ties." The effusive sentence that followed could not be mistaken for one in either Grant's or Sherman's memoirs: "Since I relieved Lieutenant [John B.] Hood on Pit River, nearly a twelvemonth before, they had been my constant companions, and the zeal with which they had responded to every call I made on them had inspired in my heart a deep affection that years have not removed." What accounted for the zealous responsiveness of his men? Did they warm to Sheridan from the start? No, they had to be won over. They did not like the change, when Sheridan relieved Hood, "but appreciative and unremitting care, together with firm and just discipline, soon quieted all symptoms of dissatisfaction and overcame all prejudice."[15]

Appreciative and unremitting care, together with firm and just discipline: Sheridan's style, or at least his representation of it, in a nutshell. Many a leader insists on discipline, often firm, not always just. Sheridan's touch was the addition of the appreciative and unremitting care, the constant vigilance for the welfare of his men and their horses. His memoirs repeated this theme throughout the first volume, with the next instance following his assumption of brigade command in Mississippi in June 1862. Again Sheridan claimed his efforts to take care of his men had won him their confidence and regard, and he added, "I had striven unceasingly to have them well fed and well clothed, had personally looked after the selection of their camps, and had maintained such a discipline as to allay former irritation."[16]

The point is not that Grant and Sherman did not care for their men; of course they did. For that matter, so did the much less effective Joseph E. Johnston and George B. McClellan. The point is that Sheridan the writer considered this aspect of his leadership significant enough to return to it throughout his narrative, as he labored to create an image of himself that would account for a large part of his celebrated success at the Battle of Cedar Creek in October 1864 or in the high-speed climax of the Appomattox Campaign six months later. Whereas neither Grant nor Sherman wrote explicitly about their men needing "the best bodily substance, and every comfort that can be provided," Sheridan told his readers he had learned from experience on the frontier that his "efforts in this direction would not only be appreciated, but requited with personal affection and gratitude; and, further, that such exertions would bring the best results." According to this formulation, Sheridan's appreciative and unremitting care for his soldiers made them affectionate and grateful, and their affection and gratitude made them more effective warriors. Grant and Sherman did not write as though the personal affection and gratitude of their men factored into their military strategies in any significant way, nor did Johnston and McClellan write like leaders who thought of personal affection and gratitude primarily as things to be converted into offensive capability. Did Sheridan calculate this way because he had also served as an effective quartermaster, or was he an effective quartermaster because he calculated this way? Either way, his fullest, most moving enunciation of the deep ties between himself and the men in his charge came in one of the great paragraphs of his memoirs, with the account of his transfer to the eastern theater in the spring of 1864:

> I at once set about obeying the order, and as but little preparation was necessary, I started for Chattanooga the next day, without taking any formal leave of the troops I had so long commanded. I could not do it; the bond existing between them and me had grown to such depth of attachment that I feared to trust my emotions in any formal parting from a body of soldiers who, from our mutual devotion, had long before lost their official designation, and by general consent were called "Sheridan's Division." When I took the train at the station the whole command was collected on the hill-sides around to see me off. They had assembled spontaneously, officers and men, and as the cars moved out for Chattanooga they waved me farewell with demonstrations of affection.[17]

Whatever the vicissitudes of the market for personal narratives, Mark Twain could not have hoped for better writing than this deft balance of historical narrative and emotional charge. The moment captured perfectly Sheridan's distinct sensibility, one that combined resolute commitment to pragmatism, realism, and discipline, on the one hand, with, on the other, loyalty, affection, and an instinctive tendency to identify closely with those working beside him. These latter impulses extended to animals, too. In his *Personal Memoirs* a reader will find far more explicit concern for horses and mules than in the two thousand pages of Grant and Sherman combined. What the same reader will not find is contradictory evidence that when it came to the Overland Campaign of 1864, the real Sheridan, not the creation of his memoirs, could be very hard on horses, too.[18]

Of course he paid close attention to horses, the response might go; he served the last year of the war as a cavalryman. But again the issue is the difference between what the cavalryman paid attention to—Grant and Sherman could not have succeeded if they had been oblivious to the condition of their horses and mules—and what the writer chose to include in his narrative. In his note

"To the Reader" at the beginning of *Look Homeward, Angel* (1929), Thomas Wolfe offered an aphoristic formulation that is relevant here: "Fiction is fact selected and understood, fiction is fact arranged and charged with purpose." If for the word "fiction" in this formulation we substitute "memoir," we can begin to get at the significance of Sheridan's selections and arrangements, as well as the purposes with which he charged them. In his account of reviewing his new command at Brandy Station, Virginia, in April 1864, for example, the purposeful charging of fact, selected and arranged, is not difficult to detect. Having reviewed the twelve thousand officers and men of the Cavalry Corps, Army of the Potomac, their new commander noted, "The corps presented a fine appearance at the review, and so far as health and equipment of the men were concerned the showing was good and satisfactory, but the horses were thin and very much worn down by excessive and, it seemed to me, unnecessary picket duty." The phrasing "excessive and, it seemed to me, unnecessary" purposefully prepared the way for the confrontation with Meade, on the next page, during which Sheridan stoutly, and possibly profanely, maintained his point of view about the most productive use of cavalry: "As the effectiveness of my command rested mainly on the strength of its horses, I thought the duty it was then performing was both burdensome and wasteful."[19]

Sheridan valued effectiveness as highly as anything, and he pushed himself tirelessly to assure it. Whoever or whatever enhanced effectiveness, he fostered and cultivated; whoever or whatever did not, he discarded without ceremony or sentiment. This ethic clearly guided his approach to leadership, and it came into play starkly and harshly in his remarks on an especially controversial phase of his Civil War service, the desolation of the Shenandoah Valley during the summer and fall of 1864. The rhetorical framing of these remarks in the memoirs was particularly significant. Unlike the ever forensic Sherman, Sheridan tended to avoid extensive primary documentation, approximating instead Grant's more modest ratio of quotation-to-narration, although he often included the order of battle for a major engagement or campaign, such as Stones River or Chickamauga or Missionary Ridge or the Overland Campaign, as well as the occasional order or letter of commendation from a superior. Usually, however, he let his story do the talking. The major exception in volume 1 was the appearance of nearly four consecutive pages of small-type excerpts at the end of the chapter on the Battle of Missionary Ridge, as Sheridan, proceeding like Sherman, worked to discredit William B. Hazen's claim that he was entitled to guns captured by Sheridan's men because his, Hazen's, had reached the crest of Missionary Ridge first.[20]

When Sheridan turned to the Shenandoah Valley Campaign, the ratio changed dramatically, especially in the case of a single, unusually long paragraph in which he stepped back to meditate on the nature of war. This paragraph ran to four pages because so many messages from Grant appeared in the footnotes, which at one point squeezed Sheridan's own account to a mere four lines at the top of a page. Sheridan did not include Grant's orders to him merely to justify his own actions in the valley or to shift from himself to Grant any blame arising from those actions. To be sure, the narrative moment was clearly a large one for the author, and its magnitude led to one of the few authorial, or editorial, stutters in the memoirs, the repeated printings, twenty pages apart, of Grant's order of August 5, 1864, to David Hunter, commander of the Department of West Virginia, which contained a key formulation that subsequently guided Sheridan: "In pushing up the Shenandoah Valley . . . it is desirable that nothing should be left to invite the enemy to return." But instead of including Grant's various orders to show that he was acting under them only as the obedient agent of destruction, not as its originator, Sheridan adopted a very different approach: "I endorsed [Grant's] programme in all its parts, for the stores of meat and grain that the valley provided, and the men it furnished for Lee's depleted regiments, were the strongest auxiliaries he possessed in the whole insurgent section."[21]

Endorsement usually flows the other way, with the commander endorsing the suggestion of a subordinate, a subordinate's endorsement of his commander wholly beside the point; it is for the subordinate to carry out the orders, not to presume to endorse them. In this case the subordinate's explicit endorsement of Grant's program, presumptuous and insubordinate as it may sound, cleared the way for a unique moment in Sheridan's narrative, his shift, in the final chapter of the first volume, to a large and memorable formulation about the nature of war. Denying that war involves only lines of men engaged in battle, amounting to nothing more than a duel, he saw war as something much worse. "Those who rest at home in peace and plenty see but little of the horrors attending such a duel, and even grow indifferent to them as the struggle goes on." Content with encouraging others to enlist, such civilians find it another matter "when deprivation and suffering are brought to their own doors." Sheridan concluded with magisterial generalization: "Death is popularly considered the maximum of punishment in war, but it is not; reduction to poverty brings prayers for peace more surely and more quickly than does the destruction of human life, as the selfishness of man has demonstrated in more than one great conflict."

What makes this wide-angle meditation especially valuable is that in addition to letting us hear yet another of the many languages Sheridan could speak—here the language of the philosopher or social critic—there is nothing else as ambitious and comprehensive in either volume of his memoirs. Unlike Grant or Sherman, Sheridan did not incline toward aerial perspectives and pronouncements. Narrating the outbreak of the war, for example, Sheridan said nothing—not a word—about the causes behind it. Whereas Grant traced these to the Mexican War and Sherman to the slavery question arising from the acquisition of California, Sheridan, the only one of the three actually in the army when the war began, remained sublimely indifferent to larger questions. Recounting his weekly climb to watch for a messenger returning from Portland, he waited "with anxiety for his coming, longing for good news" in the aftermath of First Manassas–Bull Run. The reason for anxious vigilance? "Isolated as I had been through years spent in the wilderness, my patriotism was untainted by politics, nor had it been disturbed by any discussion of the questions out of which the war grew, and I hoped for the success of the Government above all other considerations."[22]

Sheridan's claim to simple patriotism, undisturbed by any of the vast questions out of which the war grew, made all the more remarkable the vastness of his assertion that war means much more and is far worse than a duel between lines of men engaged in battle. A cousin of Sherman's famous statement of September 12, 1864, to the mayor and councilmen of Atlanta, "War is cruelty, and you cannot refine it," Sheridan's formulation focused on the strategic efficacy of enlisting human selfishness on behalf of peace. Having completed the desolation of the Shenandoah Valley in the name of such efficacy, Sheridan turned over command of the Middle Military Division to Alfred T. A. Torbert on February 28, 1865, destroyed Jubal Early's army at the Battle of Waynesboro, March 2, 1865, and set out to rejoin Grant at Petersburg, "feeling that the war was nearing its end" and desiring his cavalry "to be in at the death." By the time he turned his story to the Appomattox Campaign, Sheridan had succeeded in creating for his readers a personal, even intimate portrait of a protagonist flawed enough to be sympathetic and competent enough to be followed.[23]

The Appomattox Campaign

In the fifth chapter of his second volume, Sheridan took up narration of the Appomattox Campaign. Although at least one reader has claimed to prefer the 1883 account of the campaign published in the *North American Review*, those who have not followed Sheridan through his memoirs up to this point risk missing the sonority of accumulated echoes rolling through the 1888 version. To begin with, if Sheridan had been dutifully subordinate, in both letter and spirit, he might not have taken part in the Appomattox Campaign at all; or, to put it differently, if Sheridan had been dutifully subordinate, the Appomattox Campaign, as we know it, would not have unfolded when it did, the way it did. Instead, we might well be talking about the final, and later, Lynchburg campaign or Chatham campaign or Danville campaign. These points cannot be made too emphatically. The opening sentence of the chapter quickly established Sheridan as the initiator of his shift eastward: "The transfer of my command from the Shenandoah Valley to the field of operations in front of Petersburg was not anticipated by General Grant; indeed, the despatch brought from Columbia by my scouts, asking that supplies be sent me at the White House, was the first word that reached him concerning the move." Here Sheridan's use of the passive voice ("was not anticipated by General Grant") neatly muffled the true state of affairs, which amounted to "I wanted to be in at the death of the rebellion and moved accordingly." In case his reader missed this point, he restated it more bluntly in the final sentence of the first paragraph: "The reunited [cavalry] corps was to enter upon the campaign as a separate army, I reporting directly to General Grant; the intention being thus to reward me for foregoing, of my own choice, my position as a department commander by joining the armies at Petersburg."[24]

Archival evidence shows the handwritten words "foregoing of my own choice" inserted above a caret mark in the heavily edited typescript that succeeded Sheridan's clerk's handwritten manuscript, in which the corresponding phrase read, less pointedly, "the intention being to thus reward me for sacrificing my position." Critics of Sheridan who argue that his willful insistence on getting his own way inevitably compromised his integrity and value as a military leader have a strong case. A soldier's duty is to obey orders and, where orders are lacking, to seek them. Furthermore, the phrase "of my own choice" was misleading at best and wholly disingenuous at worst. Grant did not give Sheridan a choice between retaining command of the Middle Military Division, on the one hand, or of forfeiting it in order to transfer his force to Petersburg, on the other, in which case he was to be rewarded with autonomy apart from Meade. Sheridan made the move on his own, having acknowledged that "Grant's orders were for me to destroy the Virginia Central railroad and the James River canal, capture Lynchburg if practicable, and then join General Sherman in North Carolina wherever he might be found, or return to Winchester, but as to joining Sherman I was to be governed by the state of affairs after the projected capture of Lynchburg." Although one could maintain that Grant's orders to his subordinate were discretionary, Grant's larger intention could not have been clearer. As he wrote to Meade from City Point on February 21, 1865, "Sherman has but little over 4,000 cavalry, and Schofield none. The main object is to re-inforce Sherman in that arm of service."[25]

But fulfilling Grant's main object by moving southwest to serve Sherman was the last thing Sheridan wanted, as he recounted at length. Through ten pages of his memoirs—one-eighth of the space he devoted to the Appomattox Campaign—he fretted quite openly, especially after Sherman himself appeared on the scene at City Point to make his own case: "Well knowing the zeal and emphasis with which General Sherman would present his views, there again came into my mind many misgivings with reference to the movement of the cavalry, and I made haste to start for Grant's headquarters." The reader who has followed Sheridan from the opening of his memoirs to this point, and who recollects his account of the 1862 interview with Grant in Corinth, can anticipate the story of what followed in the shanty where Sheridan found Grant and Sherman in conversation: "My uneasiness made me somewhat too earnest, I fear, but General Grant soon mollified me, and smoothed matters over."[26]

If one needed further confirmation of Grant's superlative skills as a leader, the image of him mediating between the prickly self-interests of Sherman and Sheridan in his City Point shanty should provide it abundantly. Sheridan was unstinting in his summary praise of Grant, to whom he allotted the final two pages of the Appomattox section, giving to him the kind of encomium Grant and Sherman gave to Lincoln in their respective memoirs. By the time of his writing in 1887 or 1888, Sheridan's encomium for Grant doubled as a moving eulogy, ending with three sentences that showed keen awareness and appreciation of how Grant had managed him and others:

> During [the Overland Campaign] and in the siege of Petersburg he met with many disappointments—on several occasions the shortcomings of generals, when at the point of success, leading to wretched failures. But so far as he was concerned, the only apparent effect of these discomfitures was to make him all the more determined to discharge successfully the stupendous trust committed to his care, and to bring into play the manifold resources of his well-ordered military mind. He guided every subordinate then, and in the last days of the rebellion, with a fund of common sense and superiority of intellect, which have left an impress so distinct as to exhibit his great personality. When his military history is

> analyzed after the lapse of years, it will show, even more clearly than now, that during these as well as in his previous campaigns he was the steadfast centre about and on which everything else turned.[27]

To the everlasting credit of "the steadfast centre"—a phrase that first appeared in the typescript to replace "the planet about which everything revolved" in the clerk's manuscript—Grant's superiority of intellect and fund of common sense enabled him to know when to let Sheridan have his way. Recounting a meeting with his feisty lieutenant early in the Appomattox Campaign, Grant claimed he felt "glad to see the spirit of confidence with which he was imbued," knowing as he did "from experience, of what great value that feeling of confidence by a commander was." Spirit of confidence or insubordination? The line between them is not always clear, especially in Sheridan's case, but Grant saw the former where others might see only the latter. Critical as some may be about Sheridan's willfulness, Grant knew what he had in this particular subordinate, as he testified to, among many others, Mark Twain's daughter Susy, in memory of whom the bereaved father began "A Family Sketch" soon after her death on August 18, 1896, at the age of twenty-four: "When Susy was twelve years old General Grant described one or two of Sheridan's achievements to her, and gave his reasons for regarding Sheridan as the first general of the age." The point here is not whether everyone agrees that Sheridan was the first general of the age or whether he should have done what Grant originally wanted and gone southwest to serve under Sherman or whether his version of events is wholly reliable; the point is that Sheridan the writer could strike the rhetorical pose he adopted in his memoirs, and particularly in his narrative of the Appomattox Campaign, because he had triumphed as the hero of that campaign. He could afford to admit his tendency toward willful insubordination throughout his memoirs because, in the case of the Appomattox Campaign, it produced victory.[28]

In this respect Sheridan the writer drew heavily on credit accrued from what philosopher Thomas Nagel has called "moral luck," and specifically from one of Nagel's four types of moral luck, that pertaining to the results or outcome of one's actions or projects. Arguing that "whether we succeed or fail in what we try to do nearly always depends to some extent on factors beyond our control" and "what has been done, and what is morally judged, is partly determined by external factors," Nagel summarized his idea of moral luck this way: "Where a significant aspect of what someone does depends on factors beyond his control, yet we continue to treat him in that respect as an object of moral judgment, it can be called moral luck. Such luck can be good or bad." Nobody understood this kind of moral luck better than Abraham Lincoln, who explained in his letter to Albert G. Hodges, written April 4, 1864, exactly a year before the opening day of Sheridan's 1883 account of the Appomattox Campaign, "I claim not to have controlled events, but confess plainly that events have controlled me." This admission was not merely humility, true or false, on Lincoln's part; it was an instance of his shrewd, lawyerly appraisal of the role external factors play in moral judgments. If external factors had turned out to Lincoln's disadvantage—if in the fall of 1864, for example, Sherman had not taken Atlanta and Sheridan had not subdued the Shenandoah Valley, so that the president had lost his bid for reelection, as he fully expected to as of August 1864—the moral judgment of controversial actions such as suspending habeas corpus or issuing the Emancipation Proclamation or initiating a draft might have gone against him and his moral luck been much worse.[29]

The Sheridan of the memoirs had good moral luck, too. If we take as comparative examples the insubordination or noncompliance of two leaders, such as Sheridan before the Appomattox Campaign and Joseph E. Johnston during the later stages of Grant's Vicksburg Campaign—when Johnston failed, from Jefferson Davis's point of view, to comply with his orders and fulfill his duties as commander of the Department of the West—we tend to praise the former and condemn the latter largely on the basis of results or consequences: Sheridan's noncompliance contributed to Lee's surrender at Appomattox, Johnston's to the Confederate loss of Vicksburg. What matters most here is that if the positions were reversed—if Sheridan's noncompliance had led to Lee's escape and reunion with Johnston somewhere between Appomattox and Greensboro, or Johnston's noncompliance had led to Grant's failure to capture Vicksburg—the two generals' memoirs most likely would have turned out to be very different. Presumably, Johnston could have done something else with the many pages he spent refuting Davis's censure of his performance, and Sheridan might have had to resort to much more of the self-justifying rhetorical strategy of extensive documentation that he adopted in the chapters devoted to his tumultuous service in New Orleans as military governor of Texas and Louisiana during the early years of Reconstruction. Then again, if his noncompliance had led to Lee's escape at Appomattox, the *North American Review* might have been much less interested in publishing his account, and Mark Twain might never have suggested his writing his memoirs at all. Unlike Lincoln, however, Sheridan gave no hint in his memoirs that he spent substantial time in contemplating his subordination to external factors.[30]

A particularly urgent and complicated example of moral luck emerged in Sheridan's account of his relieving Gouverneur Warren from command of the Fifth Corps during the Battle of Five Forks, April 1, 1865: "It was therefore necessary to protect myself in this critical situation, and General Warren having sorely disappointed me, both in the moving of his corps and in its management during the battle, I felt that he was not the man to rely upon under such circumstances, and deeming that it was to the best interest of the service as well as but just to myself, I relieved him, ordering him to report to General Grant." The controversy that followed Sheridan's bold action—some have maintained it an unjust one—cast the only large shadow over the Appomattox portion of the memoirs. For seventeen pages, or between a fifth and a quarter of the whole, Sheridan told the story of the Battles of Dinwiddie Court House (March 31, 1865) and Five Forks not by focusing exclusively on his case against Warren's alleged slowness and apathy but certainly by including more than enough details along the way to explain his decision.[31]

Like everyone else involved in the race west from Petersburg, Gouverneur Warren had to cope with, among other things, the heavy rains and extreme muddiness of the roads, which almost led Grant to suspend operations—until Sheridan, in combination with John Rawlins, argued him out of doing so—and which caused Sheridan to choose over Rienzi "a powerful gray pacing horse called Breckenridge" to carry him through the immobilizing muck. Sheridan gave none of his narrative to Warren's challenges. True to form, even though by the time of writing he had succeeded Sherman as commanding general of the United States and might have rehearsed the events of April 1865 with the coolly secure detachment of that high eminence, Sheridan instead chose to describe candidly his own agitations in the moment: "That we had accomplished nothing but to oblige our foe to retreat was to me bitterly disappointing. . . . I was disappointed. . . . At last I expressed to Warren my fears. . . . when my patience was almost worn out. . . . General Warren having sorely disappointed me."[32]

What made this unguarded self-portrait of agitation particularly revealing was that it showed little or no attempt to answer controversy by pretending to level-headed objectivity. Sheridan the writer gambled that because his action against Warren was part and parcel of all the actions that led to victory on April 9, when his cavalry delayed the final Confederate push west from Appomattox long enough for lead elements of Edward O. C. Ord's Army of the James to arrive and block it, his own subjective state was justification enough for Warren's relief. The language we have seen could not have been more telling:

"deeming that it was to the best interest of the service *as well as but just to myself,* I relieved him" (emphasis added). Grant's order of March 31, 10:15 p.m., had instructed Meade to urge Warren "not to stop for anything," and Grant had given Sheridan authority to relieve Warren, as he would not have done unless he had anticipated some version of what later happened. There was something almost defiant in Sheridan's account, as though he were saying, I had the power to relieve Warren, so when he disappointed me, I relieved him, and the positive ending justified the controversial means to it.[33]

Not quite willing to let it go so brazenly at that, Sheridan sought to strengthen his position and jumped ahead to the 1879 Court of Inquiry given to Warren. This flash-forward actually took him eight years beyond the narrative boundary of his memoirs, which concluded, after many pages of what often reads like pleasure-seeking travel literature, with his return in 1871 from observing the Franco-Prussian War. Having pointed out that that the court found against Warren on two counts and for him on two counts, Sheridan took the fifty-fifty split as vindication and ended his sixth chapter of the second volume with the assertion—one that appeared neither in typescript nor in manuscript and must have been added at a later stage – "That I was justified in this is plain to all who are disposed to be fair-minded." Then, in a final clinching move tinged by some irony after the reluctance to serve under him in the spring of 1865, Sheridan gave the last word to Sherman, commanding general of the army in 1879, the authority and eloquence of whose judgment were powerfully persuasive, as Sheridan himself knew very well.[34]

Familiar to readers of his own memoirs as capable of both passionate enthusiasm and passionate disgust, Sherman delivered his opinion on Sheridan's relief of Warren with a sagacious tact and finely calibrated precision worthy of Solomon. One can imagine without difficulty that Sheridan quoted Sherman's opening statements with a firm conviction that they had been designed specifically with him in mind, as they captured his style of leadership exactly:

> "It would be an unsafe and dangerous rule to hold the commander of an army in battle to a technical adherence to any rule of conduct for managing his command. He is responsible for results, and holds the lives and reputations of every officer and soldier under his orders as subordinate to the great end—victory. The most important events are usually compressed into an hour, a minute, and he cannot stop to analyze his reasons. He must act on the impulse, the conviction, of the instant, and should be sustained in his conclusions, if not manifestly unjust. The power to

> command men, and give vehement impulse to their joint action, is something which cannot be defined by words, but it is plain and manifest in battles, and whoever commands an army in chief must choose his subordinates by reason of qualities which can alone be tested in actual conflict."[35]

Sherman's assertion that the conditions of battle compel us to subordinate judgment of a leader's actions to "the great end" of victory offered yet another version of moral luck. Where a leader's impulses, convictions, and actions combine with external events to produce victory, they "should be sustained," or judged morally acceptable. What Sherman did not say, but what his assertion left implicit, is that the same impulses, convictions, and actions could be judged unacceptable where they fail to combine with external events to produce victory. This unspoken side of the argument led one of Sheridan's early readers to call Sherman's rationale "a monstrous theory." Sheridan's account of the Appomattox Campaign was an account of nothing so much as his exertions, under extraordinary conditions, to "give vehement impulse" to the joint action of the men under his command and, by doing so, to produce victory. That Sherman did not find the effects of Sheridan's exertions "manifestly unjust" became clear in the deliberate, discriminating language of what followed: "'No one has questioned the patriotism, integrity, and great intelligence of General Warren. These are attested by a long record of most excellent service, but in the clash of arms at and near Five Forks, March 31 and April 1, 1865, his personal activity fell short of the standard fixed by General Sheridan, on whom alone rested the great responsibility for that and succeeding days.'" One might wonder what role Grant played in Sherman's understanding of the Appomattox Campaign, if such great responsibility rested on Sheridan "alone," but with or without acknowledgment of Sheridan's own subordinate position, Sherman's final word could not have been more welcome: "'My conclusion is that General Sheridan was perfectly justified in his action in this case, and he must be fully and entirely sustained if the United States expects great victories by her arms in the future.'"[36]

If "the standard fixed by General Sheridan" during the Appomattox Campaign could be compressed into one word, that word, his word, was "celerity," from the Latin for swiftness. Speed was the key to the vehement impulse Sheridan sought to give the joint actions of the men he commanded. The word "celerity" appeared five times in the two volumes of his memoirs, the first time in orders issued by Andrew A. Humphreys to James H. Wilson on June 21, 1864:

"'The success of your expedition will depend upon the secrecy with which it is commenced, and the celerity with which its movements are conducted.'" Within the next twenty pages Sheridan used the word twice more, both times in a phrase that echoed Humphreys, "celerity of movement," leading to the reasonable conclusion that quoting Humphreys brought the word to his attention and he liked it enough to employ it on his own. But even though the word did not appear in the first volume before the quotation from Humphreys, Sheridan had used it years earlier in "The Last Days of the Rebellion," specifically with respect to events of April 7, 1865: "A detachment ordered to move with the greatest celerity, via Prince Edward's Court-house, reported that Lee had crossed the Appomattox at and near Farmville, and that Crook had followed him." Sheridan's single-minded focus on celerity, swiftness, or speed found its way from his memory of 1865 into the writing of 1883, as he entrusted several adverbs, appearing on the same page, with the work of conveying the breathlessness of the pace in the last forty-eight hours of the campaign: "He immediately started. . . . I swung off to the left, and moved quickly. . . . my command was instantly turned north." In the final version of 1888, he did not retain any of these particular phrases to describe these particular moments, but he did retain the language of speed, which he now enhanced and extended over his account of April 7, 8, and 9: Crook "promptly attacked. . . . The intelligence as to the trains was immediately despatched to Crook. . . . Custer having the advance, moved rapidly. . . . These regiments set off at a gallop. . . . Without halting to look after the cars further, Custer attacked. . . . that the Confederates might have no rest. . . . after a hasty consultation. . . . but hastily galloping back. . . . I decided to attack at once."[37]

Framing and intensifying the narrative speed of these pages was an anecdote missing from the earlier 1883 version, the anecdote of what Sheridan dubbed "Lincoln's Laconic Despatch." Lincoln made only three personal appearances in Sheridan's memoirs, and none of the three constituted the stuff of mythmaking hero-worship. The first appearance came when Sheridan, newly transferred to the East in April 1864, went to see the president after an interview with Stanton, and Lincoln "wound up our short conversation by quoting that stale interrogation so prevalent during the early years of the war, 'Who ever saw a dead cavalryman?'" In the second, in August 1864, Sheridan, in company with Stanton, went to see Lincoln again, and again the connection between the soldier and president was less than lustrous: "During a short conversation Mr. Lincoln candidly told me that Mr. Stanton had objected to my assignment to General Hunter's command, because he thought me too young, and that he himself had concurred with the Secretary," although the president now had decided to back Grant's selection of Sheridan and hope for the best. Of their third and final meeting, aboard the steamer *Mary Martin* at City Point in March 1865, Sheridan sketched a telling portrait, one that showed the strain of recent events on the chief executive: "On the trip the President was not very cheerful. In fact, he was dejected, giving no indication of his usual means of diversion, by which (his quaint stories) I had often heard he could find relief from his cares." In the clerk's manuscript "dejected" replaced and softened Sheridan's original, darker word, "gloomy."[38]

Lincoln did not come through as an inspiring personal presence in any of these accounts, but with the inclusion of his "laconic despatch," sent sometime during the early hours of April 7, 1865, Sheridan suggested that the president's words played a significant part in the final push for celerity. Near midnight on April 6, Sheridan telegraphed Grant about the victory at Sailor's Creek that day, adding, "'If the thing is pressed, I think that Lee will surrender.'" Grant transmitted the message to Lincoln, who replied to Grant, simply and sufficiently, with five words that, Sheridan's narrative arrangement implied, were all the fiat he needed to hear: "'Let the thing be pressed.'" Sheridan's account did not say how he came to know of Lincoln's dispatch, nor did Grant mention it in his memoirs, but Sheridan's narrative management of the anecdote made it seem as though Lincoln were authorizing him directly. From the recounting of Lincoln's reply on, Sheridan accelerated both his actions and his descriptions of them toward the surrender at Appomattox.[39]

An especially valuable assessment of Sheridan's standard of celerity during the Appomattox Campaign came from someone who was not an unqualified supporter of his, someone who opposed and criticized his treatment of Warren. In his posthumously published *The Passing of the Armies* (1915), Joshua Lawrence Chamberlain recounted the evening of April 1, after the Battle of Five Forks, when "a compact form" emerged from the shadows "with vigorous stride unlike the measure and mood of ours, and a voice that would itself have thrilled us had not the import of it thrilled us more." It was Sheridan, come to offer his apologies for speaking harshly to some of the officers in the Fifth Corps during the battle. Having gushed, "And this is Phil Sheridan! . . . All the repressed feeling of our hearts sprang out towards him," Chamberlain settled into a paragraph comparing Sheridan's style with that to which they had been accustomed under Warren:

> We had had a taste of his style of fighting, and we liked it. In some respects it was different from ours. . . . We had a habit, perhaps, drawn from

> dire experience, and for which we had also Grant's quite recent sanction, when we had carried a vital point or had to hold one, to entrench. But Sheridan does not entrench. He pushes on, carrying his flank and rear with him—rushing, flashing, smashing. He transfuses into his subordinates the vitality and energy of his purpose; transforms them into part of his own mind and will.[40]

Brandishing an auditory bravado fully worthy of the man it described, Chamberlain's apt phrase "rushing, flashing, smashing" caught something essential about Sheridan at the height of his powers during the Appomattox Campaign. It caught the quicksilver quality of his inspired, inspiring impulsiveness and opportunism, along with the relentless destructiveness that went with it. Sheridan was not the first or only military commander to insist on speed and mobility to keep an enemy off balance. Antecedents and analogues extend from the ancient world through his Confederate counterparts Stonewall Jackson, Nathan Bedford Forrest, and John Singleton Mosby—not to mention the Indian warriors he faced in the northwest and, later, on the Plains, especially the Cheyennes, "the most warlike tribe of all"—and on to those influenced by the twentieth-century ideas of John Boyd, the fighter pilot whose presentations led to the U.S. Marines model of maneuver warfare. But Sheridan was the first commander to bring speed, mobility, and the quick reactions of self-reliant autonomy to the Army of the Potomac, as Chamberlain's testimony confirmed. Not everyone liked or admired his early prototype of maneuver warfare, which he could not have developed without Grant's understanding and support, and criticisms of Sheridan for insubordination or ill-breeding unbecoming an officer sometimes masked, and continue to mask, discomfort with the innovations he introduced and embodied. At least one of his enemies, the straight-talking artillerist Edward Porter Alexander, also recognized something undeniable about the power of "Sheridan's presence & personality," referring unequivocally to the Union cavalry commander as Grant's "best general."[41]

For all his insistence on speed, when it came to narrating the events of April 9, Sheridan the writer slowed down his pace considerably, giving eleven pages to the hours beginning with the sleepless night of April 8, during which "everybody was overjoyed at the prospect that our weary work was about to end so happily," and ending with Lee, after his meeting with Grant in the McLean house, riding "his chunky gray horse" through "the bivouac of the Army of Northern Virginia," his progress audible by the varying loudness of his soldiers' cheering. Along the way Sheridan recounted Ord's predawn arrival with news that John Gibbon's Twenty-Fourth Corps was approaching; the moment when John B. Gordon's advancing "gray lines instinctively halted" on reaching the crest from which they could "see Ord's men emerging from the woods, and the hopelessness of a further attack"; and word from George A. Custer, "'Lee has surrendered; do not charge; the white flag is up.'" After five pages devoted to the unsettled period before Grant's arrival, during which Confederates continued to fire on Sheridan and others before Sheridan managed to meet with Gordon and Cadmus M. Wilcox, the story finally brought Grant on stage.[42]

The memoirs had prepared the ground for this moment seventy pages earlier, with a sentence describing the commanding general's manner with his subordinates: "General Grant was never impulsive, and always met his officers in an unceremonious way, with a quiet 'How are you?' soon putting one at his ease, since the pleasant tone in which he spoke gave assurance of welcome, although his manner was otherwise impassive." With this brief, deft characterization, Sheridan equipped his readers to savor the understated power of this unadorned exchange near the village of Appomattox Court House: "He remaining mounted, spoke first to me, saying simply, 'How are you, Sheridan?' I assured him with thanks that I was 'first-rate,' when, pointing toward the village, he asked, 'Is General Lee up there?' and I replied, 'There is his army down in that valley, and he himself is over in that house (designating McLean's house) waiting to surrender to you.' The General then said, 'Come, let us go over,' this last remark being addressed to both Ord and me." At this weighty moment it was as though Sheridan the writer chose to surrender the rushing, flashing, smashing of Sheridan the warrior to the calm, quiet manner of Grant. The lean, spare quality of the writing amounted to an act of imitative homage, a voluntary act of authorial subordination to the composed taciturnity of the steadfast center.[43]

Proceeding from this moment, Sheridan's 1888 account omitted some details of the 1883 one in "The Last Days of the Rebellion," forgoing, for example, an inventory of U.S. officers who entered the McLean house with Grant ("as nearly as I can recollect, Ord, Rawlins, Seth Williams, Ingalls, Babcock, Parker, and myself"). The version in the memoirs also dropped the parenthetically inserted information that Sheridan bought from Wilmer McLean the "elliptical-shaped table" on which Grant had written out the terms of surrender, later presenting it to "Mrs. G. A. Custer," as well as a sentence about Robert E. Lee: "He had on his face the expression of relief from a heavy burden." A perfectly good sentence, and one that offered readers a moving glimpse of the Confederate chief, it may have struck Sheridan later as tending toward cliché or overly sympathetic attentiveness to the icon of the Lost Cause. Whatever his reason for dropping it, he did retain quotation of Lee's one direct statement to him. Earlier in the day, Sheridan had fired off two dispatches to Lee, protesting the withdrawal of a portion of the Confederate cavalry in violation of the truce agreement. Having had no time to make copies of the dispatches, Sheridan had asked to have them returned. Handing the dispatches back to Sheridan in the McLean house, Lee apologized, with the small but suggestive change from "possible" in the 1883 version and memoir manuscripts (both Sheridan's original and his clerk's copy) to "probable" in the typescript and 1888 final version: "'I am sorry. It is probable that my cavalry at that point of the line did not understand the agreement.'"[44]

Then, after the moment that ended the 1883 version, with the image of hearing the cheers for Lee on Traveller, Sheridan spent a short paragraph assessing the Confederate general before concluding his account of the Appomattox Campaign with his two pages in praise of Grant. Sixty pages earlier, Sheridan had subjected Lee to the critical second-guessing familiar to readers of the first volume: "Lee made no effort to hold Dinwiddie, which he might have done with his cavalry, and in this he made a fatal mistake." When it came to his parting assessment, however, he waived all criticism in favor of a short, matter-of-fact appraisal with which few could quarrel: "For four years his army had been the main-stay of the Confederacy; and the marked ability with which he directed its operations is evidenced both by his frequent successes and the length of time he kept up the contest." As it turned out, this relatively muted approbation—acknowledging a record of "frequent" successes was hardly the same as bowing to the unparalleled achievements of military genius—simply prepared the way for Grant to receive the last word: "Indeed, it may be said that till General Grant was matched against him, he never met an opponent he did not vanquish," a statement that dismissed Meade's victory at Gettysburg. After the summary encomium for Grant, Sheridan turned briefly to the assassination of Lincoln ("dastardly deed") and then to missing the Grand Review in Washington because of Grant's insistence that he go west immediately "to force the surrender of the Confederates under Kirby Smith." With that, Grant faded into the background of Sheridan's memoirs, which moved on to the border with Mexico during the downfall of Maximilian, New Orleans during Reconstruction, the Plains during the campaign against hostile tribes, and Europe during the Franco-Prussian War. Those interested in Sheridan primarily in the context of the Civil War may have already ended their reading with Appomattox, however.[45]

Sheridan's style of fighting may have shaped the victorious Appomattox Campaign, but his *Personal Memoirs* did not shape commercial victory for Charles L. Webster and Company. Bound in green boards to match the other works in Webster's "Great War Library," Sheridan's two volumes joined those by or about Grant, Sherman, McClellan, Samuel Crawford, Winfield Scott Hancock, and Custer. In 1891 the publisher followed a cheap, two-dollar edition of Sherman's memoirs with one of Sheridan's. By this point the financial health of the company was steadily deteriorating. For years Mark Twain had been pouring the profits into another commercial venture, the Paige Typesetting Machine. When the machine proved a failure, and when financial panic struck the markets in 1893, Charles L. Webster and Company did not survive. News of the bankruptcy, formally declared the day before, appeared in the *New York Times* on April 19, 1894. Eight years later, when Michael Sheridan brought out an enlarged edition of his brother's memoirs, continuing the story from 1871 through his death in 1888, he did so with Sherman's original publisher, D. Appleton and Company. This enlarged edition has not replaced the original in the literary and military history of the Civil War; Sheridan's original continues to maintain its independent command.[46]

7

CODA

Mark Twain and the Mississippi of Memory

WITHOUT MARK TWAIN the Civil War memory market would not have developed as it did, and without the Civil War there never would have been a Mark Twain. Some evidence for this assertion comes from chapter 21 of his *Life on the Mississippi* (1883), a heterogeneous book containing, along with much else, Twain's most extended version of Civil War memoir. Earning his pilot's license on April 9, 1859, twenty-three-year-old Samuel Clemens "dropped into casual employments" on the Mississippi until "intermittent work gave place to steady and protracted engagements." The life of a Mississippi pilot could have proven prestigious and lucrative for a young man from Hannibal, Missouri. "Time drifted smoothly and prosperously on, and I supposed—and hoped—that I was going to follow the river the rest of my days, and die at the wheel when my mission was ended," Twain continued. History had other plans for Samuel Clemens, however, as it did for millions of his contemporaries. "But by and by the war came, commerce was suspended, my occupation was gone." This efficient sentence, telescoping months of tumult into three short clauses, echoes Abraham Lincoln's four-word understatement in his Second Inaugural Address, "And the war came," before it proceeds to kill off an industry and drive the newly unemployed pilot into Nevada in search of "another livelihood." In this one-page chapter, "A Section of My Biography," Twain did not mention his brief and ambiguous service as a Confederate partisan in Marion County, Missouri, during June 1861, nor did he discuss his choice to serve neither the United States nor the Confederacy as a badly needed pilot. Instead, he bridged the two parts of *Life on the Mississippi*—the first, about his early steamboat days, had appeared in a series of seven articles in the *Atlantic* during 1875—by recounting that eventually he "became a scribbler of books, and an immovable fixture among the other rocks of New England."[1]

Concluding this abbreviated chapter with "Let us resume, now," the self-styled New England scribbler steered into the second part of *Life on the Mississippi* by flipping the calendar forward to the spring of 1882 and his return to the river for a monthlong trip with publisher James R. Osgood. Now an established author, *The Adventures of Huckleberry Finn* beginning to form in his mind, Mark Twain treated his return to the Mississippi from a variety of perspectives and modes, some more successful than others. Among them are those he explored in chapters about his encounters with the aftermath of the Civil War along the river. As he steamed first down from St. Louis to New Orleans, then back up from New Orleans to St. Paul, stopping for three nights in Hannibal, his riverine travel through space twinned with his mental travel through time. As the former pilot cruised his familiar river, memory and imagination took turns at the wheel.

But between 1861, when the outbreak of hostilities ended Samuel Clemens's career as a Mississippi pilot, and 1882, when Mark Twain returned to the river as a public figure, there was a formative moment when the not-yet-famous writer was mulling over famous public language produced by the Civil War. This moment provides another kind of evidence for the shaping influence of the war on his life and career. At the end of July 1866, thirty-year-old Samuel Clemens found himself becalmed aboard the *Smyrniote*, sailing from Honolulu to San Francisco in twenty-five days. Four months earlier the outbound trip to Pearl Harbor on the *Ajax* had taken ten. In a notebook entry for Monday, July 30, he jotted, "This is the fifth day of dead, almost motionless calm—a man can walk a crack in the deck, the ship lies so still. I enjoy it, and I believe all hands do except the d—d baby. I write 2 hours a day & loaf the balance." On assignment for the *Sacramento Union*, Clemens was putting his writing hours toward journalism, to which the *Hannibal Journal* and a few other periodicals had introduced him in the early 1850s. On the timeline of Samuel Clemens's transformation into Mark Twain, 1866 would turn out to mark the start of an important turn, as he moved toward longer forms of writing. Eventually the Sandwich Island letters for the *Union* found their way into *Roughing It* (1872), Twain's second full-length travel book. The first, *The Innocents Abroad, or the New Pilgrims' Progress*, which also included a roundtrip ocean voyage, had appeared in 1869.[2]

"The sea is fully as level as the Mississippi," Clemens observed from the deck of "the good ship *Smyrniote*," but his evocation of outward calm is misleading.

Three years before he saw his pen name on a title page, Clemens was doing more than writing for two hours and loafing the better part of twenty-two. He was thinking, and in particular he was thinking about what he called eloquence, as in this example: "Eloquence Simplicity—Lincoln's 'With malice toward none, with charity for all, & doing the right as God gives us to see the right, all may be well.[']—Very simple & beautiful." Clemens's imperfect recollection of the last sentence of the Second Inaugural Address, delivered a year before he left San Francisco for Hawaii and not yet polished by public repetition into civic scripture, may sound comically truncated, as though Tom Sawyer had suddenly mangled it; yet even his imperfect recollection, out in the Pacific "at least as smooth as the river is when ruffled by a very light breeze & swelling with a few dying steamboat waves," testifies with an eloquence of its own.

His 1866 notebook shows Mark-Twain-in-the-Making spending the enforced maritime suspension thinking hard about the kind of writer he wanted to become, about such things as voice and tone and the various effects and techniques and devices that fall under the category of rhetoric, a word he used rarely and then only pejoratively, as in his December 1881 speech in Montreal at a banquet in his honor: "But, as I have already intimated, I will close this oration with a few sentiments in the French language. I have not ornamented them, I have not burdened them with flowers of rhetoric, for, to my mind, that literature is best and most enduring which is characterized by a noble simplicity." A noble simplicity: this is what he was mulling over on the *Smyrniote*.[3]

Noble simplicity does not just happen, though, at least not always. "There are factitious aids—surroundings & circumstances which often make a passage thrillingly eloquent which inherently possesses no such attribute—for instance, how Gen. Grant's simple response to Buckner who had asked about what terms he would stipulate or agree for the surrender of Fort Donaldson used to rouse the multitude in the fierce days of the rebellion. 'Unconditional surrender! I propose to move at once upon your works!'" No experienced reader of Ulysses S. Grant would mistake the exclamation marks for his. The twelve hundred pages in the first edition of Grant's *Personal Memoirs* contain exactly ten such marks, and seven of them appear in quotations. Of the other three, those signaling Grant's own depth of feeling, this one is the most eloquent, for both what it says and what it does not: "A casualty to Sherman that would have taken him from the field that day would have been a sad one for the troops engaged at Shiloh. And how near we came to this!" What Grant actually wrote to Brigadier General Simon B. Buckner, from "Camp near Donelson, Feb.y

16th 1862," was "No terms except an unconditional and immediate surrender can be accepted. I propose to move immediately upon your works." Clemens's exclamation marks annotate the thrill stirred in him by Grant's compressed understatement.[4]

Twenty years after Ulysses S. Grant demanded the surrender of Fort Donelson with eloquent language that impressed a budding Mark Twain, Clemens found his personal past converging with the recent past of the United States. To review one meant reviewing the other. Although he did not say so then, this insight would inform his savvy assessment of the market for memoirs written in a first-person voice, which he himself was exploring in one of the preeminent literary experiments with such a voice, *The Adventures of Huckleberry Finn*. As he steamed along the Mississippi in 1882, he jotted notes showing he realized that reviewing the recent public events through the lens of his personal past meant giving more than a little thought to the blending of imagination, which complemented his visit to Vicksburg on Wednesday, April 26, 1882, and memory, which he linked with his sojourn in New Orleans from 8:00 a.m. on Friday, April 28, to 5:00 p.m. on Saturday, May 6. These two motifs, imagining the war and remembering the war, recall earlier remarks about Thomas Jefferson's classification of books and the faculties of mind employed on them. But whereas Jefferson's classifying tendency reflected his Enlightenment loyalty to analytical precision, Twain's love of humor, tall tales, and a mixing of romance and realism led him away from analytical precision toward indirect association and figurative suggestiveness. His own composite mode, located by many within the domain of literature, had much in common with the books by generals he would see through publication over the next few years.

A Changeable River

With implications for both memory and imagination, a particularly suggestive image running through *Life on the Mississippi* is the changeableness of the river's course. On the southbound trip in April, Twain's boat, the *Gold Dust*, "passed through the Plum Point region, turned Craighead's Point, and glided unchallenged by what was once the formidable Fort Pillow, memorable because of the massacre perpetrated there during the war." Twain left details of the April 1864 massacre unspoken, relying on his readers to recall that victims of the no-quarter executions were mostly Black soldiers from the Sixth United States Colored Heavy Artillery Regiment and a detachment of the Second United States Colored Light Artillery Regiment. Referring with a pilot's detailed knowledge to navigational points in the Mississippi between Arkansas and Tennessee, Twain added, in a serious tone, "Massacres are sprinkled with some frequency through the histories of several Christian nations, but this is almost the only one that can be found in American history; perhaps it is the only one which rises to a size correspondent to that huge and somber title."[5]

In both this section of *Life on the Mississippi* and the corresponding entries in his notebook, it is clear that the former steamboat pilot had on his mind history, memory, and the Civil War. Three chapters earlier, for example, he had turned his notebook version of an anecdote heard from either Lemuel or Edmund Gray, bothers who alternated pilot watches on the *Gold Dust*, into a first-person, pilot's-eye account of the Battle of Belmont, fought November 7, 1861, in Mississippi County, Missouri. In the case of Twain's remarks about Fort Pillow, however, history and memory do not agree, as it is possible to think of Fort Pillow as the only massacre in American history if one forgets or omits three and a half centuries of Native American precursors, beginning with Hernando de Soto and the 1539 Napituca Massacre in Florida. Someone who had spent as much time in the American West as Samuel Clemens did in the 1860s would not have been distant from the sites of several of them.

Memory that forgets or omits historical events, either willfully or out of ignorance, is memory that changes or reshapes history. Twain's next sentence, in a new paragraph, pivots from historical memory of massacres to memory of a particularly shifty stretch of the Mississippi. "More of the river's freaks," the paragraph opens before turning to specifics in a passage tracking closely with one in Twain's notebooks. "In times past, the channel used to strike above Island 37, by Brandywine Bar, and down towards Island 39." But Tuesday, March 7, 1876, brought one of the river's freaks. "Afterward, changed its course and went from Brandywine down through Vogelman's chute in the Devil's Elbow, to Island 39—part of this course reversing the old order; the river running *up* four or five miles, instead of down, and cutting off, throughout, some fifteen miles of distance." In honor of the year, the same that saw publication of *The Adventures of Tom Sawyer* in distant Connecticut, "All that region is now called Centennial Island." Twain did not point out that in this instance the river's freaks had legal consequences not without implications for state sovereignty, as Island 37, though on the Arkansas side of the main Mississippi channel after the river changed course, remained under the legal jurisdiction of Tennessee.[6]

The changeableness of the Mississippi is infamous. It was a problem for the young cub pilot of 1858–59, and it remains a problem today. "The Mississippi moves with such force that it eats away at its outer bends," a recent news story reported, then added, "Unimpeded, the river could move hundreds of feet a year." What Mark Twain called the river's freaks are not as unimpeded now as they used to be. Overseen by the U.S. Army Corps of Engineers, a system of locks, levees, and concrete mats slows the movement of the river, though it cannot contain it altogether. The shifting of the Mississippi River was and is a literal, practical, logistical problem. In Twain's hands it also serves as a persistently figurative image, a metaphor for the fickle topography of history and imagination and memory. Some may think the course of Civil War history set and stable, a matter of documents to be studied and facts to be mastered, but Twain's metaphor suggests that our imaginations and our memories, both individually in our own lives and collectively over the century and a half since the war ended, keep eating away at the banks of the past and changing the course of what we choose to remember and how we choose to remember it.[7]

Mark Twain's visit to Vicksburg, subject of the single chapter "Vicksburg during the Trouble," prompted him to consider the divide between people who had experienced the Civil War firsthand and people who had not. The chapter begins with an image of another change in the course of the Mississippi, this one at Vicksburg. "We used to plough past the lofty hill-city, Vicksburg, downstream," recollected the former pilot; "but we cannot do that now." Once again, the shifting Mississippi changed the navigational map, with serious economic consequences for the former port of Vicksburg. "A cut-off has made a country town of it, like Osceola, St. Genevieve, and several others." The cut-off formed on Wednesday, April 26, 1876, seven weeks after the one at Island 37. "There is currentless water—also a big island—in front of Vicksburg now." In these opening sentences Twain used the topographic change to signal the contrast between a receding Then and an immediate Now. With that signal he opened a meditation on how we who live now can make any kind of mental connection with what happened back then. This is the challenge behind any and all historical writing, whether it corresponds to what we call fiction or what we call nonfiction.[8]

A visitor to Vicksburg in April 1882 had much to help with thinking about six weeks of siege there, from May 18 to July 4, 1863. "Signs and scars still remain, as reminders of Vicksburg's tremendous war-experiences; earthworks, trees crippled by the cannon balls, cave-refuges in the clay precipices, etc." Twain focused on the caves used by the noncombatants seeking shelter during bombardment, as he tried to imagine his way into the texture of lives lived in "mere holes, tunnels, driven into the perpendicular clay bank." Even for an unusually imaginative writer the effort initially appeared to prove frustrating. "Life in Vicksburg, during the six weeks was perhaps—": here Twain abruptly, dramatically broke off his tentative groping toward what noncombatant life had been like in besieged Vicksburg. His next move revealed a new strategy: "but wait; here are some materials out of which to reproduce it."

In "Vicksburg during the Trouble," Mark Twain put his finger on the problem of writing and reading history, in this case the history of the American Civil War. How can we who were not there and did not undergo the "tremendous war-experiences" of Vicksburg ever manage to reproduce those experiences? How do we who have no firsthand memories of events reproduce them in our minds? How do historically belated stragglers move from traces of past events to accurate and effective reproductions of them in their minds? In the case of Vicksburg, Twain attempted this reproduction by means of materials he shaped into a single, long, tour-de-force sentence allotted a paragraph of its own:

> Population, twenty-seven thousand soldiers and three thousand non-combatants; the city utterly cut off from the world—walled solidly in, the frontage by gunboats, the rear by soldiers and batteries; hence, no buying and selling with the outside; no passing to and fro; no God-speeding a parting guest, no welcoming a coming one; no printed acres of world-wide news to be read at breakfast, mornings—a tedious dull absence of such matter, instead; hence, also, no running to see steamboats smoking into view in the distance up or down, and ploughing toward the town—for none came, the river lay vacant and undisturbed; no rush and turmoil around the railway station, no struggling over bewildered swarms of passengers by noisy mobs of hackmen—all quiet there; flour two hundred dollars a barrel, sugar thirty, corn ten dollars a bushel, bacon five dollars a pound, rum a hundred dollars a gallon; other things in proportion: consequently, no roar and racket of drays and carriages tearing along the streets; nothing for them to do, among that handful of non-combatants of exhausted means; at three o'clock in the morning, silence; silence so dead that the measured tramp of a sentinel can be heard a seemingly impossible distance; out of hearing of this lonely sound, perhaps the stillness is absolute: all in a moment come ground-shaking thunder-crashes of artillery, the sky is cobwebbed with the criss-crossing red lines streaming from soaring bomb-shells, and a rain of iron fragments descends upon the city; descends upon the empty streets: streets which are not

> empty a moment later, but mottled with dim figures of frantic women and children skurrying from home and bed toward the cave dungeons—encouraged by the humorous grim soldiery, who shout "Rats! to your holes!" and laugh.

Antithesis of the lean, telescoping sentence in "A Section of My Biography," this swollen run-on ranks high among the longest sentences Mark Twain wrote; it is certainly the longest he wrote about the Civil War, although it does not appear in a recent selection of his Civil War writings. Lacking a main verb, it is not even a real sentence. It is an overgrown fragment whirring away on the cogs and gears of syntactic parallelism, cataloging, and various forms of repetition, all managed by that nineteenth-century wonder of punctuation, the semicolon. What is more, the whole verbal machine, or most of it, runs on negation, listing what is absent in order to suggest, or reproduce, what is present. Most telling of all, Twain's notebook entries for the April 1882 visit to Vicksburg include no jotted memo or prototype for this incantatory, mesmerizing Mississippi River of a pseudosentence, sinuously winding, eddying, churning, and changing. Using whatever materials he had assembled before him, he cut the channel for this verbal stream later at a desk. He reproduced conditions in Vicksburg during the siege in retrospect by means of his imagination.[9]

"Those are the materials furnished by history," Twain resumed after two shorter paragraphs about Vicksburg cave dwellers. Presumably he meant, at least in part, factual materials in the form of statistics about population or the cost of various goods in the city during the siege. Those statistics he could not or did not invent. They are the kinds of things one would have to look up, unless one carried them around from wartime Vicksburg, or from contemporary reports of it, twenty years later in an excellent memory. Twain did not let the matter go at that, however; he took the opportunity to enlarge on his own treatment of materials history furnished. "From them might not almost anybody reproduce for himself the life of that time in Vicksburg?" The phrase "reproduce for himself" points to the act of converting, by means of the imagination, traces of the past into signifiers of events and conditions that can be reconstituted into a present mental version; reproducing for oneself is another version of reconstruction. The traces-turned-signifiers may be nonverbal ones, such as landscapes or photographs or artifacts or scars remaining in Vicksburg in April 1882; they may be verbal ones, such as those in newspapers, official reports, memoranda, speeches, addresses, letters, diaries, essays, or books. Whatever their type, whatever their provenance, the imaginative reproduction of the past by means of these materials is the basic activity of any student of history, whether amateur or professional. Some may say, Of course; such a statement is obvious and trivial. Others may say, Absolutely not; my historical studies have nothing to do with my imagination because my studies are detached, disinterested, and empirical.

Either way, the statement was true in 1882–83 for Mark Twain, writer of fiction and nonfiction. Either way, it tells us how he read the writings of generals he published, Ulysses S. Grant, George B. McClellan, Philip H. Sheridan, and, eventually, William T. Sherman among them, or how he would have read Joseph E. Johnston or Richard Taylor, if he ever did. Either way, it calls into question Thomas Jefferson's neat distinction—first appearing one hundred years earlier in the 1783 catalog of his second library after fire destroyed the first—between Memory and Imagination or between their respective applications to History books and Fine Arts books. It certainly calls into question what Jefferson meant by his phrase "the faculties of mind employed on them," referring to his classes of books, as Twain's next sentence confirms. "Could you, who did not experience it, come nearer to reproducing it to the imagination of another non-participant than could a Vicksburger who *did* experience it?"

In defending his suggestion that a nonparticipant might come nearer to reproducing events in Vicksburg through imagination than would a wartime citizen, Mark Twain used an image familiar to him, that of someone making a voyage. "When one makes his first voyage in a ship, it is an experience which multitudinously bristles with striking novelties; novelties which are in such sharp contrast with all this person's former experiences that they take a seemingly deathless grip upon his imagination and memory." For the man who had sailed to and from the Sandwich Islands seventeen years earlier, it felt inevitable that such a first-time voyager by "tongue or pen" could "make a landsman live that strange and stirring voyage over with him; make him see it all and feel it all." For Twain, though, the immediate problem was that the voyager might wait too long to tell the story, so vividness would dim, or go on too many subsequent voyages, so novelty would wear off. To clinch this point, he described a Vicksburger, perhaps real, perhaps invented, who started keeping a diary during the siege but gave it up after only six days, "life in terrific Vicksburg having now become commonplace and a matter of course." The many Civil War diaries left by combatants and noncombatants alike show that people did not necessarily abandon them simply because war became familiar. Nevertheless, Twain raised an issue at Vicksburg he would return to, from a different perspective, in New Orleans.

Life on the Mississippi gives New Orleans ten chapters. By the time it leaves that city for St. Louis, with its author aboard the *City of Baton Rouge*, piloted by his former instructor and Civil War naval veteran Horace Bixby, the book has used the city to blend observations, anecdotes, and digressive stories within stories. Not all of these involve the Civil War. But in the chapter titled "Southern Sports," Mark Twain returned to Civil War memory, this time focusing on the conversation of participants who lived through the war and in their talk appear to be reproducing events and conditions directly from memory, without the enhancements of imagination. "In the North one hears the war mentioned, in social conversation, once a month; sometimes as often as once a week; but as a distinct subject for talk, it has long ago been relieved of duty," the chapter opens. A new resident of Buffalo in 1870, and then of Hartford in 1871, Samuel Clemens had spent more than a decade among northeasterners by the time he returned to the Mississippi River, and he could base this sentence on conversations with them.

With the return to New Orleans in the spring of 1882, he realized, however, "The case is very different in the South. There, every man you meet was in the war; and every lady you meet saw the war." Seasoned with a dash of exaggeration—except for two weeks with the Marion Rangers, Samuel Clemens was one southern man who was not in the war—this statement appears to explain why "the war is the great chief topic of conversation," the "interest in it . . . vivid and constant," while "the interest in other topics is fleeting." For people of the South, at least as Twain represented the ones he met in New Orleans, "the war is what A. D. is elsewhere: they date from it." What *Life on the Mississippi* called southern "waw talk" inevitably "shows how intimately every individual was visited, in his own person, by that tremendous episode."

Ten chapters earlier Twain had used the adjective "tremendous," from Latin for "tremble," to describe the war experiences of Vicksburg as well. But the similarity between the Vicksburg and New Orleans episodes ends there. When it comes to the memories of firsthand participants, the New Orleans chapters appear to reach a conclusion altogether different from the Vicksburg one. According to Twain in New Orleans, war talk "gives the inexperienced stranger a better idea of what a vast and comprehensive calamity invasion is than he can ever get by reading books at the fireside." Wait a minute. Even books written by people whose imaginations and verbal skills enable them to reproduce wartime events and conditions in the imaginations of others? After Vicksburg he suggested, by means of a rhetorical question, the exact opposite. "Could you, who did not experience it, come nearer to reproducing it to the imagination of another non-participant than could a Vicksburger who *did* experience it?" What is going on here? Did Twain simply forget that he had made a contradictory statement elsewhere? Did he simply not care, hoping his readers would overlook the inconsistency?

Inconsistency thickens with immediate transition to a comic scene set in a New Orleans gentlemen's club. As Twain stages it, a companion has explained to him that southerners talk so much about the war not because they have nothing else to talk about but because in "the war, each of us, in his own person, seems to have sampled all the different varieties of human experience; as a consequence, you can't mention an outside matter of any sort but it will certainly remind some listener of something that happened during the war,—and out he comes with it." The companion then directs Twain's attention to a nearby poet talking about the moon and predicts that though "the moon is far enough from the seat of war . . . it will suggest something to somebody about the war," and "in ten minutes . . . the moon as a topic will be shelved." The prediction proves true. The poet shares his "impression that down here, toward the equator, the moonlight" is "much stronger and brighter than up North." Interruption and dispute follow, until someone remembers that "when Farragut advanced upon Port Hudson on a dark night," he had the decks of his ships painted white to give his own men "dim but valuable light," at which point in the discussion "the war got the floor again—the ten minutes not quite up yet."

Ever the master of disingenuous feigning, Twain concluded the scene by claiming, "I was not sorry, for war talk by men who have been in a war is always interesting; whereas moon talk by a poet who has not been in the moon is likely to be dull." Omit the clause following the semicolon, and the statement appears to confirm the unchallenged assumption of many: "war talk by men who have been in a war is always interesting." Retain the clause following the semicolon, and the whole thing collapses into farce. Or perhaps it does not collapse completely. Instead, the second part, about a poet who has not been to the moon, gives a wink to qualify the first. War talk by men and women who have been through war cannot always be interesting. If it could, then Mark Twain himself could not have valued *Personal Memoirs of Ulysses S. Grant* so much more than he did *McClellan's Own Story*. Even though he published both books, Twain considered Grant's a literary masterpiece while he thought McClellan's deepened and justified the "obloquy" upon his name. Such a dramatic distinction does not sound like that of someone who really believed that war talk by people who have been in a war is always interesting. It cannot be that memory of war, or intimate visitation by it in one's "own person"—Twain used this phrase twice in two pages—is itself sufficient to make war talk interesting or capable of reproducing the war in other people's imaginations.

Mark Twain's changeableness about the relative value of memory and imagination recalls his image of the Mississippi River's changeable freaks. It may be too much to claim that he deliberately changed his mind on the subject, between arrival in Vicksburg and departure from New Orleans, in order to imitate the capricious river. More likely, he partly believed what he affirmed after Vicksburg, as he partly believed what he affirmed after New Orleans. To say so is not to evade his inconsistency but rather to recognize that it points to the overlapping of memory and imagination, an overlapping Mark Twain acknowledged, even celebrated.

"ALL MODERN AMERICAN literature comes from one book by Mark Twain called *Huckleberry Finn.*" A hyperbolic stretcher of the kind Twain himself savored, this reductive pronouncement appears in the opening chapter of Ernest Hemingway's *Green Hills of Africa* (1935). "All American writing comes from that. There was nothing before. There has been nothing as good since."

Hemingway's exaggerated claims, which contain several parts tongue-in-cheek posturing on the part of his game-hunting speaker, are too outlandish to require refutation. They were not true in 1935, and they are no truer now. But they can serve a useful purpose by reminding us that all American writing comes from other writing and that in the history of Civil War writing Mark Twain stands for a moment when multiple factors converged to produce writing that still matters today, both for itself and for what else has come from it.

Divisive and destructive as it was, and on many fronts still is, the Civil War meant advancement in several areas. It advanced the standing of many African Americans. It advanced the standing of many women. It advanced medical knowledge. It advanced the reach and capacity of the telegraph and the railroads. It advanced newspaper reporting and photography. And it advanced American writing. It did not advance American writing simply by giving it new subject matter or new attitudes toward that subject matter, though it did that, too. The Civil War advanced American writing by connecting disruptive public events to personal narratives taking the form of first-person memoirs on a scale never before seen. In so doing, it demonstrated something about the way American public memory began to work in combination with personal imagination, as well as something about how Americans began to associate their absorption of public events, especially disruptive ones, with first-person memoirs circulated widely by publication markets. Arguing that all modern American literature comes from *Huckleberry Finn* cannot work, but arguing for the link between Civil War memoirs published in the late nineteenth century, among them those written by generals, and first-person memoirs published now, on topics having nothing to do with the Civil War, can.

That link matters because first-person memoirs published in the present follow the twentieth-century rise of psychotherapeutic talk therapy and the twenty-first-century rise of technologies designed to exhibit and disseminate the words and images of individual citizens. One does not have to be a leading actor in public events to command a readership or an audience of hundreds, thousands, even millions. At the same time it has become increasingly commonplace for leading actors in public events to proceed directly from public events or public office or public service to lucrative contracts for first-person memoirs. This path, now so well worn that it suggests an inevitable movement from public event to public memory of the event shaped by the memoirs of leading actors, has not always existed. It began with the Civil War memory market.

In that market the first-person memoirs of leading actors advanced the progress of memoir writing begun in 1861 by giving first-person storytelling more space to develop and more scope to explore—many generals' memoirs took Civil War remembering to Dickensian lengths—and it continues to advance the effort of anyone, historian or novelist, who sets out to reproduce the past in contemporary imaginations by telling personal stories from that past, especially first-person ones. But there is more at stake than how to write histories and novels. The ascendancy and dominance of first-person stories about the past have had the collateral effects of enshrining and sanctifying first-person points of view about the present.

Of course we enshrine first-person points of view; this is a democracy; the rights and liberties of individual citizens are sacred, among them the rights of individual citizens to broadcast first-person points of view, including first-person points of view about Civil War memory, which continues to change, like the course of the Mississippi. If my first-person point of view about Civil War memory, about relations between races or relations between the federal government and the states, leads me and people like me to speak and behave in certain ways, what of it? This is a free country.

Among the serious flaws in this reasoning, one has gone largely unremarked in public debate. The founding document celebrated in the United States every Fourth of July has nowhere in it the word "individual" or "individualism."

Nor does it have anywhere in it the first-person singular pronoun "I." Each of its eleven first-person pronouns is a plural "we." As the final sentence makes clear, this was both a declaration of independence from Great Britain and a declaration of interdependence for the sake of securing and maintaining that independence. Invoking the Declaration of Independence to maintain the supremacy of individual autonomy is a distortion and a costly misreading. It is also a distortion with a history, and that history runs though the Civil War memory market, with the sudden popularity of personal stories about public crisis, then through the skyrocketing use of the word "narcissism," launched in published writing after World War I, to our own day.[10]

Why do the memoirs of generals still matter to the history of personal points of view? In part because the generals were generalists. They saw many parts of the whole, and they saw them broadly; yet they also saw "war from the inside," in the words of Frederick L. Hitchcock's 1904 title, as vividly as any private soldier. The inside of a general's war involved not just the same rain and mud and stench and fear and fatigue and boredom and dysentery and threat of capture or wounding or death the private soldier faced; the rank of a general officer in the Civil War did not buffer him from all these. The evidence shows that Civil War generals died violently at a greater rate than common soldiers. The inside of a general's war, the inside his memoirs reveal, included many of the private soldier's specifics at the same time that it included maps and reports and logistics and politics and occupied cities to be governed and newspaper reporters to be handled and campaigns to be *strategized*, which comes from the Greek word for general. If a general's book appears to be thinner on specific nitty-gritty details of wartime service than a private's, it is because a general's book has a greater range of personal experience wedged between two covers.[11]

The word "general" is not always a bad one in English. We have general admission, general assemblies, general delivery, general elections, general practitioners, general readers, and, though not much anymore, general stores. But there is also an implicit bias against the general, especially where notions of democracy combine and clash with notions of individuality. Where value attaches to individualism, however imagined, distinction often appears to reside in being or feeling special or free from the generalizing effacement of the average, the normative, the dominant. Maya Lin's Vietnam Veterans Memorial (1982) is effective because it specifies and individuates by name 58,318 soldiers, introducing a technique Lin later used in her Civil Rights Memorial (1989) in Montgomery, Alabama, one widely imitated by many other monuments, such as the African American Civil War Memorial (1997) in Washington, D.C., and the National September 11 Memorial (2011) in New York. In classroom discussion at the University of Virginia during the fall of 2018, a student from Hanoi, whose grandfathers and great-uncles died in the American war, tried to explain to her U.S. classmates that a soldiers' memorial modeled on Lin's would be unthinkable in the former North Vietnam, and not because it would have to list more than a million names. We value the family, she said; the individual is nothing apart from the family. Since this discussion took place, the technological tailoring of news to suit polarized political views has further unraveled connections between independence and interdependence in the United States. That unraveling, often linked publicly to Civil War images, has life-and-death consequences, and not only during public health emergencies.

Juicy details, fine points, brass tacks, spell it out: American clichés reveal the hold individuation and specificity have on us. Specificity has few negative connotations; generalizing has many. Too much specificity? We miss the forest for the trees, but that is not such a crime. At least we see the trunks, the branches, the leaves. Too much generalization? Differences get ignored, distinctions get flattened, people get left out and suffer for it. Be more specific, we often say; be more general, rarely, if ever.

Something important happens, however, when the generalizations of generals meet the specificities of first-person narratives. With that combination, new possibilities emerge, along with new powers, which neither a third-person historical overview by a detached observer nor a first-person account by someone otherwise unknown can match by itself. In a general's book specificity is enlarged. Why care about the observations of the high-ranking Civil War officers who were generalists? The value of their writings cannot depend solely on their truth value. Their value also depends on their relation to many other general statements, past, passing, and to come.[12]

"The cause of the great War of the Rebellion against the United States will have to be attributed to slavery." This general statement, which opens the chapter that closes Grant's memoirs, strengthens and deepens as we place it beside his statements of twenty-four years earlier or beside statements from Lost Cause apologists writing when he did or beside statements circulated by a southern nationalist organization today or beside statements by a twenty-first-century writer asking why so few Black Americans study the Civil War. All general statements about the Civil War contribute to the general volatility against which many people have understood and continue to understand specific details of their specific lives. Part of living with the general volatility, which we have always with us, is living with at least one intractable fact:

during the second half of the nineteenth century, among men in the United States who were not primarily interested in advancing social changes lumped under the shorthand heading "emancipation" or "civil rights" or "racial equality," there were several who played prominent parts at critical moments in advancing those social changes. Whether we label them history or literature or creative nonfiction—or something else altogether—the collected stories of those changes cannot approach anything like completeness by leaving some of the stories out. Whatever the degree of general volatility around us, we cannot advance our knowledge of the past, or our debates about it, by substituting, even with the best of intentions, new omissions for old ones.[13]

ACKNOWLEDGMENTS

To come into the world sound, a book needs friends and encouragers, along with critics, compassionate but firm. This one has been fortunate in having several of each, for whom a brief expression of gratitude must serve as inadequate compensation, among them Stephen Arata, Christopher Clark, Elizabeth Maddock Dillon, Gary W. Gallagher, William I. Hitchcock, Caroline E. Janney, Ann B. Miller, Aaron Sheehan-Dean, Mark Simpson-Vos, Andrew M. Stauffer, Elizabeth R. Varon, Frank S. Walker, Joan Waugh, Cecily N. Zander, and anonymous readers for University of North Carolina Press. Deserving particular mention for archival help and expertise are Michelle Krowl, Civil War and Reconstruction Specialist, Manuscript Division, Library of Congress, and both Robert H. Hirst and Melissa Martin of the Mark Twain Papers and Project, Bancroft Library, University of California, Berkeley. For other kinds of encouragement Sandra Bain Cushman belongs in a category of her own.

Most of the chapters in this book began as lectures delivered over several years to loyal Civil War conference-goers at the Huntington Library, San Marino, California, or they took shape in an east-facing office there, thanks to Steve Hindle, Director of Research, and Stephen Rogers, generous donor of fellowship support. Debts at the Huntington are a pleasure to recognize with names known to many who have worked at the library: Juan Gomez, Natalie Serrano, and Catherine Wehrey-Miller of the Research Division; Dan Lewis, Karla Nielsen, Krystle Satrum, Clay Stalls, Stephen Tabor, and Jenny Watts, curators of library collections; and, for help with digital materials, Dana Barsuhn and Mario Einaudi.

Annual conferences at the John L. Nau III Center for Civil War History, University of Virginia, have tested claims and arguments. Since its inception the center has provided support and gratitude, which are much appreciated, as are the efforts of managing director William B. Kurtz.

Finally, some chapters or parts of chapters have appeared elsewhere in earlier versions as "Sheridan's *Personal Memoirs* and the Appomattox Campaign," in *The Appomattox Campaign*, edited by Caroline E. Janney (Chapel Hill: University of North Carolina Press, 2018); "Surrender according to Johnston and Sherman," in *Civil War Writing: New Perspectives on Iconic Texts*, edited by Gary W. Gallagher and Stephen Cushman (Baton Rouge: Louisiana State University Press, 2019); "Lincoln Teaches Grant to Write," in *Critical Insights: Abraham Lincoln* (Amenia, N.Y.: Salem Press, 2020); and "George McClellan's Many Turnings," in *Civil War Witnesses and Their Books: New Perspectives on Iconic Works*, edited by Gary W. Gallagher and Stephen Cushman (Baton Rouge: Louisiana State University Press, 2021).

NOTES

Chapter 1

1. For a graph showing the increase in appearances of the phrase "Civil War memory" in English-language books, consult the Google Books Ngram Viewer at https://books.google.com/ngrams (accessed January 29, 2020). For an example of "another Civil War," see "How to Stop a Civil War," *Atlantic*, special issue, December 2019.

2. For background on Alfred E. Mathews, see Mary Sayre Haverstock, Jeanette Mahoney Vance, Brian L. Meggitt, and Jeffrey Weidman, *Artists in Ohio, 1787–1900: A Biographical Dictionary* (Kent, Ohio: Kent State University Press, 2000), 581. See also the Alfred Edward Mathews Papers (WH1679), Western History and Genealogy Department, Denver Public Library, https://history.denverlibrary.org/news/e-mathews-papers.

3. For useful background, see Ann Fabian, *The Unvarnished Truth: Personal Narratives in Nineteenth-Century America* (Berkeley: University of California Press, 2000), esp. chap. 4, "Prisoners of War"; and, though brief, Sarah E. Gardner, "Civil War Memoir," in *A History of American Civil War Literature*, ed. Coleman Hutchison (New York: Cambridge University Press, 2016), 151–64.

4. For Stephen Crane's complaint, see Corwin K. Linson, *My Stephen Crane* (Syracuse, N.Y.: Syracuse University Press, 1958), 37.

5. Elizabeth Keckley, *Behind the Scenes: Or, Thirty Years a Slave, and Four Years in the White House* (New York: G. W. Carleton, 1868), 133–34. For a chronological list of North American slave narratives, see *Documenting the American South*, University Library, University of North Carolina at Chapel Hill, https://docsouth.unc.edu/neh/chronautobio.html#1860 (accessed November 15, 2019).

6. The bibliography for the history of American book publishing is vast. A partial list of useful studies in the present context includes Helmut Lehmann-Haupt, *The Book in America: A History of the Making, the Selling, and the Collecting of Books in the United States* (New York: Bowker, 1939); Donald H. Sheehan, *This Was Publishing: A Chronicle of the Book Trade in the Gilded Age* (Bloomington: Indiana University Press, 1952); Charles Madison Allen, *Book Publishing in America* (New York: McGraw-Hill, 1966); John William Tebbel, *A History of Book Publishing in the United States*, 4 vols. (New York: Bowker, 1972–81); Madeleine B. Stern, *Books and Book People in Nineteenth-Century America* (New York: Bowker, 1978); Madeleine B. Stern, ed., *Publishers for Mass Entertainment in Nineteenth-Century America* (Boston: G. K. Hall, 1980); Scott Casper, Joanne D. Chaisson, and Jeffrey D. Groves, *Perspectives on*

American Book History: Artifacts and Commentary (Amherst: University of Massachusetts Press, 2002); Trish Loughran, *The Republic in Print: Print Culture in the Age of U.S. Nation Building, 1770–1870* (New York: Columbia University Press, 2007); Scott E. Casper et al., eds., *The Industrial Book, 1840–1880,* vol. 3 of *The History of the Book in America*, ed. David D. Hall, 5 vols. (Chapel Hill: University of North Carolina Press, 2007–10); John Hruschka, *How Books Came to America: The Rise of the American Book Trade* (University Park: Pennsylvania State University Press, 2012); and Michael Winship, "The American Book Trade and the Civil War," in Hutchison, *History of American Civil War Literature*, 17–32.

7. For recent work on memoirs by Jubal A. Early, John B. Gordon, and Edward P. Alexander, see essays respectively by Kathryn Shively, Keith S. Bohannon, and Gary W. Gallagher in Gary W. Gallagher and Stephen Cushman, eds., *Civil War Writing: New Perspectives on Iconic Texts* (Baton Rouge: Louisiana State University Press, 2019). See also Elizabeth R. Varon, "*From Manassas to Appomattox*: James Longstreet's Memoir and the Limits of Confederate Reconciliation," and Gary W. Gallagher, "Proximity and Numbers: Walter H. Taylor Shapes Confederate History and Memory," both in *Civil War Witnesses and Their Books: New Perspectives on Iconic Works*, ed. Gary W. Gallagher and Stephen Cushman (Baton Rouge: Louisiana State University Press, 2021).

8. For statistics on best sellers, see Frank Luther Mott, *Golden Multitudes: The Story of Best Sellers in the United States* (New York: Macmillan, 1947), app. A, 303–15. In compiling his statistics, Mott considered a best seller any book "believed to have had a total sale equal to one percent of the population of the continental United States . . . for the decade in which it was published." To make the list a book published in the 1860s, for example, needed a sale of 300,000 copies; in the 1880s, 500,000; and in the 1890s, 625,000. These figures make clear one reason for the growth in the book-publishing industry. For Mark Twain's bragging about the success of Grant's book, see Samuel Clemens to William Smith, February 3–4, 1887, Union Catalog of Clemens Letters 03522, Mark Twain Papers and Project, Bancroft Library, University of California. I am grateful to Robert Hirst and Melissa Martin for a transcript of this letter.

9. John Keegan, *The Mask of Command* (New York: Viking, 1987), 202.

10. *Mark Twain Speaking*, ed. Paul Fatout (Iowa City: University of Iowa Press, 1976), 226; Library of America, https://www.loa.org/about (accessed November 26, 2019).

11. James Gilreath and Douglas L. Wilson, eds., *Thomas Jefferson's Library: A Catalog with the Entries in His Own Order* (Washington, D.C.: Library of Congress, 1989), ix, 33, 113–14, 125, 132–33. For a digitized copy of Thomas Jefferson's 1783 manuscript catalog of the 2,640 books he owned as of March 1783, see this site maintained by the Massachusetts Historical Society: http://www.masshist.org/thomasjefferson papers/catalog1783/ (accessed January 14, 2020). For the chronology and description

of all Jefferson's book lists, see this site maintained by Monticello: http://tjlibraries.monticello.org/about/lists.html (accessed January 14, 2020). On the table of contents page in the 1783 catalog, Jefferson wrote, "Books may be classed from the Faculties of the mind, which being / I. Memory II. Reason III. Imagination / are applied respectively to / I. History II. Philosophy III. Fine Arts." The formulation "Books may be classed according to the faculties of the mind employed on them" introduced the catalog printed in 1815 and reprinted in Gilreath and Wilson, *Thomas Jefferson's Library*, ix.

12. Francis L. Miksa, *The Development of Classification at the Library of Congress*, Graduate School of Library and Information Science Occasional Papers, no. 164 (Champaign: University of Illinois Press, 1984), esp. 45; available at https://www.ideals.illinois.edu/bitstream/handle/2142/3957/gslisoccasionalpv00000i00164.pdf (accessed November 26, 2019).

13. Winfield Scott, *Memoirs of Lieut.-General Scott, LL.D.* (New York: Sheldon, 1864), xix.

14. Noah Webster, *An American Dictionary of the English Language*, 2 vols. (New York: S. Converse, 1828), 1:105. The definition of "imagination" remained the same in the revised 1841 edition, published in New York by White and Sheffield.

15. Henry David Thoreau, *Walden*, ed. Jeffrey S. Cramer (New Haven, Conn.: Yale University Press, 2004), 1.

16. George S. Patton Jr., preface to "War as I Knew It in Eight Chapters," George S. Patton Collection, Huntington Library, San Marino, Calif., call number mssPatton-collection, box labeled HM 63825-63841, 1942–1945. I am grateful to Christopher Clark for bringing this manuscript to my attention. In its published form, edited by Patton's wife, Beatrice Ayer Patton, *War as I Knew It* (Boston: Houghton Mifflin, 1947) omitted the general's opening apology for the frequent appearance of the first-person pronoun. In the acknowledgments it did include Beatrice Patton's expression of indebtedness to Douglas Southall Freeman, "whom my husband held in honor as the greatest military biographer of our time." Freeman's brief introduction to the volume is particularly suggestive in the context of the present discussion. According to Freeman, Patton's book corresponds "to the memoirs that Jubal A. Early, John B. Ho[o]d, Richard Taylor, and Joseph E. Johnston issued a few years after the collapse of the Southern Confederacy, with the happy difference that Patton had no defeat to excuse, no grievance to vent." Looking ahead prophetically to "about 1960," Freeman continued, "Americans may expect more deliberate works of a character similar to the memoirs of Grant, of Sherman, and of Sheridan" (xvii–xviii).

17. Translation of Rousseau's French by Christopher Kelly in Jean-Jacques Rousseau, *The Confessions and Correspondence, Including the Letters to Malesherbes*, ed. Christopher Kelly, Roger D. Masters, and Peter G. Stillman, vol. 5 of *The Collected Writings of Rousseau*, 14 vols. (Hanover, N.H.: University Press of New England, 1990–2010), 5. The textual history of Rousseau's *Confessions* is too complicated to treat

here. Those interested in the different manuscripts and editions of this work should see "Note on the Text" in this edition (xxxv–xxxvi). The date 1782 is that of first publication of an abridged version of part 1.

18. A manuscript version of the paragraph beginning, "At the time I was so relieved," in *Memoirs of William T. Sherman*, 2 vols. (New York: Appleton, 1875), 1:214, contains the following, inserted between the first and second sentences of the 1875 published version: "And the matter was to my family the more painful by reason of the fact that my mother's brother Charles Hoyt was then insane and that insanity was inherent in that Branch of the family was in an Insane Asylum." Sherman drew a line through everything from "Charles Hoyt" through "that Branch of the family." The phrase "was in an Insane Asylum" was added between the canceled lines. William T. Sherman, Memoirs: manuscript, 4 vols., HM 822, Huntington Library, San Marino, Calif., 1:67. I am grateful to Jenny Watts, Curator of Photography and Visual Culture, Huntington Library, for bringing this manuscript, formerly uncataloged, to light.

19. Abraham Lincoln, *The Collected Works of Abraham Lincoln*, ed. Roy P. Basler, 8 vols. with index and suppl. (New Brunswick, N.J.: Rutgers University Press, 1953–55), 7: 282; Thomas Carlyle, *On Heroes, Hero-Worship, and the Heroic in History*, ed. Michael K. Goldberg, Joel J. Brattin, and Mark Engel (Berkeley: University of California Press, 1993), 3. Carlyle's fifth lecture, "The Hero as Man of Letters," delivered Tuesday, May 19, 1840, discussed Samuel Johnson, Jean-Jacques Rousseau, and Robert Burns. Of Rousseau, Carlyle wrote, "He is not what I would call a strong man." He continued in this vein, "The fault and misery of Rousseau was what we easily name by a single word, *Egoism*" (158–59).

20. Henry James referred to "the romantic privilege of the 'first person'" in his preface to *The Ambassadors* (1903).

Chapter 2

1. See *The War of the Rebellion: A Compilation of the Official Records of the Union and Confederate Armies*, 128 vols. (Washington, D.C.: Government Printing Office, 1880–1901) (hereafter cited as *OR*), ser. 1, vol. 46, pt. 1, 1277–79, for "Tabular statement of officers and men of the Confederate Army paroled at Appomattox Court-House" (28,231 total), and series 1, vol. 47, pt. 1, 1066, for "Tabular statement of officers and men of the Confederate Army paroled at Greensborough, N.C., and other points, in accordance with the military convention of April 26, 1865" (39,012 total). For totals reported by Schofield and Wilson, see William T. Sherman, *Memoirs of General William T. Sherman*, 2 vols. (New York: D. Appleton, 1875), 2:370. Johnston's General Orders No. 22, his farewell address to the Army of Tennessee, May 2, 1865, appear on a short obelisk erected in May 1985 near the location of the wartime rail depot in Greensboro. See *OR*, ser. 1, vol. 47, pt. 1, 1061; for paroles of Johnston and his staff, see *OR*, ser. 1, vol. 47, pt. 3, 379–80. A manuscript duplicate of the parole for Johnston

and his staff is in the Joseph E. Johnston Papers, Huntington Library, San Marino, Calif., mssJO 1–525, box 7, folder 449. It consists of a single sheet, with the names of Johnston and his staff on the recto and the parole language, signed by Schofield and Johnston, on the verso.

2. William T. Sherman to John M. Schofield, May 5, 1865, in *Sherman's Civil War: Selected Correspondence of William T. Sherman, 1861–1865*, ed. Brooks D. Simpson and Jean V. Berlin (Chapel Hill: University of North Carolina Press, 1999), 887.

3. Sherman to Schofield, May 5, 1865. For Johnston's remarks about desertions from his army, see Joseph E. Johnston, *Narrative of Military Operations, Directed, during the Late War between the States, by Joseph E. Johnston, General C.S.A.* (New York: D. Appleton, 1874), 410: "It was very commonly believed among the soldiers that there was to be a surrender, by which they would be prisoners of war, to which they were very averse. This apprehension caused a great number of desertions between the 19th and 24th of April—not less than four thousand in the infantry and artillery, and almost as many from the cavalry; many of them rode off artillery horses, and mules belonging to the baggage-trains."

4. Landmark books in popular Civil War memory contain little about Johnston's surrender to Sherman. In *Battle Cry of Freedom* (New York: Oxford University Press, 1988), James McPherson included nothing about either the negotiations between Johnston and Sherman, eventually concluded on April 26, or the surrender of Confederate arms in Greensboro during the first days of May. In the third volume of his massive trilogy *The Civil War* (New York: Random House, 1958–74), Shelby Foote narrated the April negotiations between the two generals in the Bennett farmhouse, but as soon as he concluded them, he turned to the capture and death of Booth and never returned to the surrender at Greensboro. In *Joseph E. Johnston: A Civil War Biography* (New York: W. W. Norton, 1992), Craig L. Symonds moved in nine lines from the conclusive meeting between the generals on April 26 to Johnston's farewell to his army six days later, giving no details of the surrender proceedings in Greensboro. Those who want further details of the proceedings must turn to more specialized books of the past twenty years, such as Mark L. Bradley's *This Astounding Close: The Road to Bennett Place* (Chapel Hill: University of North Carolina Press, 2000); Robert M. Dunkerly's *Confederate Surrender at Greensboro: The Final Days of the Army of Tennessee, April 1865* (Jefferson, N.C.: McFarland, 2013) and *To the Bitter End: Appomattox, Bennett Place, and the Surrenders of the Confederacy* (El Dorado Hills, Calif.: Savas Beatie, 2015); Eric J. Wittenberg's *We Ride a Whirlwind: Sherman and Johnston at Bennett Place* (Burlington, N.C.: Fox Run, 2017); and David Silkenat's *Raising the White Flag: How Surrender Defined the American Civil War* (Chapel Hill: University of North Carolina Press, 2019). The three volumes of Rick Atkinson's trilogy are *An Army at Dawn: The War in North Africa, 1942–43* (New York: Henry Holt, 2002); *The Day of Battle: The War in Sicily and Italy, 1943–44* (New York: Henry Holt, 2007); and *The Guns at Last Light: The War in Europe, 1944–1945* (New York: Henry

Holt, 2013). On the nuances and complexities of Appomattox mythmaking, see, e.g., Elizabeth R. Varon, *Appomattox: Victory, Defeat, and Freedom at the End of the Civil War* (New York: Oxford University Press, 2013), esp. "Epilogue: The Apple Tree," 244–58. One could argue that the friendship between Ulysses S. Grant and James Longstreet, begun before the war and resumed after it, offered the public something comparable to the friendship between Johnston and Sherman. But although many admired Longstreet for putting aside wartime animosity in the name of forgiveness, many founders of Lost Cause orthodoxy reviled Longstreet for his readiness to reconcile with his former enemy, whereas almost no one reviled Johnston for his connection with Sherman.

5. *The American Heritage Dictionary of the English Language*, ed. William Morris (Boston: Houghton Mifflin, 1969), s.v. "surrender"; Ulysses S. Grant, *Personal Memoirs of Ulysses S. Grant*, 2 vols. (New York: Charles L. Webster, 1885–86), 2:489, or in the recent edition cited in subsequent notes, John F. Marszalek, David S. Nolen, and Louie P. Gallo, eds., *The Personal Memoirs of Ulysses S. Grant: The Complete Annotated Edition* (Cambridge, Mass.: Belknap Press of Harvard University Press, 2017), 721 (hereafter cited as *Personal Memoirs of U. S. Grant*). For the development of Joshua Lawrence Chamberlain's accounts of the surrender ceremony at Appomattox, see Stephen Cushman, *Belligerent Muse: Five Northern Writers and How They Shaped Our Understanding of the Civil War* (Chapel Hill: University of North Carolina Press, 2014), 147–63.

6. *Personal Memoirs of U. S. Grant*, 720. Thomas M. Cook, "The Rebellion: Views of General Robert E. Lee," *New York Herald*, April 29, 1865, 5. "Mr. Thomas M. Cook's Despatch" was dated April 24, 1865. This issue of the *New York Herald* should not be confused with that of the *New York Weekly Herald* published the same day, which contained extensive coverage of "Obsequies to Abraham Lincoln," including the funeral procession in New York, as well as coverage of Sherman's negotiations with Johnston in North Carolina and the rejection of their agreement by Andrew Johnson and his cabinet. For transcriptions of three postwar "conversations" with Lee, see Gary W. Gallagher, ed., *Lee: The Soldier* (Lincoln: University of Nebraska Press, 1996), 3–34.

7. For background on D. Appleton and Company, see Grant Overton, *Portrait of a Publisher and the First Hundred Years of the House of Appleton* (New York: D. Appleton, 1925); D. Appleton-Century Company, *The House of Appleton-Century* (New York: D. Appleton-Century, 1936); and Gerald R. Wolfe, *The House of Appleton: The History of a Publishing House and Its Relationship to the Cultural, Social, and Political Events That Helped Shape the Destiny of New York City* (Metuchen, N.J.: Scarecrow Press, 1981). See especially Wolfe's chapter "New Pastures and the Civil War Memoirs" (145–64).

8. See Symonds, *Joseph E. Johnston*, 364. Compare Douglas Southall Freeman's assessment in *The South to Posterity: An Introduction to the Writing of Confederate*

History (1939), intro. Gary W. Gallagher (Baton Rouge: Louisiana State University Press, 1998), 72: "[Joseph E. Johnston's] *Narrative of Military Operations*, published in 1874, was written vigorously and unsparingly and, of course, was read with high interest; but it cannot be said to have increased his reputation as a soldier. His grievance against President Davis, whom he accused of overslaughing him [passing him over], was too manifest for objective or even for effective presentation of his defence." No doubt many read Johnston with high interest, especially those who expected to find themselves in his narrative, but their interest did not translate into high sales. For sales of Sherman's book, see William Tecumseh Sherman, *Memoirs of General W. T. Sherman*, ed. Charles Royster (New York: Library of America, 1990), 1112. In *Portrait of a Publisher*, Overton called Sherman's book "an enormous success" and a "gigantic success" (20, 64). He did not mention Johnston's book at all.

9. Sherman, *Memoirs*, 2:47, 49.

10. *OR*, ser. 1, vol. 47, pt. 1, 32; see also Sherman, *Memoirs*, 2:348.

11. Sherman, *Memoirs*, 1:181, 328.

12. Sherman, 2:299.

13. For the conversations with Johnston and, subsequently, Hood, see Sherman, 2:39–41.

14. See Douglas Southall Freeman, *R. E. Lee: A Biography*, 4 vols. (New York: Charles Scribner's Sons, 1934–35), 4:520–21.

15. See Edward G. Longacre, *Worthy Opponents: William T. Sherman and Joseph E. Johnston: Antagonists in War—Friends in Peace* (Nashville, Tenn.: Rutledge Hill, 2006), 319–22.

16. Sherman, *Memoirs*, 2:151–52.

17. Johnston, *Narrative*, 317, 318, 329, 344, 358.

18. Johnston, 402–3.

19. Johnston, 403. For Sherman's official account of his dealings with Johnston, see his long report of May 9, 1865, which is vintage Sherman and a tour de force, including such memorable formulations as "To push an army whose commander had so frankly and honestly confessed his inability to cope with me were cowardly and unworthy the brave men I led"; "As for myself I know my motives, and challenge the instance during the past four years where an armed and defiant foe stood before me that I did not go in for a fight, and I would blush for shame if I had ever insulted or struck a fallen foe"; and "I have my opinions on the questions involved, and I will stand by the memorandum; but this forms no part of a military report." This last sentence provides a textbook example of the rhetoric of paralipsis, or making an assertion by announcing that one is withholding the assertion. Sherman's report is in *OR*, ser. 1, vol. 47, pt. 1, 32–35. One familiar way of explaining Sherman's overstepping of his military authority is to say that he was simply trying to do what he thought Lincoln wanted him to do after the final meeting of the two men on the *River Queen* at City Point, Virginia, on Monday and Tuesday, March 27 and 28, 1865. But Sherman's inclination to follow victory

with magnanimity and generosity outside his jurisdiction had already emerged in his treatment of the citizens of Jackson, Mississippi, after Johnston evacuated the city in July 1863. In the first of two letters he wrote to Grant from Jackson on July 21, 1863, he asked permission to "promise mayor and committee of citizens, say, 200 barrels of flour and 100 barrels of salt pork, if they will send for it to Big Black Bridge and give me pledges that it shall be devoted to pure charity?" In the second he sought authorization to establish trade with local civilians: "Would I be justified in making a distinct proposition to the people that if Johnston or President Davis will agree that no Confederate soldiers or guerrillas will operate west of Pearl River, we will establish at Big Black River railroad bridge a kind of trading depot, where the people of Mississippi may exchange their cotton, corn, and produce for provisions, clothing, and family supplies?" In the next paragraph, despite an initial disclaimer about his detachment from politics, Sherman went on to offer Grant his opinion on the larger strategy of reconstructing Mississippi: "I profess to know nothing of polities, but I think we have here an admirable wedge which may be encouraged without committing the President or War Department. If prominent men in Mississippi admit the fact of being subdued, it will have a powerful effect all over the South." Grant's reply, which does not appear in the *OR*, apparently checked his friend's eagerness and brought him back to his merely military authority. Sherman's next letter, written on July 22, 1863, acknowledged as much: "All right about trade. I will not promise or do anything except to relieve the immediate wants of suffering humanity." This correspondence shows that Sherman's conversations with Lincoln on the *River Queen*, or his understanding of them, merely confirmed tendencies he already exhibited. See *OR*, ser. 1, vol. 24, pt. 2, 530–31. A recent narrative of the surrender negotiations between Johnston and Sherman appears in James Lee McDonough's biography *William Tecumseh Sherman: In the Service of My Country: A Life* (New York: W. W. Norton, 2016), 625–36. McDonough's account of the surrender negotiations, while admirably readable, adds no new information, and it contains nothing about the Greensboro phase of the surrender, having left North Carolina with Sherman after the final meeting with Johnston. Subsequently, McDonough includes nothing about Johnston at Sherman's funeral. See also Robert L. O'Connell's *Fierce Patriot: The Tangled Lives of William Tecumseh Sherman* (New York: Random House, 2014), 181–83. In reconstructing the surrender negotiations, O'Connell adopts a vernacular mode to cast Sherman as the unwitting dupe of Johnston, "another cagey strategist" (181), and John Breckenridge, "the wily former U.S. vice president and currently Confederate secretary of war." Describing the first agreement between Sherman and Johnston as "a sweetheart of a deal" for people from the South, O'Connell offers this formulation: "Earlier, Sherman was described as tipsy on himself; this document reflects serious inebriation" (182). O'Connell does not mention the Greensboro phase of the surrender.

20. Sherman, *Memoirs*, 2:349; William T. Sherman Papers, Library of Congress, Washington, D.C., box 105 or reel 49. For further discussion of Sherman's description

of his first meeting with Johnston, see Cushman, *Belligerent Muse*, 105–6, 111. A second manuscript of Sherman's *Memoirs*, presumably later and the one he submitted to Appleton and Company, is in the Huntington Library. In that manuscript Sherman's insertion of "in large drops" has been adopted by the clerk who made the copy; William T. Sherman, Memoirs: manuscript, 4 vols., HM 822, Huntington Library, San Marino, Calif., 1:67. I am grateful to Jenny Watts, Curator of Photography and Visual Culture, Huntington Library, for bringing this manuscript, formerly uncataloged, to light.

21. Joseph E. Johnston, "My Negotiations with General Sherman," *North American Review*, August 1886, 189.

22. Quoted by Stanley P. Hirshson, *The White Tecumseh: A Biography of General William T. Sherman* (New York: John Wiley and Sons, 1997), 304–5.

23. *OR*, ser. 1, vol. 47, pt. 3, 257, 265, 286. Johnston and Sherman had exchanged letters not quite two years earlier, in July 1863 during the second campaign against Jackson, Mississippi. After complaints from Confederate major general John C. Breckenridge that the unburied bodies of U.S. soldiers in front of his position at Jackson were becoming "offensive" in the oppressive heat and causing sickness among his men, Johnston wrote Sherman to ask for a truce during which Confederate burial parties could do their work. Sherman thanked Johnston and granted the truce, albeit a brief one. The two short letters from Johnston and one from Sherman are respectful, but quite understandably they do not yet show the mutual admiration of the April 1865 correspondence. See *OR*, ser. 1, vol. 24, pt. 2, 538–39, and pt. 3, 1002–3.

24. *OR*, ser. 1, vol. 47, pt. 3, 266.

25. *OR*, ser. 1, vol. 47, pt. 3, 287, 293, 294, 320.

26. *OR*, ser. 1, vol. 47, pt. 3, 336–37.

27. "On the Way to His Rest: New-York's Sad Farewell to the Great Soldier," *New York Times*, February 20, 1891, 1.

28. Symonds, *Joseph E. Johnston*, 380; "Gen. Joe Johnston Dead: One of the Last of the Confederate Leaders," *New York Times*, March 22, 1891, 1; "Gen. Joseph E. Johnston Is Dead," *Chicago Sunday Tribune*, March 22, 1891, 2; "Gen. Jos. E. Johnston: Death of the Brave Old Leader of the Late Confederacy," *Washington Post*, March 22, 1891, 1; "Joseph E. Johnston: The Confederate General Who Became Sherman's Friend," *Los Angeles Times*, March 22, 1891, 1; "General Joseph E. Johnston," *Harper's Weekly*, April 4, 1891, 252.

29. Robert M. Hughes, *General Johnston* (New York: D. Appleton, 1893), 288; *American Heritage Dictionary*, s.v. "cold"; "Common Cold" in *The Merck Manual of Medical Information* (Whitehouse Station, N.J.: Merck Research Laboratories, 1997), 913; Symonds, *Joseph E. Johnston*, 380–81; Longacre, *Worthy Opponents*, 322. Symonds cites Gilbert E. Govan and James W. Livingood, *A Different Valor: The Story of General Joseph E. Johnston, C.S.A.* (Indianapolis, Ind.: Bobbs-Merrill, 1956), 397, and Longacre cites Symonds, among others.

30. Oliver Otis Howard, *Autobiography of Oliver Otis Howard*, 2 vols. (New York: Baker and Taylor, 1907), 2:553–54. In 1891 competing editions of *Memoirs of Gen. W. T. Sherman* appeared, a third edition from Appleton and Company, the original publisher, and a fourth edition from Mark Twain's Charles L. Webster and Company, which had published a third edition of its own in 1890. Both the competing editions contained appended accounts of Sherman's funeral. Willis Fletcher Johnson wrote the account for the Appleton edition, which announced on its title page that Fletcher's account was carefully reviewed by Major General O. O. Howard, U.S.A. The preface to the Webster and Co. fourth edition explained that Sherman's family compiled the added material, which was then reviewed by James G. Blaine, Benjamin Harrison's secretary of state at the time; Blaine added a personal tribute to Sherman to this edition as well. The story of Johnston refusing to put on his hat does not appear in the accounts of either edition.

31. Lloyd Lewis, *Sherman: Fighting Prophet* (1932; repr., New York: Harcourt, Brace, 1958), 669n, 652.

32. Howard, *Autobiography*, 2:473.

Chapter 3

1. Douglas Southall Freeman, *The South to Posterity: An Introduction to the Writing of Confederate History* (1939), intro. Gary W. Gallagher (Baton Rouge: Louisiana State University Press, 1998), 72–73, 84–87, 219–20.

2. Freeman, 86; Frederick Law Olmsted, *The Cotton Kingdom: A Traveller's Observations on Cotton and Slavery in the American Slave States; Based upon Three Former Volumes of Journeys and Investigations* (1861), ed. Arthur M. Schlesinger Sr. (New York: Modern Library, 1984), 248, 259.

3. Freeman, *South to Posterity*, xxxiii.

4. Richard Taylor, *Destruction and Reconstruction: Personal Experiences of the Late War* (New York: D. Appleton, 1879), 223–24. Because pagination is the same in the more readily available reprint, edited by T. Michael Parrish under a slightly altered title, subsequent references are to *Destruction and Reconstruction: Personal Experiences of the Civil War* (New York: Da Capo, 1995). Parrish's edition begins with an excellent introduction, but it contains no annotations, whereas Richard B. Harwell's differently paginated edition, which retains Taylor's original title (New York: Longmans, Green, 1955), includes useful endnotes about contemporary people and events. Harwell's notes do not attempt to tackle annotation of Taylor's frequent references to literature and military history. For the chronology of composition and publication of *Destruction and Reconstruction*, see the introductions by Harwell (xxx–xxxi) and Parrish (xv–xvi).

5. *Destruction and Reconstruction*, 39, 64, 72.

6. The best and most comprehensive biographical treatment of Richard Taylor is

T. Michael Parrish's *Richard Taylor: Soldier Prince of Dixie* (Chapel Hill: University of North Carolina Press, 1992). See chaps. 1–3 (5–123) for background summarized in this paragraph. An older, and much shorter, introduction to Taylor's life and career can be found in Charles L. Dufour's *Nine Men in Grey* (1963), intro. Gary W. Gallagher (Lincoln: University of Nebraska Press, 1993). Much of Dufour's narrative paraphrases *Destruction and Reconstruction*, but it includes references to and quotations from other useful documents as well.

7. *Destruction and Reconstruction*, 13.

8. *Destruction and Reconstruction*, 30.

9. Freeman, *South to Posterity*, 84–87.

10. Edmund Wilson, *Patriotic Gore: Studies in the Literature of the American Civil War* (1962; repr., New York: Oxford University Press, 1966), 299–307. Freeman did discuss Edward Porter Alexander's *Military Memoirs of a Confederate* (1907), commenting that Alexander was "restrained in his criticism," could have said much that he felt "improper to print," and "did not pretend to literary style" (*South to Posterity*, 177–78). But as Gary W. Gallagher has shown, *Military Memoirs of a Confederate* and *Fighting for the Confederacy* are very different books. See Gallagher's introduction to *Fighting for the Confederacy: The Personal Recollections of General Edward Porter Alexander* (Chapel Hill: University of North Carolina Press, 1989), esp. xx–xxiii. Freeman's nomination for writing by a Confederate general "second only to 'Dick' Taylor" was G. Moxley Sorrell's *Recollections of a Confederate Staff Officer* (1905). Freeman's endorsement of Sorrell's "easy style" suggests that he would also have endorsed Alexander's style in *Fighting for the Confederacy* as well (*South to Posterity*, 176–77).

11. *Destruction and Reconstruction*, 43.

12. *Destruction and Reconstruction*, 75; Douglas Southall Freeman, *Lee's Lieutenants: A Study in Command*, 3 vols. (New York: Charles Scribner's Sons, 1942–44), 3:819; quoted in Parrish, *Soldier Prince of Dixie*, 494. Freeman's narrative of the Valley Campaign appears in 1:362–469; James McPherson, *Battle Cry of Freedom: The Civil War Era* (New York: Oxford University Press, 1988), 454.

13. *Destruction and Reconstruction*, 43, 129, 135, 144, 146, 147.

14. *Destruction and Reconstruction*, 136–37.

15. *Destruction and Reconstruction*, 26, 41, 43, 44, 66, 71, 80.

16. Line 343, my translation. Many translations of this line render "*punctum*" literally as "point," but Horace was probably referring to the point made on a tablet in order to cast a vote for a particular candidate. See *Cassell's Latin Dictionary*, rev. D. P. Simpson (New York: Funk and Wagnalls, 1968), s.v. "pungo."

17. *Destruction and Reconstruction*, 15.

18. *Destruction and Reconstruction*, 41.

19. See Parrish, *Soldier Prince of Dixie*, 1–21.

20. *Destruction and Reconstruction*, 22, 25, 99, 232, 239, 240.

21. *Destruction and Reconstruction*, 193–95.

22. *Destruction and Reconstruction*, 265.

23. The casualty figure for the Valley Campaign is based on the total of Peter Cozzens's numbers for fighting at Kernstown, McDowell, Front Royal, Winchester, Harrisonburg, Cross Keys, and Port Republic, May 23–June 10, 1862. See Peter Cozzens, *Shenandoah, 1862: Stonewall Jackson's Valley Campaign* (Chapel Hill: University of North Carolina Press, 2008), 215, 273–74, 307, 377, 439, 477, 499. Because Richard Ewell's Second Division, which included Richard Taylor's Eighth Brigade, did not participate in the Battles of Kernstown and McDowell, the total casualty figure for fighting described in *Destruction and Reconstruction* would be closer to 6,200, although Taylor does refer to Kernstown and McDowell. For commentary on the Dark War focus in Civil War historiography, see Gary W. Gallagher, "The Dark Turn," *Civil War Times*, August 2016, 14, 16.

24. *Destruction and Reconstruction*, 73–74.

25. *Destruction and Reconstruction*, 58; Richard Taylor, "Stonewall Jackson and the Valley Campaign," *North American Review*, March–April 1878, 238–61. For the mistaken date of Port Republic and Jackson's "usual low voice," see Taylor, "Stonewall Jackson," 257.

26. *Destruction and Reconstruction*, 56.

27. *Destruction and Reconstruction*, 37. Because the manuscript of *Destruction and Reconstruction* has disappeared (see Parrish, *Soldier Prince of Dixie*, 492n), it is difficult to demonstrate conclusively that Taylor added to "Stonewall Jackson and the Valley Campaign" to produce "The Valley Campaign." Instead, he may have reinstated passages cut in order to fit the requirements of the *North American Review*. Even if this were the case, however, one can still make the kinds of comparisons between the two that are being made here, as these comparisons do not depend on the chronology of composition.

28. *Destruction and Reconstruction*, 44–46. For more on William T. Sherman's *Memoirs* and travel writing, see Stephen Cushman, *Belligerent Muse: Five Northern Writers and How They Shaped Our Understanding of the Civil War* (Chapel Hill: University of North Carolina Press, 2014), 83–98 passim.

29. See Christopher Hussey, *The Picturesque: Studies in a Point of View* (London: G. Putnam and Sons, 1927), 14. Discussion of the picturesque began in English with William Gilpin's *Observations on the river Wye, and several parts of South Wales, &c. Relative chiefly to picturesque beauty; made in the summer of the year 1770* (London: Printed for R. Blamire, sold by B. Law and R. Faulder, 1782). According to Hussey, Uvedale Price, in *An essay on the picturesque, as compared with the sublime and the beautiful; and on the use of studying pictures, for the purpose of improving real landscape* (London: Printed for J. Robson, 1794), added the picturesque as a third category to the sublime and the beautiful. The phrase "roughness and sudden variation joined to irregularity of form" is Hussey's approximation of Price's original wording, "I am therefore persuaded, that the two opposite qualities of roughness, and of sudden variation, joined

to that of irregularity, are the most efficient causes of the picturesque" (61). In a footnote to this sentence, Price explained, "I have followed Mr. Gilpin's example in using roughness as a general term." My text of Price is not the first edition but a slightly later one (London: Printed for J. Robson, 1796).

30. *Destruction and Reconstruction*, 62–63.

31. *Destruction and Reconstruction*, 46–47.

32. See Mark Grimsley, *The Hard Hand of War: Union Military Policy toward Southern Civilians, 1861–1865* (Cambridge: Cambridge University Press, 1995), 185–86. Grimsley does not discuss Richard Taylor, but he does point out Swinton's comparison of Sheridan's campaign in the Shenandoah Valley to the 1689 campaign against the Palatinate, citing William Swinton, *Campaigns of the Army of the Potomac*, reprint ed. (Secaucus, N.J.: Blue and Gray Press, 1988), 560. See also John Childs, *Armies and Warfare in Europe, 1648–1789* (New York: Holmes and Meier, 1982), 152, cited by Grimsley.

33. For background on devastation of the Palatinate, see John A. Lynn, *The Wars of Louis XIV, 1667–1714* (New York: Longman, 1999), 129–30, 193–99; and Childs, *Armies and Warfare in Europe*, 151–52. Like William Swinton, neither Lynn nor Childs mentions an apology by Louis XIV. The only remark that suggests any misgiving on the king's part appears in Lynn's narrative of the 1674 devastation by Turenne: "Louis worried that Turenne's actions would so infuriate German princes that new allies would join the emperor" (130).

34. *The War of the Rebellion: A Compilation of the Official Records of the Union and Confederate Armies*, 128 vols. (Washington, D.C.: Government Printing Office, 1880–1901) (hereafter cited as *OR*), ser. 1, vol. 43, pt. 1, 57–58. See also Philip H. Sheridan, *Personal Memoirs of P. H. Sheridan*, 2 vols. (New York: Charles L. Webster, 1888), 1:484–88. For more on Grant's instructions to Sheridan, see Mark E. Neely Jr., *The Civil War and the Limits of Destruction* (Cambridge, Mass.: Harvard University Press, 2007), 115–16, 135–39. Neely in turn builds on the work of William G. Thomas, "Nothing Ought to Astonish Us: Confederate Civilians in the 1864 Shenandoah Valley Campaign," in *The Shenandoah Valley Campaign of 1864*, ed. Gary W. Gallagher (Chapel Hill: University of North Carolina Press, 2006), 222–56.

35. Ulysses S. Grant to Philip H. Sheridan, August 26, 1864, *OR*, ser. 1, vol. 43, pt. 1, 917; Sheridan, *Personal Memoirs*, 1:486; Ulysses S. Grant to Henry Halleck, July 14, 1864, *OR*, ser. 1, vol. 40, pt. 3, 223; Philip H. Sheridan's report to Ulysses S. Grant, October 7, 1864, *OR*, ser. 1, vol. 43, pt. 1, 31; "Advanced Sheets of 'Reminiscences of Secession, War, and Reconstruction,' by Lieutenant-General Richard Taylor," *Southern Historical Society Papers* 5, no. 3 (March 1878): 136–40 (supposed quotation of Sheridan appears at 137).

36. For his assessment of Zachary Taylor as commander in Mexico, see Ulysses S. Grant, *Personal Memoirs of U. S. Grant*, 2 vols. (New York: Charles L. Webster, 1885–86), 1:138–39; or John F. Marszalek, David S. Nolen, and Louie P. Gallo, eds., *The*

Personal Memoirs of Ulysses S. Grant: The Complete Annotated Edition (Cambridge, Mass.: Belknap Press of Harvard University Press, 2017), 93–94. For Richard Taylor's account of Grant during their 1865 meetings in Washington, see *Destruction*, 242; and Parrish, *Soldier Prince of Dixie*, 452.

37. Grimsley, *Hard Hand of War*, 185–86. For Neely's corrective revision of the persistent myth that Sheridan burned the Shenandoah Valley, see *Limits of Destruction*, 109–30, esp. 109–11.

38. *Destruction and Reconstruction*, 13, 21.

39. *Destruction and Reconstruction*, 80.

40. *Destruction and Reconstruction*, 30, 79, 96.

41. Wilson, *Patriotic Gore*, 305.

42. Henry Wadsworth Longfellow, *The Divine Comedy of Dante Alighieri* (1867), 4 vols. (Boston: C. T. Brainard, 1909), 1:147–98. I am grateful to my colleague J. Daniel Kinney for suggesting this source. Richard Taylor also may have had in mind the transformation of Cadmus into a serpent in book 4 of Ovid's *Metaphorphoses*, to which Dante referred shortly after this passage (Longfellow, 1:149). It is less likely that Taylor knew of Zahhāk, the Serpent King of Iranian mythology, who in Ferdowsi's epic poem the Shāhnāma (ca. 1000 CE) had a snake growing out of each shoulder. There is also Typhon, of Greek mythology, who according to Hesiod had a hundred snake heads on his shoulders. But none of these images matches Taylor's invention exactly.

43. Charles Royster, *The Destructive War: William Tecumseh Sherman, Stonewall Jackson, and the Americans* (New York: Vintage Books, 1993), 41.

44. *Destruction and Reconstruction*, 252, 270.

45. *Destruction and Reconstruction*, 80, 81–82; Jubal Anderson Early Papers, Library of Congress, box 16, folder titled "J. A. Early Addresses and Papers." I am grateful to Gary W. Gallagher and Kathryn Schively for providing me with a copy of Early's review. In patiently answering persistent questions about the exact location of this "fine old mansion," two deeply knowledgeable historians of Orange County, Virginia, where Taylor is a common surname, have been most generous with their expertise and their time. They are Frank S. Walker, who made valuable suggestions on a draft of this chapter, and Ann B. Miller, who having consulted John Tranver Graham, president of the Orange County Historical Society, reported that the campsite of Taylor's Louisiana Brigade was south of Gordonsville just over the Louisa County line. From this information Ann Miller, Research Scientist for Virginia Department of Transportation, has conjectured that the mansion may have been Greenwood, known after the war as Conistone and now called Buckland. The house, built circa 1848 and purchased in 1850 by Edward Taylor, still stands near Gordonsville, less than a mile up the old Blue Ridge Turnpike, modern Route 231 North, from Route 33.

46. *Destruction and Reconstruction*, 82.

Chapter 4

1. William Dean Howells, "Editor's Study," *Harper's New Monthly Magazine*, March 1886, 649. A revised version of the review appears in William Dean Howells, *Criticism and Fiction* (New York: Harper and Brothers, 1891), 89–90. In the revised version Howells dropped "common, even" and changed "is a great piece of literature" to "form a great piece of literature," treating "Personal Memoirs" as the plural subject of "form." For more recent discussions of *Personal Memoirs of U. S. Grant*, which have helped this one, see James M. Cox, "U. S. Grant: The Man in the *Memoirs*," in *Recovering Literature's Lost Ground: Essays in American Autobiography* (Baton Rouge: Louisiana State University Press, 1989), 97–120; Henry M. W. Russell, "The Memoirs of Ulysses S. Grant: The Rhetoric of Judgment," *Virginia Quarterly Review* 66, no. 2 (1990): 189–209; Elizabeth D. Samet, "'Adding to My Book and to My Coffin': The Unconditional Memoirs of Ulysses S. Grant," *PMLA* 115, no. 5 (October 2000): 117–24; and Elizabeth D. Samet, "Why Grant Should Stand Proud at West Point," *American Scholar* 88, no. 4 (Autumn 2019): 18–29.

2. Henry Nash Smith, William M. Gibson, and Frederick Anderson, eds., *Mark Twain—Howells Letters: The Correspondence of Samuel L. Clemens and William D. Howells, 1872–1910*, 2 vols. (Cambridge, Mass.: Belknap Press of Harvard University Press, 1960), 2:545; Mark Twain, *Mark Twain's Notebooks and Journals*, ed. Frederick Anderson, Michael Frank, and Kenneth M. Sanderson, 3 vols. (Berkeley: University of California Press, 1975–79), 3:217. When quoting from this edition, or from transcriptions of unpublished letters, I have omitted anything Twain canceled, along with the editorial symbols marking these cancellations.

3. Thomas Wentworth Higginson, "Grant," *Atlantic Monthly*, March 1886, 385; "Grant's Memoirs: Second Volume," *Atlantic Monthly*, September 1886, 420. Later Higginson reworked the two reviews into a single essay, "Ulysses Simpson Grant," in *The Works of Thomas Wentworth Higginson*, 7 vols. (Cambridge, Mass.: Riverside Press, 1900 [c. 1899]), 2:302–28. This essay, uncited and apparently little known, remains an excellent introduction to Grant's *Personal Memoirs*.

4. Mark Twain, *Autobiography of Mark Twain*, ed. Benjamin Griffin, Harriet Elinor Smith, et al., 3 vols. (Berkeley: University of California Press, 2010–15), 2:71–72; *Mark Twain's Notebooks and Journals*, 3:160.

5. John F. Marszalek, David S. Nolen, and Louie P. Gallo, eds., *The Personal Memoirs of Ulysses S. Grant: The Complete Annotated Edition* (Cambridge, Mass.: Belknap Press of Harvard University Press, 2017), 112 (hereafter cited as *Personal Memoirs of U. S. Grant*); originally published as Ulysses S. Grant, *The Personal Memoirs of Ulysses S. Grant*, 2 vols. (New York: Charles L. Webster, 1885–86). Grant was referring to events of September 1845 and October 1848.

6. The late Marie Borroff summarized simplicity in language with two basic

observations: "The most obvious objective correlative of 'simplicity' in language is word length—the frequency, or instance, of lines made up wholly of monosyllables, and a corresponding infrequency of words of three syllables or more," and "A more interesting factual reflection of 'simplicity' or 'difficulty' in language may be found in word origins." To these two observations we might add a third: simplicity in writing usually corresponds to sentence length. The longer the sentence, the more phrases and clauses it will have to complicate it. See Marie Borroff, *Language and the Poet: Verbal Artistry in Frost, Stevens, and Moore* (Chicago: University of Chicago Press, 1979), 23, 24. For the *Kansas City Star* style sheet, see, e.g., http://www.lostgeneration.com/includes/Hemingwaystylesheet.pdf (accessed September 11, 2019).

7. For a series of 1866 entries in which Samuel Clemens, not yet widely known as Mark Twain, referred to models of eloquence, among them Grant's message to Simon Buckner, see *Mark Twain's Notebooks and Journals*, 1:132–47, as well as further discussion in chapter 7 below. For Grant's own treatment of his correspondence with Buckner, see *Personal Memoirs*, 216–17.

8. *Personal Memoirs of U. S. Grant*, 116; Higginson, "Grant," *Works*, 2:308, 310. For a recent commentator who refers to Grant's humor in passing, see Russell, "Memoirs of Ulysses S. Grant."

9. Ulysses S. Grant, *The Papers of Ulysses S. Grant*, ed. John Y. Simon, 32 vols. (Carbondale: Southern Illinois University Press, 1967–2012), 1:5–6; *Personal Memoirs of U. S. Grant*, 14.

10. *Personal Memoirs of U. S. Grant*, 473.

11. *Personal Memoirs of U. S. Grant*, 146, 153; Abraham Lincoln, *The Collected Works of Abraham Lincoln*, ed. Roy P. Basler, 8 vols. with index and suppl. (New Brunswick, N.J.: Rutgers University Press, 1953–55), 3:16.

12. *Personal Memoirs of U. S. Grant*, 30, 33, 34–35.

13. *Personal Memoirs of U. S. Grant*, 487–88.

14. *Personal Memoirs of U. S. Grant*, 681.

15. *Personal Memoirs of U. S. Grant*, 750–51. For documents relating to Grant's drinking, see *Papers of U. S. Grant*, 7:275n, 308n, 8:322n–25n, 9:80n, 82n, 223n, 475n–76n. See also Henry Van Ness Boynton, "Grant's Liquor Drinking," *New York Sun*, January 23, 1887, 1; Boynton's long article runs down the right column of the front page, the first and second columns of the second page, and ends at the top of the third column. For William T. Sherman's response, see Ronald L. Fingerson, "A William Tecumseh Sherman Letter," *Books at Iowa*, November 1965, 34–38. Excerpts from Sherman's letter appear in *Papers of U. S. Grant*, 8:323n–24n. On the previous page appears a letter written to Grant by John Rawlins, June 6, 1863, a copy of which appeared in Boynton's article. These sentences from Rawlins's letter give the Irishman's pledge in Lincoln's story a particular resonance: "You have *full* control of your appetite and can let drinking alone. Had you not pledged me the sincerity of your honor early last March that you would drink no more during the war, and kept that pledge during

your recent campaign, you would not to-day have stood first in the world's history as a successful military leader. Your only salvation depends upon your strict adherence to that pledge. You cannot succeed in any other way."

16. Compare John Keegan's brief but suggestive remarks in his introduction to *The Mask of Command* (New York: Viking, 1987), 11: "The leader of men in warfare can show himself to his followers only through a mask, a mask that he must make for himself, but a mask made in such form as will mark him to men of his time and place as the leader they want and need." Keegan is not interested in the mask of writing, in this case Grant's in his memoirs. As for Samuel Clemens's exploration of literary masking as Mark Twain, consider the implications of his headnote to the excerpt "An Adventure of Huckleberry Finn," published in *Century Magazine*, December 1884, 268: "Readers who have met Huck Finn before (in 'Tom Sawyer') will not be surprised to note that whenever Huck is caught in a close place and is obliged to explain, the truth gets well crippled before he gets through."

17. Gertrude Stein, "Grant," in *Four in America*, intro. Thornton Wilder (New Haven, Conn.: Yale University Press, 1947), 44, 62; Higginson, "Grant," in *Works*, 2:315.

18. Samuel Clemens to Henry Ward Beecher, September 11, 1885, Elmira, N.Y., MS, draft: Union Catalog of Clemens Letters 03288, Mark Twain Papers and Project, Bancroft Library, University of California at Berkeley. I am grateful to Robert Hirst and Melissa Martin for a transcript of this letter, as for the one below. Biographers and scholars do not agree on the date of the first meeting of Mark Twain and Ulysses S. Grant. In the opening sentence of his chapter on Grant, for example, Edmund Wilson's 1881 date is much too late; Wilson seems to have confused the date of first meeting with that of Twain's first discussions with Grant about writing his memoirs. In *Mr. Clemens and Mark Twain: A Biography* (New York: Simon and Schuster, 1966), 121, Justin Kaplan suggests July 1870, probably also too late. By contrast, Gregg Camfield, in *The Oxford Companion to Mark Twain* (New York: Oxford University Press, 2003), 244, gives the date as 1867, which may be a year too early. Claiming an even earlier date of 1866 are Mark Perry, *Grant and Twain: The Story of a Friendship That Changed America* (New York: Random House, 2004), 36; and Christ Mackowski and Kristopher D. White, *Grant's Last Battle: The Story behind the Memoirs of Ulysses S. Grant* ([El Dorado Hills, Calif.]: Savas Beatie, 2015), 35. In using January 15, 1868, I am following Gary Scharnhorst, *Life of Mark Twain: The Early Years* (Columbia: University of Missouri Press, 2018), 457. In Twain's letter "Mark Twain in Washington," dated January 16, 1868, published in *Alta California* (San Francisco) on February 14, 1868, he reported of "Grant's Reception," "We went there, last night."

For Twain's efforts to sell Grant's book, see Samuel Charles Webster, ed., *Mark Twain Business Man* (Boston: Little, Brown, 1946), chap. 29, "General Grant's 'Memoirs,'" 312–24; John Tebbel, *A History of Book Publishing in the United States*, 4 vols. (New York: R. R. Bowker, 1972–81), 2:524–26; and Walter A. Friedman, *Birth of a*

Salesman: The Transformation of Selling in America (Cambridge, Mass.: Harvard University Press, 2004), chap. 2, "Selling Ulysses S. Grant: The Art of the Canvasser," 34–55. For scattered remarks about Grant's *Personal Memoirs* in the larger context of Twain's relation to the U.S. publishing industry, see the index to Bruce Michelson, *Printer's Devil: Mark Twain and the American Publishing Revolution* (Berkeley: University of California Press, 2006).

19. Clemens to Beecher, September 11, 1885.

20. Higginson, "Grant," *Works*, 2:310; *Personal Memoirs of U. S. Grant*, 626. Among biographical studies that discuss Grant's final illness, in addition to titles already cited above, are John F. Marszalek, David S. Nolen, Louie P. Gallo, and Frank J. Williams, *Hold On with a Bulldog Grip: A Short Study of Ulysses S. Grant* (Jackson: University of Mississippi Press, 2019); Ron Chernow, *Grant* (New York: Penguin, 2017); Ronald C. White, *American Ulysses: A Life of Ulysses S. Grant* (New York: Random House, 2016); Charles Bracelen Flood, *Grant's Final Victory: Ulysses S. Grant's Heroic Last Year* (Cambridge, Mass.: Da Capo, 2011); Joan Waugh, *U. S Grant: American Hero, American Myth* (Chapel Hill: University of North Carolina Press, 2009); Jean Edward Smith, *Grant* (New York: Simon and Schuster, 2001); and William S. McFeely, *Grant* (New York: W. W. Norton, 1981). For two older accounts, see Hamlin Garland, *Ulysses S. Grant; His Life and Character* (New York: Doubleday and McClure, 1898), which gives the final twenty pages to Grant's illness and death (504–24); and Owen Wister, *Ulysses S. Grant* (Boston: Small, Maynard, 1900), which has three pages on Grant's end (137–39).

21. Mark Twain, *Mark Twain Speaking*, 87, 131, 136, 173; *Papers of U. S. Grant*, 31:296n; Ronald C. White, *American Ulysses*, 590; Hilton Obenzinger, "Americans in the Holy Land, Israel, and Palestine," in *The Cambridge Companion to American Travel Writing*, ed. Alfred Bendixen and Judith Hamera (Cambridge: Cambridge University Press, 2009), 146; *Mark Twain's Notebooks and Journals*, 3:152.

22. *Mark Twain's Notebooks and Journals*, 3:105, 105n, 152, 152n.

23. Gary Scharnhorst provides a guide to both sides of the disagreement in *Life of Mark Twain: Early Years*, 135, 578–79n; *Mark Twain's Letters*, ed. Albert Bigelow Paine, 2 vols. (New York: Harper and Brothers, 1917), 1:52. For recent work on Mark Twain and the Civil War that has been helpful for this discussion, see Harold K. Bush, *Mark Twain and the Spiritual Crisis of His Age* (Tuscaloosa: University of Alabama Press, 2007), esp. chap. 5, "Mark Twain's Civil War: Civil Religion and the Lost Cause," 161–204; David Rachels, ed., *Mark Twain's Civil War* (Lexington: University of Kentucky Press, 2007), esp. the introduction, 1–17; Jerome Loving, *Confederate Bushwhacker: Mark Twain in the Shadow of the Civil War* (Hanover, N.H.: University Press of New England, 2013); Neil Schmitz, "Mark Twain," in *A History of Civil War Literature*, ed. Coleman Hutchison (New York: Cambridge University Press, 2016), 272–87. Among older works, especially useful have been James Cox, "Walt Whitman, Mark Twain, and the Civil War," *Sewanee Review* 69, no. 2 (April–June 1961):

185–204; and James Cox, *Mark Twain: The Fate of Humor* (1966; repr., Columbia: University of Missouri Press, 2002), esp. chap. 8, "The Campaign That Failed," 185–97.

24. John Russell Young, *Around the World with General Grant: A Narrative of the Visit of General U. S. Grant, Ex-President of the United States, to Various Countries in Europe, Asia, and Africa in 1877, 1878, 1879*, 2 vols. (New York: American News, 1879), 1:339–40.

25. Julia Dent Grant, *The Personal Memoirs of Julia Dent Grant*, ed. John Y. Simon (Carbondale: Southern Illinois University Press, 1975), 236; *Papers of U. S. Grant*, 28:349, 350.

26. Mark Twain, *The Innocents Abroad, or the New Pilgrims Progress* (Hartford, Conn.: American Publishing, 1870), 584.

27. *Personal Memoirs of U. S. Grant*, 240.

28. *Mark Twain's Notebooks and Journals*, 3:11; Mark Twain, *Life on the Mississippi* (New York: Oxford University Press, 1996), 25, 454 (photographic facsimile of the first American edition [Boston: James R. Osgood, 1883]).

29. Grant referred to phrenology again in a letter of May 1, 1861, when he mentioned to Julia his "bump of order" (*Papers of U. S. Grant*, 2:16). The following year L. M. Smith published *The Great American Crisis: Or Cause and Cure of the Rebellion* (Cincinnati, Ohio: Johnson, Stephens, 1862). Calling himself a "Practical Phrenologist," Smith asked, "Why has no Great General, capable of leading our armies to victory, been born to this generation? and why is it that the Administration, in whom the combined Wisdom and Energy of the Nation ought to be centred, has shown itself so inefficient in the conduct of the War, and in meeting the requirements of the present Crisis?" (6). Smith answered by examining and interpreting "the phrenological characters" of Abraham Lincoln, his leading generals through George B. McClellan, and his cabinet officers. After a few preliminary illustrations, the author asserted that a "Great General . . . should possess a large brain with an active vivacious temperament; large intellectual faculties all around; large Firmness, Self-Esteem, Hope, Cautiousness, Combativeness, and Destructiveness. Hope, Cautiousness and Combativeness particularly, should be as nearly balanced as possible; as any great predominance either way, might, in many instances, prove fatally disastrous" (7). None of the U.S. generals up to and including McClellan fulfilled this description, and Smith did not publish anything later about Ulysses S. Grant or William T. Sherman. Smith's remarks on the two most famous Confederate generals went this way: "We have no generals who will compare *with* Rebel General Lee for strategy and natural military genius. I pointed him out as the strongest man on either side, long before he was brought out, and wondered why a man with such a giant intellect should be kept back in obscurity. All of his intellectual faculties are immensely developed, but his moral organization is decidedly *bad*. Stonewall Jackson's brain is not so large, but the organs are all *sharp* and *pointed*, hence his great activity and celerity of movement! Lee probably does the planning of his raids, and he executes them" (7n–8n). As for Grant and Charles Dickens's 1842

American tour, Grant's West Point account book shows that in June 1842, the month Dickens left the United States to return to England, Grant paid for "Subscription to the Phila. Sat Courier" (U. S. Grant account book, call number HM975, Huntington Library, San Marino, Calif.). The timing may be coincidence, or the famous Dickens tour may have played a role in prompting the young cadet to subscribe to a periodical that published Edgar Allan Poe, for example.

30. *Papers of U. S. Grant*, 1:24; *Personal Memoirs of Julia Dent Grant*, 34, 52.

31. For a study of nineteenth-century love letters as a genre of their own, see Karen Lystra, *Searching the Heart: Women, Men, and Romantic Love in Nineteenth-Century America* (New York: Oxford University Press, 1992). For a selection of Grant's letters to Julia, see Ulysses S. Grant, *My Dearest Julia: The Wartime Letters of Ulysses S. Grant to His Wife*, intro. Ron Chernow (New York: Library of America, 2018).

32. *Papers of U. S. Grant*, 2:173; *Personal Memoirs of U. S. Grant*, 185.

33. *Papers of U. S. Grant*, 2:294, 300–301.

34. *Papers of U. S. Grant*, 2:295.

35. See Robert L. Thompson, *Wiring a Continent: The History of the Telegraph Industry in the United States, 1832–1866* (Princeton, N.J.: Princeton University Press, 1947); James W. Carey, *Communication as Culture: Essays on Media and Society*, rev. ed. (New York: Routledge, 2009), esp. chap. 8, "Technology and Ideology: The Case of the Telegraph"; Annteresa Lubrano, *The Telegraph: How Technology Innovation Caused Social Change* (New York: Garland, 1997); Tom Standage, *The Victorian Internet: The Remarkable Story of the Telegraph and the Nineteenth-Century's On-Line Pioneers* (New York: Walker, 1998); and David Paull Nickles, *Under the Wire: How the Telegraph Changed Diplomacy* (Cambridge, Mass.: Harvard University Press, 2003).

36. *Personal Memoirs of U. S. Grant*, 609; United States Military Telegraph, War Department, Sent, Jany. 21, 1864–Dec. 7, 1865, Thomas Eckert Papers, "Decoding the Civil War" (digital collection), Huntington Library, mssEC 181 p155; *Collected Works of Abraham Lincoln*, 7:499, 514. I am grateful to Mario Einaudi, Huntington Library, for help with locating and decoding this telegram. For background on Anson Stager and his route-cipher system, see William Rattle Plum, *The Military Telegraph during the Civil War in the United States: With an Exposition of Ancient and Modern Means of Communication, and of the Federal and Confederate Cipher Systems; Also a Running Account of the War between the States*, 2 vols. (Chicago: Jansen, McClurg, 1882). See also John Emmet O'Brien, *Telegraphing in Battle: Reminiscences of the Civil War* (Scranton, Pa.: Raeder Press [Wilkes-Barre, Pa.], 1910); and Grant's remarks on "the use made of the telegraph and signal corps" by the Army of the Potomac during the Overland Campaign, *Personal Memoirs of U. S. Grant*, 532–33; as well as Keegan, *Mask of Command*, 210–12. Finally, see Grant's letter of "testimony" to his telegrapher, Samuel H. Beckwith, February 14, 1866, in *Papers of U. S. Grant*, 16:61.

37. *Personal Memoirs of U. S. Grant*, 21–22. See *Papers of U. S. Grant*, 1:11, for correspondence in which Grant ordered "illustrated editions" of Charles Lever's *Charles*

O'Malley (1841) and *Harry Lorrequer* (1839), both "comic novels of military life in the period of the Napoleonic Wars" (*Papers of U. S. Grant*, 1:11n). In letters of May and October 1845, Grant referred to translated works by French novelist Eugène Sue (*Papers of U. S. Grant*, 1:44, 60). In a letter to Julia, date February 2, 1854, Grant wrote from Fort Humboldt, California, "I do nothing here but set in my room and read and occasionally take a short ride on one of the public horses" (*Papers of U. S. Grant*, 1:316). He did not give the titles of anything he read during this period, but at some time he must have become familiar with Laurence Sterne's novel *The Life and Opinions of Tristram Shandy, Gentleman*, 9 vols. (1759–67). He alluded indirectly to this novel in a letter to Julia, dated August 10, 1861, written from Ironton, Missouri. The editors of *Papers of U. S. Grant* do not annotate the allusion, but those of *My Dearest Julia* do. Grant also read Charles Dickens and alluded to *David Copperfield* in a letter to Elihu B. Washburne, dated August 16, 1864 (*Papers of U. S. Grant*, 12:17). See the index in White, *American Ulysses* ("reading by" under "Grant, Ulysses S."), for helpful background. According to White, Grant and his wife went to hear Charles Dickens read in Washington at Carroll Hall in 1868 (455). For more on Dickens's lucrative tour, see Jillian Martin, "Making It in America: How Charles Dickens and His Cunning Manager George Dolby Made Millions from a Performance Tour of the United States, 1867–1868" (M.A. thesis, Georgia State University, 2014), https://scholarworks.gsu.edu/communication_theses/112 (accessed February 13, 2020).

38. See unsigned review of Frank Wilkeson, *Recollections of a Private in the Army of the Potomac* (New York: G. P. Putnam's Sons, 1887), in "Books of the Month," *Atlantic Monthly*, April 1887, 575.

39. *Papers of U. S. Grant*, 8:323n–324n.

40. *Personal Memoirs of U. S. Grant*, 121–22.

41. *Personal Memoirs of U. S. Grant*, 238–39. Although Grant revised his article "The Battle of Shiloh" for *Personal Memoirs*, the paragraph about the "unendurable" sight in the log house, aside from minor differences in punctuation, remained unchanged.

42. *Personal Memoirs of U. S. Grant*, 330–32.

43. *Personal Memoirs of U. S. Grant*, 361.

44. *Personal Memoirs of U. S. Grant*, 580.

45. *Personal Memoirs of U. S. Grant*, 575–80.

46. *Personal Memoirs of U. S. Grant*, 367, 580–81.

47. *Papers of U. S. Grant*, 22n–23n, 27n.

48. *Personal Memoirs of U. S. Grant*, 717–19.

49. Ulysses S. Grant Papers, Library of Congress, Series 4, Personal Memoirs, 1884–1885; 1885; mss23333, reel 6, digital image 402, https://www.loc.gov/resource/mss23333.006_0008_0501/?sp=402&r=0.018,0.556,1.112,0.409,0 (accessed October 15, 2019); *Personal Memoirs of U. S. Grant*, 81, 409.

50. *Personal Memoirs of U. S. Grant*, 723; *Papers of U. S. Grant*, 11:371. The writing Grant did during the Overland and Appomattox Campaigns has been published

in *Papers of U. S. Grant* and *The War of the Rebellion: A Compilation of the Official Records of the Union and Confederate Armies*, 128 vols. (Washington, D.C.: Government Printing Office, 1880–1901); yet another vivid image of his wartime writing load comes from the four boxes and 345 manuscript items in Grant's hand in the collection of his correspondence, from May 1864 through April 1865, in the Huntington Library, call numbers mssHM 3210-3536 and HM 25063-25080. As Grant wrote Julia on June 9, 1862, from Corinth, Mississippi, "People in civil life have no idea of the immense labor devolving on a commander in the field" (*Papers of U. S. Grant*, 5:140).

51. For an earlier version of Grant's statement "though that cause was, I believe, one of the worst for which a people ever fought, and one for which there was the least excuse," see letter to Julia, May 13, 1864: "The enemy were really whipped yesterday but their situation is desperate beyond anything heretofore known. To loose this battle they loose their cause. As bad as it is they have fought for it with a gallantry worthy of a better" (*Papers of Ulysses S. Grant*, 10:444). The battle "yesterday" to which Grant referred would have been that of May 12, 1864, at the Bloody Angle of the Mule Shoe salient at Spotsylvania.

52. Douglas Southall Freeman, *R. E. Lee: A Biography*, 4 vols. (New York: Charles Scribner's Sons, 1934), 4:521–22. For Grant's letter to Julia about the loss of his dentures, dated February 11, 1863, from near Vicksburg, see *Papers of U. S. Grant*, 7:311.

53. "Wars produce many stories of fiction, some of which are told until they are believed to be true," Grant wrote of "the story of the famous apple tree" (*Personal Memoirs of U. S. Grant*, 720). He worked to correct or clarify such stories of fiction until the end of his life. Five days before his death, on July 18, 1885, Charles L. Webster presented him with a bound prospectus of advance sheets from his memoirs. According to a note signed by Webster and pasted into the prospectus, "This prospectus is the ONLY SPECIMEN of his book seen by General Grant, and the penciled marginal notes were written by him four days before he died." The penciled marginal notes appear on what is page 30 in the prospectus. On this page Grant inserted an asterisk above a carat after "garb," in the phrase "in about the garb Mr. Jefferson Davis was wearing subsequently, when he was captured"; the phrase describes how Edwin Stanton was dressed on one occasion when Grant went to see him and does not appear in the memoirs. Then, starting along the right-hand margin, Grant wrote, "Fiction, poetry or truth / clothed Mr x x . [Jefferson Davis] I do not know myself [then a pencil line across page, running diagonally from upper right to lower left, down to bottom margin for continuation] how Mr. Davis was dressed on this occasion. His position was such as to justify any means of escape. His life was cried out for. The President of the U. S. had been assassinated and [then a pencil line, running across page from lower right to upper left, up to top margin] Mr. Davis was held responsible" (U. S. Grant, "Prospectus" accompanied by *Personal Memoirs* (1885–86), Huntington Library, call number 26479).

Chapter 5

1. Mark Twain, *The Love Letters of Mark Twain*, ed. Dixon Wecter (New York: Harper, 1949), 249. For evidence that Twain tried to secure book publication rights for the Battles and Leaders series, see Samuel Charles Webster, ed., *Mark Twain, Business Man* (Boston: Little, Brown, 1946), 307. Twain was unsuccessful in his attempt; Robert Underwood Johnson and Clarence C. Buel edited the four volumes of *Battles and Leaders of the Civil War*, which Century Company published in 1887. Had Twain been successful, Charles L. Webster and Company would have published all the Confederate writers included in these volumes. For background on the Grand Army of the Republic, see, e.g., Mary R. Dearing, *Veterans in Politics: The Story of the G.A.R.* (Baton Rouge: Louisiana State University Press, 1952); Stuart McConnell, *Glorious Contentment: The Grand Army of the Republic, 1865–1900* (Chapel Hill: University of North Carolina Press, 1992); and James Marten, *Sing Not War: The Lives of Union and Confederate Veterans in Gilded Age America* (Chapel Hill: University of North Carolina Press, 2011).

2. George McClellan, *McClellan's Own Story: The War for the Union, the Soldiers Who Fought in It, The Civilians Who Directed It, and His Relations to It and to Them* (New York: Charles L. Webster, 1887), 327; Theodore Roosevelt, "At the Unveiling of the Statue to Major-General George B. McClellan at Washington, May 2, 1907," in *Presidential Addresses and State Papers*, 8 vols. (New York: Review of Reviews, 1910), 6:1231–32. A bill for the appropriation of $50,000, "for the preparation of a site and erection of a pedestal for statue of late Major-General George B. McClellan," was introduced in the House of Representatives by George Washington Ray, Republican of New York and a Civil War veteran, as H.R. 8072 on February 5, 1900, and in the Senate as S. 3272 on February 21, 1900. The Senate amended the bill with the addition, "Provided, That said statue shall not be located in the grounds of the Capitol or Library of Congress." The amended bill having passed the Senate on February 6, 1901, it became H.R. 14018, referred to the Committee on Appropriations and ordered to be printed on February 13, 1901. For copies of these bills and their accompanying reports, see *McClellan Statue at Washington* [Washington, D.C.: Government Printing Office, 1900–1901], the binder's title of a slim volume in the Huntington Library, San Marino, Calif., call number E467.1.M2 U5. The other eight equestrian statues are those of generals Ulysses S. Grant, Winfield Scott Hancock, John A. Logan, James B. McPherson, Winfield Scott, Philip H. Sheridan, William T. Sherman, and George H. Thomas.

3. Theodore Roosevelt, "At the Unveiling," in *Presidential Addresses*, 6:1229.

4. Peter S. Michie, *General McClellan* (New York: D. Appleton, 1901), 472.

5. Nathaniel Hawthorne, "Chiefly about War-Matters, by a Peaceable Man," *Atlantic Monthly*, July 1862, 43, 51–52. For a reading of this essay and the self-awareness

shown in Hawthorne's fictionalized editorial notes, see James Bense, "Nathaniel Hawthorne's Intention in 'Chiefly about War Matters,'" *American Literature* 61, no. 2 (May 1989): 200–220.

6. Thomas J. Rowland, *General George B. McClellan and Civil War History: In the Shadow of Grant and Sherman* (Kent, Ohio: Kent State University Press, 1998), 16–18. Rowland opens his survey of diagnoses, in a chapter tellingly titled "A Foray into the Twilight Zone," with the sentence, "Clearly, the most damaging flaw attributed to George McClellan is that he labored under innate psychological defects so severe as to preclude him from ever attaining excellence as a military leader." From there Rowland proceeds to inventory writings by Irving Stone, Kenneth P. Williams, Allan Nevins, T. Harry Williams, Stephen W. Sears, Harold Holzer, and Joseph T. Glatthaar.

7. For recent treatments of Simon Cameron and Edwin Stanton, see Paul Kahan, *Amiable Scoundrel: Simon Cameron, Lincoln's Scandalous Secretary of War* (Lincoln, Nebr.: Potomac Books, 2016); and William Marvel, *Lincoln's Autocrat: The Life of Edwin Stanton* (Chapel Hill: University of North Carolina Press, 2015). For a discussion of how much Lincoln had learned as commander in chief by the spring of 1862, see Gary W. Gallagher, "'You Must Either Attack Richmond or Give Up the Job and Come to the Defence of Washington': Abraham Lincoln and the 1862 Shenandoah Valley Campaign," in *The Lincoln Forum: Rediscovering Abraham Lincoln*, ed. John Y. Simon, Harold Holzer, and Dawn Ruark (New York: Fordham University Press, 2002), 34–47. Gallagher argues that Lincoln reacted admirably to Jackson's campaign, showing a sound grasp of strategy and none of the nervous panic sometimes attributed to him. There still remains the question of why McClellan retreated to Harrison's Landing after his victory at Malvern Hill. Brian K. Burton has argued that he was "following the train of thought that haunted him for months. He had insisted that the Confederates outnumbered him, and he had decided he should not risk the army." See Burton, *Extraordinary Circumstances: The Seven Days Battles* (Bloomington: Indiana University Press, 2001), 366–68.

8. Stephen W. Sears, *George B. McClellan: The Young Napoleon* (New York: Ticknor and Fields, 1988), 403–6; Stephen W. Sears, "The Curious Case of General McClellan's Memoirs," *Civil War History* 34, no. 2 (June 1988): 101–14.

9. George B. McClellan, *Letter of the Secretary of War, Transmitting Report on the Organization of the Army of the Potomac, and of Its Campaigns in Virginia and Maryland, under the Command of Maj. Gen. George B. McClellan, from July 26, 1861, to November 7, 1862* (Washington, D.C.: Government Printing Office, 1864); subsequently published with an additional section on the West Virginia campaign as *Report on the Organization and Campaigns of the Army of the Potomac, to Which Is Added an Account of the Campaign in Western Virginia, with Plans of Battle-Fields* (New York: Sheldon, 1864). For McClellan's somewhat coy letter to William C. Prime about translation of this report into French, see Stephen W. Sears, ed., *The Civil War Papers*

of George B. McClellan: Selected Correspondence, 1860–1865 (New York, Ticknor and Fields, 1989), 567: "It is immaterial to me whether it is translated or not—tho' I suppose it would be very well to have it circulate in as many languages as possible, not omitting Sanscrit & Chinese."

10. Sears, "Curious Case," 109, 110, 113. The phrases quoted in the following sentence are at 109 and 111.

11. Samuel L. Clemens to P. T. Barnum, February 3, 1875, in *Letters, 1874–1875*, ed. Michael B. Frank and Harriet Elinor Smith, vol. 6 of *Mark Twain's Letters: A Publication of the Mark Twain Project of the Bancroft Library*, ed. Robert H. Hirst, 8 vols. (Berkeley: University of California Press, 2002), http://www.marktwainproject.org/xtf/view?docId=letters/UCCL01188.xml;query=p.t.barnum;searchAll=;sectionType1=;sectionType2=;sectionType3=;sectionType4=;sectionType5=;style=letter;brand=mtp#1 (accessed February 20, 2020).

12. McClellan, *McClellan's Own Story*, 22, 23.

13. Sears, "Curious Case," 108, 109; McClellan, *McClellan's Own Story*, 27; Candace Shy Hooper, *Lincoln's Generals' Wives: Four Women Who Influenced the Civil War—for Better and for Worse* (Kent, Ohio: Kent State University Press, 2016), 145.

14. Edmund Wilson, *Patriotic Gore: Studies in the Literature of the American Civil War* (1962; repr., New York: Oxford University Press, 1966), 329; Gary Gallagher, intro. to *Recollections and General Robert E. Lee by His Son Captain Robert E. Lee* (Wilmington, N.C.: Bradfoot, 1988), n.p. The sentence summarizing opinions of Freeman, Connelly, Harwell, and Johannsen borrows heavily from and is wholly indebted to Gallagher's introduction.

15. This translation is by Albert Cook and appears in *The Classic Line: A Study in Epic Poetry* (Bloomington: Indiana University Press, 1966), 123; Cook's translation of Homer's *Odyssey* was published in New York by W. W. Norton in 1967.

16. William Starr Myers, ed., *The Mexican War Diary of George B. McClellan* (Princeton, N.J.: Princeton University Press, 1917), 1. For more on McClellan's 1855–56 European tour, see Sears, *George B. McClellan: The Young Napoleon*, 44–49; and Matthew Moten, *The Delafield Commission and the American Military Profession* (College Station: Texas A&M University Press, 2000), on which Ethan S. Rafuse has based his subsequent treatment in *McClellan's War: The Failure of Moderation in the Struggle for the Union* (Bloomington: Indiana University Press, 2005), 61–66.

17. *McClellan's Own Story*, 331; Fitzhugh Lee, *General Lee: A Biography of Robert E. Lee* (1894), intro. Gary Gallagher (New York: Da Capo, 1994), 166.

18. Rafuse, *McClellan's War*; John C. Waugh, *Lincoln and McClellan: The Troubled Partnership between a President and His General* (New York: Palgrave Macmillan, 2010); Chester G. Hearn, *Lincoln and McClellan at War* (Baton Rouge: Louisiana State University Press, 2012).

19. Michie, *General McClellan*, 50.

20. Joseph E. Johnston, *Narrative of Military Operations, Directed, during the Late War between the States, by Joseph E. Johnston, General C.S.A.* (New York: D. Appleton, 1874), 496.

21. Sears, *George B. McClellan: The Young Napoleon*, 106–7; Rowland, *George B. McClellan and Civil War History*, 26, 28; Rafuse, *McClellan's War*, 27, 81.

22. Myers, *Mexican War Diary*, 3–4.

23. *McClellan's Own Story*, 172, 450.

24. Fitzhugh Lee, *General Lee*, 220; Myers, *Mexican War Diary*, 3.

25. *McClellan's Own Story*, 463–64.

26. Robert E. Lee to Mary Anna Randolph Custis Lee, November 15, 1856, Lee Family Digital Archive, http://leefamilyarchive.org/papers/letters/transcripts-adams/a045.html (accessed February 20, 2020). For original source, see Ely-DeButts Papers, Library of Congress, transcribed in Francis Raymond Adams Jr., "An Annotated Edition of the Personal Letters of Robert E. Lee, April, 1855–April, 1861" (Ph.D. diss., University of Maryland, 1955), 204–8.

27. *McClellan's Own Story*, 358, 360, 554.

28. *McClellan's Own Story*, 35.

29. Fitzhugh Lee, *General Lee*, 220. One of the newest and best additions to the vast and growing literature on hard war and the ethical considerations it raised is D. H. Dilbeck's study of the Lieber Code, *A More Civil War: How the Union Waged a Just War* (Chapel Hill: University of North Carolina Press, 2016). See especially the pages under the entry "Christianity and Just War Ideas" in the index.

30. *McClellan's Own Story*, 37, 445.

31. *McClellan's Own Story*, 295.

32. *McClellan's Own Story*, 487–88. Many have commented on McClellan's attraction to the military theories of Antoine-Henri Jomini; see, e.g., Rafuse, *McClellan's War*, 3, 34; and Sears, *George B. McClellan: The Young Napoleon*, 36, 99, 130, 241, 390. While it is true that McClellan learned about Jomini at West Point under Dennis Hart Mahan, visited Jomini in 1868, and published the essay "General Jomini" in the *Galaxy* 7 (June 1869): 876–88, nothing in Jomini's best-known writings anticipated McClellan's Harrison Landing letter. In *The Art of War*, an English translation of Jomini's *Précis de l'art de la guerre* (1838) published the year of the Peninsula Campaign, the word "Christian" appears six times and never in the context of ethics; see *The Art of War*, trans. George H. Mendell and William P. Craighill (Philadelphia: Lippincott, 1862), 362–81. Meanwhile, Jomini's name never appears in *McClellan's Own Story* or in Sears, *Civil War Papers of George B. McClellan*. This absence supports the argument—that Jomini's influence has been overestimated—in Carol Reardon, *With a Sword in One Hand and Jomini in the Other: The Problem of Military Thought in the Civil War North* (Chapel Hill: University of North Carolina Press, 2012).

33. *McClellan's Own Story*, 488. See also Mark Grimsley, *The Hard Hand of War: Union Military Policy toward Southern Civilians, 1861–1865* (New York: Cambridge

University Press, 1995), 86–87. For McClellan's report on the Peninsula Campaign, see *The War of the Rebellion: A Compilation of the Official Records of the Union and Confederate Armies*, 128 vols. (Washington, D.C.: Government Printing Office, 1880–1901), ser. 1, vol. 11, pt. 1, 5–105; the Harrison's Landing letter appears at 73–74. For a public version of McClellan's testimony before the Committee on the Conduct of the War, see *New York Times*, May 3, 1863, 2–3. This testimony did not mention the letter, but the paper did publish the full text of the Harrison's Landing letter eight months later; see *New York Times*, January 5, 1864, 5. The letter subsequently had wide circulation during the 1864 presidential campaign. It is included, for example, with a bound volume of 1864 campaign documents in the Huntington Library. This copy of the letter was published by E. B. Patten, 35 Park Row, New York, call number 36370.

34. *McClellan's Own Story*, 488–89. In his essay "A Civil War Watershed," Gary W. Gallagher points to a letter by Charles Sumner, dated August 5, 1862, connecting passage of the Second Confiscation Act to "pressures from our reverses at Richmond." Gallagher comments, "Had McClellan been the victor in July 1862, he certainly could have pressed his case for a softer policy more effectively." See Charles Sumner, *The Selected Letters of Charles Sumner*, ed. Beverly Wilson Palmer, 2 vols. (Boston: Northeastern University Press, 1990), 2:122; and Gary W. Gallagher, ed., *The Richmond Campaign of 1862: The Peninsula and the Seven Days* (Chapel Hill: University of North Carolina Press, 2000), 16–17, 26n23.

35. *McClellan's Own Story*, 105.

36. In the heat of one moment, for example, McClellan wrote to Edwin M. Stanton from Savage's Station at 12:20 a.m. on June 28, 1862, "Had I twenty thousand (20,000), or even ten thousand (10,000), fresh troops to use to-morrow, I could take Richmond"; see *McClellan's Own Story*, 101–5, 424.

37. *McClellan's Own Story*, 346.

38. *McClellan's Own Story*, 604, 608.

39. *McClellan's Own Story*, 236; *Report on the Organization and Campaigns of the Army of the Potomac*, 107. McClellan's invocation of Fitz John Porter was not without complexity: it was Porter who did not want to commit his Fifth Corps reserves to the fighting on the left flank at Sharpsburg-Antietam. See Stephen W. Sears, *Landscape Turned Red: The Battle of Antietam* (1983; repr., New York: Warner Books, 1985), 322–23.

40. John Keats to George and Thomas Keats, December 22, 1817, in *Letters of John Keats to His Family and Friends*, ed. Sydney Colvin (London: Macmillan, 1925), 48; *McClellan's Own Story*, 346.

41. *McClellan's Own Story*, 648, 650.

42. Michael Shaara, *The Killer Angels* (1974; repr., New York: Ballantine Books, 1975), 124, 166; Phil Leigh, "Making 'Killer Angels,'" *New York Times*, June 28, 2013, https://opinionator.blogs.nytimes.com/2013/06/28/making-killer-angels.

43. Robert L. Chapman, ed., *American Slang*, 2nd ed. (New York: HarperCollins, 1998), 32–33; *McClellan's Own Story*, 567; Sears, *Civil War Papers*, 435.

44. Robert E. Lee Jr., *Recollections and Letters of General Robert E. Lee* (New York: Doubleday, 1904), 89; *McClellan's Own Story*, 453–54.

45. *McClellan's Own Story*, 458–59.

46. The phrase "emotional self-interest" appears in Arlie Russell Hochschild, *Strangers in Their Own Land: Anger and Mourning on the American Right* (New York: New Press, 2016), 228; for Google Ngram searches of "human interest," "human interest story," and "soft news," consult the Google Books Ngram Viewer at https://books.google.com/ngrams (accessed December 2, 2020).

Chapter 6

1. William T. Sherman, *Memoirs of General William T. Sherman*, 2 vols. (New York: D. Appleton, 1875); Ulysses S. Grant, *The Personal Memoirs of U. S. Grant*, 2 vols. (New York: Charles L. Webster, 1885–86); Philip H. Sheridan, *Personal Memoirs of P. H. Sheridan*, 2 vols. (New York: Charles L. Webster, 1888), 1:xiii.

2. Mark Twain, *Mark Twain's Notebooks and Journals*, ed. Frederick Anderson, Michael Frank, and Kenneth M. Sanderson, 3 vols. (Berkeley: University of California Press, 1975–79), 3:388n, 430n.

3. Samuel L. Clemens to Philip H. Sheridan, December 26, 1884. The manuscript of this letter is number 7.60 in Series B of the Samuel L. Clemens Papers, Vassar College Archives and Special Collections Library. It has been published in Samuel Charles Webster, ed., *Mark Twain: Business Man* (Boston: Little, Brown, 1946), 288, where Webster introduced it with the statement, "The following letter seems not to have been delivered." Clearly, some subsequent version of the letter must have been delivered, or Webster and Company would not have published Sheridan's *Memoirs*. I am grateful to Robert H. Hirst, General Editor, Mark Twain Papers, Bancroft Library, University of California at Berkeley, and to Dean Rogers, Special Collections Assistant, Vassar College Archives and Special Collections Library, for their generous assistance; Philip H. Sheridan, "The Last Days of the Rebellion," *North American Review*, July 1883, 8–18.

4. *Mark Twain's Notebooks and Journals*, 3:212; Mark Twain, *Adventures of Huckleberry Finn (Tom Sawyer's Comrade)* (New York: Charles L. Webster, 1885). This copy resides in the Albert and Shirley Small Special Collections, University of Virginia. Twain's inscription to "the General's boys" raises some questions, because Sheridan had three daughters and only one son, Philip Jr., who was born in 1880 and who wrote his name in pencil on the rear fly-leaf. It may well be that Twain was referring to Sheridan's soldiers or some other group identified with him; Frank A. Burr and Richard J. Hinton, *"Little Phil" and His Troopers: The Life of Gen. Philip H. Sheridan: Its Romance and Reality: How an Humble Lad Reached the Head of an Army* (Providence, R.I.: J. A. and R. A. Reid, 1888), 3–4.

5. Jubal A. Early, *A Memoir of the Last Year of the War for Independence, in the Confederate States of America: Containing an Account of the Operations of His Commands*

in the Years 1864 and 1865 (Toronto: Lovell and Gibson, 1866), 97n; Edward A. Pollard, *The Lost Cause: A New Southern History of the War of the Confederates* (New York: E. B. Treat, 1866), 590.

6. Paul Andrew Hutton, *Phil Sheridan and His Army* (Lincoln: University of Nebraska Press, 1985), 371; George B. McClellan, *McClellan's Own Story: The War for the Union, the Soldiers Who Fought in It, the Civilians Who Directed It and His Relations to It and to Them* (New York: Charles L. Webster, 1887); Philip H. Sheridan to Charles L. Webster, December 7, 1886, number 30.35, Series HH, Samuel L. Clemens Papers, Vassar College Archives and Special Collections Library.

7. Philip H. Sheridan to Charles L. Webster, December 21, 1886, number 30.43, Series HH, Samuel L. Clemens Papers, Vassar College Archives and Special Collections Library; Sheridan, *Memoirs,* 1:20, 102, 106.

8. Sheridan, *Memoirs,* 1:254, 315.

9. Sheridan, 1:96–97.

10. Walt Whitman, "So Long!," in *Complete Poetry and Collected Prose* (New York: Library of America, 1982), 611; Sheridan, *Memoirs,* 1:17, 39, 64, 199, 288, 368–69, 2:43. The theme of swearing reappeared in Sheridan's account of observing the Battle of Gravelotte (August 18, 1870) during the Franco-Prussian War. In that account he described King Wilhelm I of Prussia, whom he called "William," berating fugitive German soldiers with an energy that reminded Sheridan "forcibly of the 'Dutch' swearing that I used to hear in my boyhood in Ohio" (Sheridan, *Memoirs,* 2:377). In November 1888, *Scribner's Magazine* published an excerpt from Sheridan's *Personal Memoirs* titled "From Gravelotte to Sedan" (515–35). The publication of this excerpt resulted from contractual wrangling between Webster and Scribner's. For background on negotiations between the two publishers, see *Mark Twain's Notebooks and Journals,* 3:387n. The excerpt in *Scribner's Magazine* includes an illustration, at 524, of Wilhelm I, in Sheridan's words, "dressing down" the shirkers. Frederick C. Newhall, one of Sheridan's principal staff officers in the Appomattox Campaign, tried to dispel the "popular idea" that his commander "was an exceedingly profane man," admitting that he could use "some lusty oaths" to "buffet back the panic and retrieve disorder" of men in combat. See Frederick C. Newhall, *With Sheridan in the Final Campaign against Lee* (1866), ed. Eric J. Wittenberg (repr., Baton Rouge: Louisiana State University Press, 2002), 2–3.

11. Sheridan, *Memoirs,* 1:152, 191, 200, 303, 375. Sheridan's second volume included two extended self-justifications, one with respect to the controversies arising from his relieving Gouverneur Warren from command of the Fifth Corps during the Battle of Five Forks, April 1, 1865 (*Memoirs,* 2:154–70), the other from his collision with Andrew Johnson over the implementation of the Reconstruction Laws in New Orleans after a riot there, July 30, 1866 (*Memoirs,* 2:233–80). See note 20, below.

12. Sheridan, *Memoirs,* 1:11–12; see Eric J. Wittenberg, *Little Phil: A Reassessment of the Civil War Leadership of General Philip H. Sheridan* (Washington, D.C.: Brassey's,

2002), 171, for criticism of Sheridan's "wide streak of insubordination." Although I agree with Wittenberg about the width of that streak, it should be apparent that I cannot agree wholly about what he calls Sheridan's "hypocrisy" about his insubordination. As shown here, his memoirs suggest considerable self-awareness and candor about his tendency toward insubordination.

13. Sheridan, *Memoirs*, 1:134–35, 182; Grant, *Personal Memoirs*, 1:402; see also John F. Marszalek, David S. Nolen, and Louie P. Gallo, eds., *The Personal Memoirs of Ulysses S. Grant: The Complete Annotated Edition* (Cambridge, Mass.: Belknap Press of Harvard University Press, 2017), 275 (hereafter cited as *Personal Memoirs of U. S. Grant*).

14. Not everyone has celebrated Sheridan or his leadership. George Crook, who first appeared in Sheridan's narrative at Fort Reading in California in 1855 (*Memoirs*, 1:37), later fought beside him in the Shenandoah Valley as head of the Army of West Virginia. Resenting the credit he felt Sheridan took for his, Crook's, achievements at the Battles of Cedar Creek and Winchester, Crook fumed retrospectively, in a diary entry for December 26, 1889, "The adulations heaped upon him by a grateful nation for his supposed genius turned his head, which, added to his natural disposition, caused him to bloat his little carcass with debauchery and dissipation, which carried him off prematurely." See George Crook, *General George Crook: His Autobiography*, ed. Martin Schmitt (Norman: University of Oklahoma Press, 1946), 134n; and David Coffey, *Sheridan's Lieutenants: Phil Sheridan, His Generals, and the Final Year of the Civil War* (Lanham, Md.: Rowman and Littlefield, 2005), 142–43. In the booklet-sized *Notes on the Personal Memoirs of P. H. Sheridan* (St. Paul, Minn.: Press of William L. Banning, Jr., 1889), Carswell McClellan, who served on the staff of Andrew A. Humphreys and was a first cousin of George B. McClellan, challenged many moments in Sheridan's memoirs from the Wilderness on, as in *The Personal Memoirs and Military History of U. S. Grant versus the Record of the Army of the Potomac* (Boston: Houghton, Mifflin, 1887) he had challenged many moments in Grant's. In *Glory Enough for All: Sheridan's Second Raid and the Battle of Trevilian Station* (Washington, D.C.: Brassey's, 2001), 304–9, Eric J. Wittenberg summarizes various negative assessments of Sheridan's performance in that battle. But Wittenberg also admits, "In spite of their commander's poor performance, Sheridan had a true gift for inspiring the men who served under him" (308–9). Wittenberg has continued his bracing though balanced critique of Sheridan in *Little Phil*.

15. Sheridan, *Memoirs*, 1:93.

16. Sheridan, 1:153.

17. Sheridan, 1:153–54, 340.

18. See, e.g., Wittenberg, *Little Phil*, specifically these sentences from Sheridan's report of operations from April 6 to August 4, 1864, which Wittenberg reprints as appendix A (176–95): "The horses which failed were shot by the rear guard, as they could have been easily recuperated and made serviceable to the enemy. I think the actual

number lost would not exceed 300, perhaps not more than 250" (183). Although Sheridan claimed, "We lost but few horses, considering their condition when we started" (183), the official numbers of horses sent to him strongly suggest that this policy of shooting failed horses, here carried out during his raid on Richmond (May 9–24, 1864), could not have been an isolated one. Consider Henry W. Halleck's letter of June 4, 1864, written from Washington, D.C., to Ulysses S. Grant: "In the month of May we sent to the Army of the Potomac 6,683 cavalry horses in addition to the cavalrymen remounted here. About 1,000 more cavalry horses are being shipped to White House." For Halleck's letter, see *The War of the Rebellion: A Compilation of the Official Records of the Union and Confederate Armies*, 128 vols. (Washington, D.C.: Government Printing Office, 1880–1901) (hereafter cited as *OR*), ser. 1, vol. 36, pt. 3, 569. Sheridan started the Overland Campaign with twelve thousand mounted cavalrymen, so the need for 7,700 new horses would suggest a loss of 64 percent. I am grateful to Robert E. L. Krick for pointing out his letter.

19. Thomas Wolfe, *Look Homeward, Angel* (1929; repr., New York: Charles Scribner's Sons, 1957), xv; Sheridan, *Memoirs*, 1:353–54.

20. Sheridan, *Memoirs*, 1:320–24. Defending his actions, Sheridan included documentation related to the relieving of Warren during the Battle of Five Forks and to the implementation of the Reconstruction Laws in New Orleans. See note 11, above.

21. Sheridan, 1:465, 484–88.

22. Sheridan, 1:123. I have compared Grant's and Sherman's accounts of causes of the war in *Belligerent Muse: Five Northern Writers and How They Shaped Our Understanding of the Civil War* (Chapel Hill: University of North Carolina Press, 2014), 166–67, 170–72.

23. Sheridan, *Memoirs*, 2:119.

24. In a note to his reprinting of Sheridan's 1883 essay "The Last Days of the Rebellion" in *Battles and Leaders of the Civil War*, vol. 6 (Urbana: University of Illinois Press, 2004), 526–35, editor Peter Cozzens offered this puzzling judgment: "This account of the Appomattox Campaign is longer, markedly superior to, and much more personal than Sheridan's treatment of the subject in his memoirs" (598). In fact, the 1883 version, which corresponds to Sheridan, *Memoirs* 2:175–202, is shorter than the later version (approximately 4,300 words to 5,800); it omits a description of the Battle of Sailor's Creek, April 6, 1865; and it leaves out Lincoln's "laconic despatch" of April 7, 1865, to Sheridan. In fairness to Cozzens, the earlier version included two or three colorful touches that did not make it into the memoirs, such as a jocular quip by Confederate Cadmus M. Wilcox at Appomattox: "'Here, Sheridan, take these saddlebags; they have one soiled shirt and a pair of drawers. You have burned everything else I had in the world, and I think you are entitled to these also'" ("Last Days of the Rebellion," 17). But otherwise it would be hard to defend as "markedly superior" locutions such as "sanguinary engagement" ("Last Days of the Rebellion," 13) to "spirited fight" (Sheridan, *Memoirs*, 2:190) or "'I am very well, thank you'" (Sheridan's

response to Grant's "'Sheridan, how are you?'" in "Last Days of the Rebellion," 17) to "I assured him with thanks that I was 'first-rate'" (Sheridan, *Memoirs*, 2:200). Finally, it is unclear how such passive constructions in the earlier version as "Orders were at once given to General Crook" and "Orders were given to complete the formation" ("Last Days of the Rebellion," 8, 15) helped to make it "much more personal" than the first-person, active constructions Sheridan used later in the memoirs. At one point Cozzens undertook to correct Sheridan's Latin, changing *in statu quo* ("Last Days of the Rebellion," 17) to "in status quo" (*Battles and Leaders*, 6:533). Sheridan's version is grammatically correct. Cozzens has published two volumes supplementing the original four volumes of *Battles and Leaders of the Civil War*, ed. Robert Underwood Johnson and Clarence Clough Buel, 4 vols. (New York: Century, 1887–88); vol. 5 (Urbana: University of Illinois Press, 2002); Sheridan, *Memoirs*, 2:124–25.

25. Philip Henry Sheridan Papers, Library of Congress, box 104, reel 98, shelf no. 19,308. In the letter of December 21, 1886, cited above, Sheridan asked Webster to send him a check for one hundred dollars each month to pay his clerk for work on the memoirs. The clerk's manuscript followed Sheridan's handwritten first draft, which is often difficult to read. All subsequent discussion of changes in the typescript or the clerk's manuscript refers to this microfilm reel; *OR*, ser. 1, vol. 46, pt. 2, 609. For background on Grant's repeated attempts to get Sheridan to destroy the Virginia Central Railroad, and Sheridan's noncompliance, see Morris, *Sheridan*, 222–37; and Sheridan, *Memoirs*, 2:112–13.

26. This was another moment revised in the clerk's manuscript, where "I fear" has been inserted above a caret mark and "earnest" has replaced "emphatic"; Sheridan, *Memoirs*, 2:131, 133.

27. Sheridan, 2:204.

28. Grant, *Personal Memoirs*, 2:438, or *Personal Memoirs of U. S. Grant*, 690; Mark Twain, Livy Clemens, and Susy Clemens, *A Family Sketch and Other Private Writings*, ed. Benjamin Griffin (Oakland: University of California Press, 2014), 40. Even Wittenberg concedes that the Appomattox Campaign was Sheridan's "finest moment" and showed him "at his best"; see Wittenberg, *Little Phil*, 149.

29. Thomas Nagel, "Moral Luck" in *Mortal Questions* (Cambridge: Cambridge University Press, 1979), 25–26; Abraham Lincoln to Albert G. Hodges, April 4, 1864, in *Collected Works of Abraham Lincoln*, ed. Roy P. Basler, 9 vols. (New Brunswick, N.J.: Rutgers University Press, 1953–55), 7:282. For Lincoln's expectation that he would lose the election of 1864, see his "Memorandum Concerning His Probable Failure of Re-Election," August 23, 1864, in *Collected Works*, 7:514.

30. For a balanced discussion of Johnston's performance as commander of the Department of the West and Davis's censure of that performance, see Craig Symonds, *Joseph E. Johnston: A Civil War Biography* (New York: W. W. Norton, 1992), 187–218; Sheridan, *Memoirs*, 2:235–80.

31. An especially passionate defender of Warren has been Eric J. Wittenberg, who

dedicated his edition of Newhall's *With Sheridan in the Final Campaign against Lee* to "the brave men" of the Armies of the Potomac and Northern Virginia and "to the memory of Maj. Gen. Gouverneur K. Warren, whose many contributions to the Union victory in the Civil War have been largely forgotten by history as the result of an injustice" (v). Wittenberg reprinted as appendix B to this edition Warren's 1866 pamphlet defending his actions, "An Account of the Operations of the Fifth Corps, Commanded by Maj. Gen. G. K. Warren, at the Battle of Five Forks, April 1, 1865, and the Battles and Movements Preliminary to It, by G. K. Warren, Late Major General Volunteers" (147–88); Sheridan, *Memoirs*, 2:165.

32. Sheridan, *Memoirs*, 2:143–45, 158, 160, 161, 165. Sheridan explained that he named his horse Breckenridge "from its capture from one of Breckenridge's staff-officers at Missionary Ridge." He was referring to John C. Breckinridge, whose name he misspelled consistently throughout his memoirs. It is curious, and perhaps indicates a limited concern with details about Confederate leaders, that neither Mark Twain nor anyone else at Webster and Company caught the mistake.

33. Sheridan, *Memoirs*, 2:155, 160.

34. Sheridan, 2:169.

35. Sheridan, 2:169–70.

36. McClellan, *Notes on the Personal Memoirs of P. H. Sheridan*, 54; Sheridan, *Memoirs*, 2:170.

37. Sheridan, *Memoirs*, 1:441, 458, 459, 2:188–93; Sheridan, "Last Days of the Rebellion," 11.

38. Sheridan, *Memoirs*, 1:347, 463–64, 2:130.

39. Sheridan, 2:187.

40. Joshua Lawrence Chamberlain, *The Passing of the Armies: An Account of the Final Campaign of the Army of the Potomac, Based Upon Personal Reminiscences of the Fifth Army Corps* (1915; repr., New York: Bantam Books, 1993), 115–16.

41. Sheridan, *Memoirs*, 2:287. For background on John Boyd, see Grant T. Hammond, *The Mind of War: John Boyd and American Security* (Washington, D.C.: Smithsonian Institution Press, 2001); and Robert Coram, *Boyd: The Fighter Pilot Who Changed the Art of War* (Boston: Little, Brown, 2002). See esp. Hammond's chapter "From Patterns of Conflict to Maneuver Warfare" (136–54), which includes this formulation: "Two concepts underlie Boyd's analysis and synthesis of warfare. They are time and movement, or, more precisely, speed and maneuver. If one moves and constantly presents an opponent with a changing situation and does so quickly, one has a tremendous advantage" (151). Boyd contrasted maneuver warfare with attrition warfare, which students of the Appomattox and Overland Campaigns can readily associate with Sheridan and Grant, respectively. Edward Porter Alexander, *Fighting for the Confederacy: The Personal Recollections of General Edward Porter Alexander*, ed. Gary W. Gallagher (Chapel Hill: University of North Carolina Press, 1989), 512.

42. Sheridan, *Memoirs*, 2:191, 192, 194, 202.

43. Sheridan, 2:126, 200.

44. Sheridan, "Last Days of the Rebellion," 17–18; Sheridan, *Memoirs*, 2:201.

45. Sheridan, *Memoirs*, 2:130, 202, 205, 209.

46. *Mark Twain's Notebooks and Journals*, 3:612n, 614n. Webster and Company had been selling a third edition of Sherman's memoirs since September 1890, and a fourth edition followed in 1891. For background on the failure of the company, see Webster, *Mark Twain: Business Man*, vii–viii; and Albert Bigelow Paine, *Mark Twain: A Biography*, 3 vols. (New York: Harper and Brothers, 1912), 2:983–87. News of the bankruptcy appeared in the *New York Times*, April 19, 1894, 9. For the later edition of Sheridan's book, see Philip H. Sheridan, *Personal Memoirs of P. H. Sheridan*, 2 vols., enlarged ed., ed. Michael V. Sheridan (New York: D. Appleton, 1902). The only available print editions of this book seem to be the products of companies that sell digital scans of public domain material.

Chapter 7

1. Mark Twain, *Life on the Mississippi* (Boston: James R. Osgood, 1883), 246. My text is the facsimile reproduction of this edition, published in the *Oxford Mark Twain*, ed. Shelley Fisher Fishkin (New York: Oxford University Press, 1996).

2. For quotations from Mark Twain's notebook in this and the following paragraphs, see *Mark Twain's Notebooks and Journals*, ed. Frederick Anderson, Michael Frank, and Kenneth M. Sanderson, 3 vols. (Berkeley: University of California Press, 1975–79), 1:132–47. When quoting from this edition, I have omitted anything Twain canceled, along with the editorial symbols marking these cancellations. For biographical background on his voyage aboard the *Smyrniote*, see Gary Scharnhorst, *The Life of Mark Twain: The Early Years, 1835–1871* (Columbia: University of Missouri Press, 2018), 343–44.

3. Mark Twain, *Mark Twain Speaking*, ed. Paul Fatout (Iowa City: University of Iowa Press, 1976), 160.

4. Ulysses S. Grant, *The Papers of Ulysses S. Grant*, ed. John Y. Simon, 32 vols. (Carbondale: Southern Illinois University Press, 1967–2012), 4:218; John F. Marszalek, David S. Nolen, and Louie P. Gallo, eds., *The Personal Memoirs of Ulysses S. Grant: The Complete Annotated Edition* (Cambridge, Mass.: Belknap Press of Harvard University Press, 2017), 235 (hereafter cited as *Personal Memoirs of U. S. Grant*).

5. Along with the two USCT regiments, the Thirteenth Tennessee Cavalry, a regiment of white Unionists also at Fort Pillow, suffered many casualties after surrendering. See Clayton Butler, "'A Terrible Retribution': West Tennessee Unionists at Fort Pillow," *Tennessee Historical Quarterly* (forthcoming).

6. Twain, *Life on the Mississippi*, 311; *Mark Twain's Notebooks and Journals*, 2:533, 537; Guy Lancaster, "Island 37," *Encyclopedia of Arkansas*, Central Arkansas Library

System, https://encyclopediaofarkansas.net/entries/island-37-5081 (accessed January 8, 2020).

7. Todd C. Frankel, "Taming the Mighty Mississippi," *Washington Post*, March 14, 2018, https://www.washingtonpost.com/graphics/2018/national/mississippi-river-infrastructure/.

8. See Twain, *Life on the Mississippi*, 375–86, for all quotations from the chapter "Vicksburg during the Trouble."

9. For excerpts from *Life on the Mississippi* in his edition of *Mark Twain's Civil War* (Lexington: University Press of Kentucky, 2007), 37–46, David Rachels chose "The Pilot's First Battle," about the Battle of Belmont, and a section from Twain's visit to New Orleans, discussed at greater length below.

10. For "narcissism," consult the Google Books Ngram Viewer at https://books.google.com/ngrams.

11. Figures for mortality of general officers are based on tables in Ezra Warner, *Generals in Gray: Lives of the Confederate Commanders* (Baton Rouge: Louisiana State University Press, 1959), xix; and Ezra Warner, *Generals in Blue: Lives of the Union Commanders* (Baton Rouge: Louisiana State University Press, 1964), xx–xxi. According to these tables, there were 425 Confederate and 583 Union generals, for a total of 1,008. Of these, 77 Confederate and 47 Union generals were killed in action or died of wounds, for a total of 124 and a combat-related mortality rate of just over 12 percent. The rate for Confederate generals alone was 18 percent, for Union generals 8 percent. The combat-related mortality rate for all soldiers and sailors in the Civil War was probably between 7 and 9 percent. This figure assumes that (1) the total number of soldiers and sailors for both sides was somewhere between 2.75 and 3.5 million; (2) the total number of deaths is somewhere between 700,000 and 750,000; and (3) the total number of combat-related deaths is one-third of the total number of deaths, most of which resulted from sickness and disease. The combat-related mortality rate for Union generals was about the same as that for all soldiers and sailors. For one perspective on the mortality rate for Confederate generals, see the comment of George St. Leger Grenfell quoted in Arthur James Lyon Fremantle, *Three Months in the Confederate States: April–June, 1863* (1864), intro. Gary W. Gallagher (Lincoln: University of Nebraska Press, 1991), 159: "Colonel Grenfell told me that the only way in which an officer could acquire influence over the Confederate soldiers was by his personal conduct under fire. . . . Colonel Grenfell's expression was, 'every atom of authority has to be purchased by a drop of your blood.'"

12. Ulysses S. Grant to Julia Dent Grant, May 6, 1861, in *Papers of Ulysses S. Grant*, 2:24.

13. *Personal Memoirs of Ulysses S. Grant*, 756; League of the South, leagueofthesouth.com (accessed November 26, 2019); Ta-Nehisi Coates, "These Are the Last Days of U. S. Grant," *Atlantic*, June 29, 2010, https://www.theatlantic.com/entertainment/archive

/2010/06/these-are-the-last-days-of-us-grant/58879; Ta-Nehisi Coates, "Why Do So Few Blacks Study the Civil War?," *Atlantic*, Special Commemorative Issue on the Civil War, December 5, 2011, https://www.theatlantic.com/magazine/archive/2012/02/why-do-so-few-blacks-study-the-civil-war/308831. In "These Are the Last Days of U. S. Grant," Coates writes that he came away very sad from reading Grant's memoirs while calling Grant "splendid." With respect to the fact that many U.S. generals who advanced emancipation did so without particular interest in the cause, the case of Philip H. Sheridan is instructive. In July 2019 the city council of Charlottesville, Virginia, voted unanimously to establish Liberation and Freedom Day on March 3, 2020. This new city holiday commemorates the occupation of Charlottesville by Philip H. Sheridan's force and the subsequent emancipation of fourteen thousand people. Here is all of Sheridan's own account of this event from *Personal Memoirs of P. H. Sheridan*, 2 vols. (New York: Charles L. Webster, 1888), 2:118: "Custer [leading Sheridan's vanguard] reached Charlottesville the 3d [March 3, 1865], in the afternoon, and was met at the outskirts by a deputation of its citizens, headed by the mayor, who surrendered the town with medieval ceremony, formally handing over the keys of the public buildings and of the University of Virginia. But this little scene did not delay Custer long enough to prevent his capturing, just beyond the village, a small body of cavalry and three pieces of artillery."

INDEX